T0246042

HAPPY TRAILS

HAPPY TRAILS

Andrew Lauder's Charmed Life
and High Times in the
Record Business

ANDREW LAUDER
and MICK HOUGHTON

WHITE
RABBIT

First published in Great Britain in 2023 by White Rabbit,
an imprint of The Orion Publishing Group Ltd
Carmelite House, 50 Victoria Embankment
London EC4Y 0DZ

An Hachette UK Company

1 3 5 7 9 10 8 6 4 2

A CIP catalogue record for this book is
available from the British Library.

ISBN (Hardback) 9781474623599
ISBN (Trade Paperback) 9781474623605
ISBN (eBook) 9781474623629
ISBN (Audio) 9781474623636

Printed in Great Britain by Clays Ltd, Elcograf S.p.A.

MIX
Paper from
responsible sources
FSC
www.fsc.org   FSC® C104740

www.whiterabbitbooks.co.uk
www.orionbooks.co.uk

For Judith

Contents

Foreword
by Richard Williams

Many people who love music – or think they do – aspire to the A&R role. Some are chosen. Very few succeed. Hardly any succeed as significantly and consistently as Andrew Lauder, who also earned another rare distinction, that of being a successful person who even his rivals in the music business liked as well as admired during the years when his instincts and intuition helped shape the musical tastes of a generation.

There's a passage in this fascinating autobiography where Andrew describes going to see a new band managed by a friend who has been pestering him to sign them up. A special performance is arranged in a rehearsal room, where he will be an audience of one. They've set up a chair for him in front of the band. 'I never sit down at gigs,' he writes, 'so I stood at the back, hardly inconspicuous, watched and listened.'

That's one of Nature's A&R people for you. Standing at the back of a gig, watching and listening, hoping to be transported by the music but prepared for the possibility of disappointment, storing first impressions, assessing potential, and not particularly wanting to be noticed in case rivals are alerted, inflating the commercial value of something that might become the object of a bidding war.

For forty years, Andrew was an A&R man on whom those rivals kept the closest of eyes (I know that for certain because for a while I was one of them, and saw how good he was). Without making a fuss, without bothering – unlike so many – about raising his own public profile, he applied his knowledge and enthusiasm to the business of identifying interesting musicians and helping them to reach an audience.

Mostly it was only people within the industry who knew of the part he played in bringing a succession of important artists to public attention. The British bands in his debt included the Groundhogs, Brinsley Schwarz, Hawkwind, Dr Feelgood, the Stranglers, Buzzcocks and the Stone Roses. His love of the blues and American roots music lay behind his enthusiasm for Canned Heat, Creedence Clearwater Revival and Captain Beefheart in their early days, at a time when he was reaching a position to get their music heard more widely, and later enabled him to give new life to the careers of John Lee Hooker, J.J. Cale and John Hiatt.

Andrew was also responsible for bringing the music of the first generation of important German rock bands to the attention of British audiences, at a time when the idea of an important German rock band would have seemed to most people like a contradiction in terms and to promote them invited ridicule: the enormously influential Can, in particular, along with their contemporaries Amon Düül II and Neu!

Andrew landed at the right time. Born in 1947, he grew up in the 1950s with a wind-up gramophone in the family home in West Hartlepool, listening to his mother's Edmundo Ros 78s. Then Lonnie Donegan's 'Rock Island Line' and Bill Haley's 'Rock Around the Clock' changed his world. At boarding school he acquired a guitar and joined a band, playing Shadows and Ventures instrumentals, as so many of us did. But Fats Domino and Little Richard had given him a taste of the real thing, and soon he was listening to the more exotic sounds of R&B, both the originals and the versions by young British musicians – the

Rolling Stones, the Pretty Things, the Yardbirds – who were only two or three years older than him. At 17, with one O level and the conviction that Howlin' Wolf's 'Smokestack Lightning' was 'the greatest thing of all time', he headed for London and the music business.

When he secured his first job in the first week of 1965, as a clerk at a music publisher, it was in Denmark Street, London's Tin Pan Alley. This was a world then inhabited by the type described by the author Robert Hunter in his 1958 pulp novel *The A&R Man*, in the words of its protagonist: 'The letters A&R stand for Artists and Repertoire Manager, a pompous title for a comparatively simple job. My primary function is to discover new talent for the company. Once I've found them I nurse them, dress them, straighten their noses, fix their teeth, improve their accents, get them publicity, find them TV spots, plug their records on the radio, and select the songs best suited to their often limited musical talent.'

A new generation was about to blow the dust and the cynicism out of Tin Pan Alley, and Andrew became one of them. They spent their nights at venues like the Marquee, the 100 Club or Klook's Kleek, listening to the Who, John Mayall's Bluesbreakers and Rod Stewart with the Hoochie Coochie Men and visiting American R&B stars like Larry Williams and Sugar Pie DeSanto. For a while Andrew managed a band and learned a few lessons on the way before joining the newly formed UK subsidiary of Liberty Records, where a poorly defined job description allowed him to slide into an A&R role, dealing with Family, the Bonzo Dog Doo Dah Band and Hapshash and the Coloured Coat (with the Heavy Metal Kids), a project brought to him by Guy Stevens, another inspired A&R man.

The Groundhogs were his first real success, popular with college and festival audiences – and John Peel – during a British blues boom that laid the foundation for the rock era. In the early

'70s he worked with bands such as Brinsley Schwarz, Man and Cochise before a night in 1974 when, at Nick Lowe's suggestion, he went along to a West London pub and was blown away by a spiky, hard-hitting band from Canvey Island, playing R&B with a brand new attitude. 'I had to pinch myself,' he writes. 'Dr Feelgood captured everything that got me into music in the first place . . . from day one, I just wanted to make a record with them. I never sat around worrying if anyone was going to buy it. I didn't care if they did or not. I always thought there'd be someone who loved it in the same way I did.'

But there had to be more to it than just enthusiasm and confidence. In a commercial environment, that kind of idealism has to find a way of coming to terms with the real world, which is what A&R is about. As well as his love of their music, Andrew brought his imagination. In this case it was the idea of including a shrink-wrapped seven-inch 45 along with the first 10,000 copies of *Stupidity*, the Feelgoods' third album, released in 1976. It was enough to provide the initial sales impetus that gave them their first UK No 1.

Their rise, and that of others, is described by Andrew in a way that explains how effectively all the hard-earned knowledge of the recording process – about studios, producers, engineers, about songs, and about the delicate psychology of when to offer musicians firm guidance, when to let them have their heads and when to let them go – was applied to the benefit of so many bands.

His further adventures with the Radar, F-Beat, Demon, Edsel and Silvertone labels – finding new artists and introducing older ones to new audiences – present us a portrait of the UK music business at its most individualistic, vibrant and creative, a combination of qualities that inevitably could lead not just to success but to explosive disputes. And sometimes failures, as in his description of a short and unhappy period at Island Records,

which must have seemed like a perfect home but was definitely
no such thing. Clashes of talent and ego, of ambition and delu-
sion are endemic to the industry and are not avoided here.

He's out of it all now, which means he can reflect without fear
or favour on the extraordinary cast of characters he met along
the way, including Lemmy (who, you might have guessed, 'could
be a handful'); Jake Riviera, his fellow conspirator at F-Beat,
with his fondness for annoying people; Stacia, Hawkwind's
unforgettable 'spontaneous dancer', and many, many more. As
you read these stories, you might be hearing a favourite record
that he helped to bring into the world. It could be Hawkwind's
'Silver Machine', or Can's 'Vitamin C', Brinsley Schwarz's
'Surrender to the Rhythm', Dr Feelgood's 'She Does It Right',
Nick Kent's 'My Flamingo', Department S's 'Is Vic There?', John
Hiatt's 'Lipstick Sunset', Peter Blegvad's 'King Strut', the Stone
Roses' 'Fool's Gold'.

This is a man who harboured, as he puts it, 'a disdain for
image and being hip', who never grabbed a producer credit or
tried to persuade an artist to record a song he'd just written.
He's just the guy who, after starting Silvertone thirty years ago,
put out a couple of newly recorded albums by the legendary
blues singer and guitarist John Lee Hooker, then in his seventies. One of the albums won Hooker his only Grammy, and
the other had sold almost three quarters of a million copies by
the time Andrew left the label. It was no accident. It was the
product of love, care and vision. And that, like everything in this
book, is a story worth telling.

PART ONE
Mr Lucky, 1947–1967

Chapter 1
A Charmed Life Begins

I was born in the Cameron Hospital in West Hartlepool, County Durham, a forbidding old-fashioned Victorian building. My mother had been in the kitchen department of Binns' chain store when she felt she was going into labour. She always said I was born at nine o'clock precisely that evening. Dr Cameron apparently muttered that I was a bit blue. It wasn't fatal and I arrived on 22 May 1947, defied the odds and managed to stick around.

My father was thirty-nine when I was born and my mother was thirty-seven, which was considered a risky age for childbirth. She'd had two miscarriages after the war and I was probably the last throw of the dice. Dad had been a regular soldier in the Durham Light Infantry before the outbreak of war and rose to the rank of lieutenant colonel. He spent six years serving in Delhi, India, where he was head of searchlights, anti-aircraft and air defences. When he returned home in 1945 my brothers didn't know what he looked like. They all went to meet him at Southampton and were asking, 'Which one's Dad?'

My two brothers had arrived well ahead of me in December 1936 and April 1938. It was a long-standing family tradition that the first-born son was called Robert, although he was always known by his middle name Nigel. My middle brother is Simon Neville Lauder, the Neville after my uncle on my mother's side. Dad missed them growing up and thankfully my parents decided they wanted another child. I was named Andrew Justus Lauder. Justus was my Swedish grandfather's name. We had a Scottie dog called Angus at the time I was born. Mum told me it was a toss-up whether I was going to be called Angus or the dog. Luckily the dog won out. Either way it was a good Scottish name befitting the family's significant Scottish heritage.* Scottish roots were particularly important to my dad. My great-grandfather moved down to Hartlepool from Scotland. He was Colonel Robert Lauder, who was born in Dundee in 1851, but my grandfather and then my father were born in Hartlepool. Dad was born in 1908.

Mum was born in 1910 and brought up in Edgbaston, although her father was Swedish. Her mother – whose maiden name was O'Neill – was Liverpool Irish, born in Southport. Mum was Hilda Jeanetta Sjogren before marrying my dad, but she was always known as Biddy. Her father had become a wealthy man working for Sandvik Steel. The original company was based in Sandviken in Sweden and adopted Sandvik as a brand name. It dated back to 1862; my grandfather had arrived in England thirty years later, working his way up to running the Sandvik works in Halesowen, outside Birmingham, just before the First World War. He was obviously a bit of a character and represented Sweden as a figure skater in the Summer Olympics in London in 1908 where winter sports first took place at Prince's Skating Club in Knightsbridge.

Mum was brought up in a large house in Edgbaston with extensive grounds. It was near the Warwickshire Cricket Ground, which was one of her favourite hang-outs. I became

---

* The Scottish family of Lauder were Royalists and Lairds of the Bass and extensive landowners in East Lothian. The Bass Rock, a volcanic island in the Firth of Forth, was in the Lauder family for nearly six centuries. It's recorded that in 1057 the island was given to Sir Robert de Laverdre by King Malcolm III of Scotland for helping him recover his crown from Macbeth. The tradition of naming the first son Robert began then.

seriously interested in cricket when I was ten and through poring over *Wisden* I knew the names of past county players, including the celebrated Warwickshire leg spinner Eric Hollies. I was impressed when Mum said she briefly went out with him.*

Mum's brother Neville was at school with my father, which is how they met. They were married in 1935 and lived in West Hartlepool. They had a house, named Always, specially built for them on my grandfather's land. It was a beautiful property that looked like something out of an episode of *Poirot* with a deco facade, all white with rounded doors that were bright red, a flat roof and an ornate balcony. It was ready for them when they got married, but they had to move out for the duration of the war because Hartlepool's shipyards made the town a prime target for enemy bombers. My mother took my brothers to live with her parents, who'd moved to what was laughingly referred to as a cottage but was actually a big house off the beaten track on the side of the Malvern Hills in Worcestershire. It was beautiful, with a stream running through the garden.

Dad's father passed away at the start of the war so, as the eldest son, he took over the firm on his return from India. Robert Lauder & Company had around sixty employees. Dad even had his own lorry with our name on the side – that was a great source of pride for me. They imported timber from Norway, Sweden and Canada. The company had its own joinery works and sawmill where it manufactured windows, doors, staircases, roof timbers and the like during the extended post-war building boom. Our timber yard had a direct rail line to the port; they'd unload timber off the boat onto a shunting engine and it would

---

* Hollies played for England and famously bowled out the great Australian batsman Sir Don Bradman for a duck in his final test at the Oval in 1948, denying him a career average of 100 in Tests.

come straight from the docks to our yard for unloading, then turn in a big circle and head back to the docks.

West Hartlepool and Hartlepool were originally two separate towns, although you couldn't tell where one town started and the other finished. There was the old town of Hartlepool which went back to AD 900 and was a seaside port built on a headland that made it easy to defend from all sides. West Hartlepool didn't emerge till the Industrial Revolution. It was effectively a new town established by Ward Jackson, who had a plan for attracting and encouraging industries, developing shipbuilding and bringing in timber. The two towns became one town – Hartlepool – in 1967, and even though West Hartlepool had the larger population it ceased to exist.

The port was very busy until unemployment kicked in in the late fifties after shipbuilding fell away; over the years the familiar horizon of shipyard cranes from my boyhood just disappeared.* We weren't really impacted by the severe unemployment because there was still so much housebuilding going on. It would never have crossed my mind that I was in any way privileged. I had nothing to compare my upbringing to and most of my parents' friends were professional people. I knew little about the hardships others were suffering. Even the kids in my first school were mostly from better-off families.

When I was four, my parents decided Always wasn't big enough to accommodate the family, so they sold it to a local butcher and we moved into my late grandfather's house on the same land. My granny had been rattling around in this

---

* Film director Ridley Scott went to West Hartlepool College of Art. His first short film, *Boy on a Bicycle*, was shot in the early sixties. It showed his younger brother Tony cycling round the shipyards and steelworks and nearby Seaton Carew beach. The old steelworks foundries are said to have influenced the look of *Blade Runner*.

huge three-storey property with six bedrooms. They renamed
it Always, and I lived there from 1951 to 1962. It overlooked
Ward Jackson Park, on the edge of the countryside, the nearest
properties all essentially farm buildings, the surrounding fields
stretching out to small villages. It was also adjacent to the West
Hartlepool Cricket Ground.

Granny's old house was a great place to grow up. It had two
orchards, a rose garden, a tennis court, two double garages and
a massive garden to get lost in. We had one pet chicken left from
when, during rationing, they constructed chicken coops in the
tennis courts. They didn't have the heart to dispatch the last
surviving chicken, which used to wander into the house as freely
as Angus the dog. It never became the Sunday roast, at least as
far as I knew.

There was a bomb shelter at the end of the garden where I
used to play with Jane Stonehouse, the girl next door. We had a
little gang and, depending on numbers, would pretend we were
the Famous Five or the Secret Seven. After nursery school I
went to Rosebank High School. It only took in about 130 kids
and was within walking distance of the house. All my friends
went there too, up until the summer of 1957 when I was packed
off to boarding school.

Dad would often take me out after work. He wasn't a big
television watcher so after the news we'd drive to the Docks and
to the old town. I used to love seeing the mothball fleet. After
the Second World War, many Royal Navy destroyers and cruisers
were laid up in Hartlepool docks with the more exposed, rust-
prone areas sealed off or wrapped in brown plastic, which looked
like some kind of eerie cocoon in the evening light.

One time Dad heard about a fire at the North of England
Match Factory in Swainson Dock, a huge building employing over
a hundred workers, most of them women. I was only seven. We
watched it burning from a safe distance. Thick black smoke was

billowing upwards in a column. The fire continued late into the night, gutting the building, and all that remained the next day was a shell where all the windows had been burnt out. I remember photos in the papers of huge crowds gathered in Church Street to watch the blaze, with a dozen fire engines lined up in the street and even tugboats spraying water from the docks.

I spent a lot of time in Dad's various cars. The first one I remember was a classic cream-coloured pre-war Jaguar with big headlamps and running boards. But it was the car that my grandfather had owned since the 1920s that really captured my imagination. That was an immaculate Armstrong Siddeley. Grandad didn't drive any more, so whenever he took us out, he had a chauffeur. It was during those early car journeys that I first began to display signs of an enquiring mind by shouting out the name of every car or lorry we passed. Dad used to get *Autocar* and *The Motor*, and I would read them from cover to cover. For someone who has never driven a car, it seems strange now. The collector in me was probably born then too. I had a collection of Dinky Toys which had been passed down to me by my brothers. Once I started collecting them myself, I always took care to put them back in their boxes.

That fastidiousness may be explained by one of my earliest memories. My brothers had a Hornby Dublo train set, which was usually laid out across the ping-pong table in the games room, and Nigel had saved up to buy a wagon that carried a load of timber. Realising it was special, I'd seized upon it as I was being taken out in a pram by our Swedish au pair Inger Britt. Nigel was convinced I was going to lose it overboard, but I clung onto it for dear life and wouldn't let it out of my clutches. When I finally relinquished it, he was so relieved. It stuck with me how important it is to look after things. A few years later, while Simon was away doing National Service, I'd play his records and I used to care for them better than he did, putting them back

8

in their paper and card sleeves, mindful not to bend the corners of the jackets or scratch the records. That carefulness is a habit that has stayed with me my whole life.

As a family we were very rarely all together in the same place, largely because of our age differences. Nigel was eleven and Simon nine and a half years older than me. They were away at school during the fifties when I was growing up, and then both did two years' National Service. I'd been packed off to school myself by then. Nigel and Simon both attended Bradfield College in Pangbourne, near Reading, Berkshire, which was the same school my father and Uncle Neville attended. My name was put down to follow in their footsteps as soon as I was born, but things didn't go to plan.

After National Service, Nigel went on to join the Territorial Army and he became a second lieutenant, but he had to abandon further military service in order to accept his destiny; Dad packed him off to Sweden for six months to learn about all things timber. Simon was much more like me. We both loved cricket and he'd bowl at me for hours on end in the garden; he was into music too. He hated every moment of National Service though he ended up teaching basic literacy at Catterick Camp in North Yorkshire for most of his stint.

I was lucky in having two much elder bothers; so much was handed down to me from Nigel and Simon: board games, books, annuals, toys, comics, football scrapbooks, cigarette cards and more. They were really great to me. Nigel used to build model airplanes, so he'd help me assemble my Airfix kits and he built me a tree house in the orchard. Also, with them not around, I was effectively an only child and as a result I was spoilt, especially by my mother.

At the age of ten, if asked what I wanted to be, I'd have said a cricketer. I loved playing cricket in the garden, executing immaculately imagined cover drives, sweeps and cuts, but cricket appealed just as much to my thirst for facts and statistics. I'd get *Wisden* and the *Playfair* annuals every year and memorise everything I could – all the county teams, second teams and minor county teams, the grounds where they played, bowling figures and batting averages. Dad would take me to see Durham, then one of the minor counties in the North Yorkshire– South Durham Cricket League, which included a few games at the nearby West Hartlepool ground. The first county game he took me to see was Worcestershire playing at the Worcester County Ground when we visited Mum's old home in West Malvern. I was able to get Yorkshire and England fast bowler Fred Trueman's autograph at the Scarborough Festival. I barely came up to his waist but somehow he noticed me shrouded in clouds of smoke billowing from his pipe. It was the only autograph I ever collected as a kid.

Watching England against the Windies at Edgbaston in 1957 on television sealed my obsession, but I'd get frustrated when the cricket cut to regular programmes. Mum discovered *Test Match Special* which began that year on the Third Programme. I was hooked by the chattering ball-by-ball radio commentary. I even asked Mum if we could have our lunch at the same time as the players, between 1 and 1.40. She lovingly obliged.

Mum's prized possession was a wind-up HMV gramophone. Of an afternoon, she'd often play 78s in the breakfast room where we ate all our meals. George Formby stuck with me the most; his songs were silly and simplistic and traded on his goofy accent and naughty lyrics that were lost on an innocent four-year-old. Mum always sang along. She loved the popular dance bands of the day, and later Latin and South American samba music. Edmundo Ros was her favourite. She could tell I was really taken with the music but, watching her through the bars of my playpen, I was also fascinated by the way she'd wind up the gramophone between each record and the fiddly business of changing the needle. The old 78s later served as toys; I was captivated by the different coloured labels; the George Formby records sported a red-and-gold label I later found out was Regal Zonophone; others were dark blue or black and gold – or had a unique little drawing or logo like Nipper the dog on HMV records.

She'd have the radio on in the kitchen all day, usually tuned to the BBC Light Programme. *Housewife's Choice* and *Music While You Work* mapped out the mornings, then variety shows like *Worker's Playtime* came on around lunchtime. At weekends I'd listen to Uncle Mac's *Children's Favourites* on a Saturday morning. I was one of several generations who'd tune in to hear Derek McCulloch – aka Uncle Mac – say 'Hello children everywhere' and play the same records week after week: novelty songs such as 'Nellie the Elephant' and 'The Laughing Policeman', the smooth-voiced Burl Ives singing 'I Know an Old Lady (Who Swallowed a Fly)', Danny Kaye's epic 'The Ugly Duckling', and best of all, 'Sparky's Magic Piano', the first time any of us born in the post-war years heard sounds being modified on Sparky's 'talking piano'.

The most telling musical influence came through my brother Simon. He was mad about New Orleans trad jazz and particularly Chris Barber. He even started to learn the trombone. I'd hear these strange farting noises coming out of his bedroom, but he never really mastered it; I couldn't get any sound out of it at all. By 1955 we had an electric Bush record player in the breakfast room. My parents thought we should have some LPs to play so they bought the soundtracks to popular musicals like *South Pacific*, *The King and I*, *Oklahoma!*, *West Side Story* and *High Society*, which were the big sellers of the day. I enjoyed the act of putting on the LPs as much as singing along to classic show tunes, and of course *High Society* featured Louis Armstrong and his band.

Simon had one 10-inch LP I really loved – Chris Barber's Jazz Band and Skiffle Group's *New Orleans Joys* on Decca. It featured the Lonnie Donegan skiffle group playing 'John Henry' and 'Rock Island Line' – this was well before it was a hit. I thought it was fantastic and learned 'Rock Island Line' parrot fashion. I probably drove Mum mad singing it around the house. Simon bought everything by the Chris Barber Band. I liked Ottilie Patterson singing the blues as much as Lonnie Donegan's folky skiffle. Simon started buying original US trad records by George Lewis, Kid Ory and Louis Armstrong as well. One of the first records I bought was 'Petite Fleur' by Monty Sunshine with Chris Barber's Jazz Band, a surprise No. 1 hit in 1959.

When 'Rock Island Line' was released as a single in 1956 it caused the sensation which launched the skiffle craze. Bill Haley's 'Rock Around the Clock' was a hit the same year after driving teenagers wild during the opening credits for *The Blackboard Jungle*. I went on about it so much that Mum bought 'Rock Around the Clock', although she bought the wrong version, by American Gospel group the Deep River Boys. White British harmony vocal groups – like the Dallas Boys and the King Brothers – all did watered-down covers of American rock 'n' roll hits and were staples of radio variety shows. They were as close to rock 'n' roll as the BBC allowed.

Bill Haley did have a big impact. It was strange that this overweight, balding, middle-aged bloke was so popular. We had a competition among our gang to get the best Bill Haley kiss curl. He had hit after hit and when he arrived in Britain in February 1957 it was front-page news in the *Daily Express*. Thousands of fans mobbed him at Waterloo station, where a special train had been laid on from Southampton. A year earlier I remember the *Daily Express* front page with just the words BRITAIN IS GREAT AGAIN in huge type; it was at the beginning of the Suez crisis. Nigel was serving in Aden, much to my mum's distress.

At age ten I discovered there was more to rock 'n' roll than Lonnie Donegan and Bill Haley. They gave way to the wilder, more exciting sounds I heard on Radio Luxembourg. In summer

1957, we were driving back from holiday in Cornwall and once we'd crossed into Yorkshire Dad gave in to me twiddling the knobs on the radio. I landed on a record I liked and a voice, a broad drawling accent that announced: 'This is 208 Radio Luxembourg'. It was definitely not a polished BBC accent. As soon as we got home, I went straight to the radio to find Luxembourg on the Medium Wave. It featured all sponsored shows, the best of which was Tony Hall's Decca show. Sure, the signal was patchy, but that didn't matter; I heard things like Larry Williams' 'Bony Maronie', Fats Domino's 'I'm Walkin'', and later, Buddy Knox singing 'I Think I'm Gonna Kill Myself' which Mum really hated me singing around the house. In June 1957 the Light Programme launched *Saturday Skiffle Club*, which immediately followed *Children's Favourites. Saturday Club* became an absolute must-listen programme stretching long into the 1960s.

I started buying singles myself in 1957, the first few by Little Richard and Jerry Lee Lewis. They were more like it than Bill Haley – whatever 'it' was. They were thrilling and primal even to a ten-year-old's ears. I'd seen clips of Little Richard and Jerry Lee Lewis both treating their pianos with extreme disrespect. Hearing Buddy Holly was a different kind of revelation with his softer vocals and melodic, rhythmic guitars. Buddy Holly and the Crickets were another big favourite.

I didn't see a lot of pop on television before the end of the summer, aside from *Six-Five Special* where the BBC acknowledged there was such a thing as rock 'n' roll. It was presented in a really stuffy format and featured unconvincing acts like the Dallas Boys and fast-singing Don Lang and his Frantic Five – who were awful; as was Britain's so-called answer to Elvis, Tommy Steele. His cheeky, grinning performances did nothing for me. He showed his true colours within a couple of years as a cheeky Cockney singing novelty hits 'Little White Bull' and 'What A Mouth'.

Pop television improved when the commercial channel's *Oh Boy* brought genuine British rockers like Billy Fury, Marty Wilde, and Cliff Richard into the front room. They all looked and sounded more like the real thing. By then I was in boarding school and could only catch up during the holidays. I must have been home from school when I saw Buddy Holly and the Crickets on *Sunday Night at the London Palladium* performing 'Peggy Sue' and 'That'll Be the Day' sometime in March 1958. I'd seen photos before but seeing the Crickets with their Fender guitars was immediately striking, while seeing Buddy Holly's thick, black-framed glasses made me feel better about having to wear glasses myself. I used to walk around singing 'Peggy Sue' – it wasn't hard to learn all the words and imitate Holly's hiccupping vocal style. For me, 1957 was the year the penny dropped. I'd been drawn to music through my mum, then trad and skiffle through Simon, but rock 'n' roll was something else. It was my own thing. I was surely the only ten-year-old boy in West Hartlepool who knew about it.

That same year I also discovered Hartlepools United Football Club. They made the third round of the FA Cup in January 1957 and were drawn at home to Manchester United. I'd never been into football that much because my father was a rugby player. Rugby Union, of course. Football was frowned upon. I didn't even know we had a local football team in town. Dad played rugby for Durham County – Simon has a cigarette card of him. His best friend played for West Hartlepool and Durham, and even captained England six times. This was Uncle Carl. He wasn't a real uncle, but we called a lot of my parents' friends aunt and uncle, whether they were relatives or not. Carl Aarvold was born in Hartlepool and was another lieutenant colonel who served in India when Dad was there. He was a barrister who later became the senior judge at the Old Bailey, even presiding over the Kray twins' trial in 1965.

At Rosebank High School we played football and I had my Stanley Matthews football boots. I loved playing, but my dad wouldn't tolerate any sport unless it was amateur. He was very much a product of that Gentlemen vs Players era, subscribing to the view you shouldn't be paid for playing sport. He took me to Twickenham to see Durham play Middlesex one time, and to Hartlepool Rovers vs West Hartlepool, the big local derby. When I said I'd like to go to a soccer match he just grimaced. As far as he was concerned the best team in England was Bishop Auckland, a local amateur team. In 1961 he took me to Wembley for the Amateur Football Cup Final to see another local village team, West Auckland Town, beat Walthamstow Avenue 2–1.

I'd discovered that my brothers had some football scrapbooks and annuals, mostly from the golden era of Newcastle Untied winning the FA Cup three years out of four in the early 1950s. They had a lot of stuff about Hartlepools United, who were doing very well in the Third Division North in 1957. Hartlepools nearly went up at the end of the season that year. Only one team was promoted from each of the North and South Divisions, and they came second to Derby County. So we just missed making the Second Division for what would have been the only time in the club's history.*

There was huge excitement in the town about the FA Cup match with Manchester United; this was the all-conquering Busby Babes. Another unrelated 'Uncle Harry' was the chairman of Hartlepools United and he lived in the big house across the way.

_____

* It wasn't until 22 August 1960 that I finally got to see Hartlepools United play against newly promoted Peterborough United, playing their first ever away game. My team had found themselves in Division Four after the North and South regional leagues were scrapped in the 1958/9 season and replaced by two national leagues. Hartlepools United dropped the 's' in 1968 and it was just Hartlepool until the 'United' was restored in 1977. It's been Hartlepool United ever since.

I was allowed to ride my bike round his yard as long as I stayed off the flower beds. We could have got tickets from him, but my dad was disinterested and Mum was convinced there'd be trouble because of overcrowding. The game went ahead without me.

Officially, 17,265 people were there, the club's biggest-ever crowd, and it was a legendary match. We went 3–nil down after thirty minutes, pulled one back before half time and then it was 3–3 with fifteen minutes to go. Manchester United won 4–3. People were hanging off cranes in the dockyard to watch and it's still one of the major events in the town's history. I made up my mind that day that I was going to be a Hartlepools United fan. I stood outside Uncle Harry's gate on my bike and swore allegiance to his team.*

My own life had changed by the start of the next season. My mum hadn't wanted me to be sent away to school at too young an age, but when I turned ten she had to give in to my father's wishes. Having tried to put it out of my mind all summer, the reality of being sent to boarding school caught up with me. Going to W.G. Allen's Gentleman's Outfitters in Harrogate to get kitted out with the uniform made it horribly real. I didn't want my idyllic life to be interrupted. I had a record collection building up and everything else I collected or cared about or was interested in – including cricket and now football – was at home. In 1957 all those interests coalesced just as boarding school was about to bring the shutters down on everything that mattered to me – all my things, my friends and my family.

---

* On the front page of the late Saturday evening edition of the *Hartlepool Mail* there'd always be a cartoon of the Docker. He wore a flat cap and stood on a log suspended from a crane overlooking the ground. If we lost, the Docker was glum-faced, his thumb down; if his hand was level we'd drawn, and if we won his thumb pointed upwards. I'm looking at a picture of the Docker on my wall right now – celebrating the 'Pools' 10–1 win over Barrow in April 1959.

16

Chapter 2
The Best and Worst Days of Your Life

I'd never been away from home before so there was nothing to
prepare me for boarding school. What I knew came from reading
Tom Browne's School Days and various Charles Dickens tales
of deprivation and degradation at the hands of brutal teachers.
That was my rather jaundiced impression, and I was filled with
foreboding. When I got there it was an even more horrendous
experience than I could have imagined. I was sent to Corchester
Boys Preparatory School in Corbridge, a market town in North-
umberland, very close by Hadrian's Wall and only 45 miles from
home. The school was in an imposing Victorian building that was
Dickensian in its bleakness and in the attitudes of the teachers.
I found living in a dormitory especially hard to adjust to after
the comforts of my own room. At night it was like lockdown in a
black-and-white POW film.

The washbasins weren't plumbed in, so every morning at 6
a.m. the bowls were filled from a pitcher of cold water by the
grim-faced female staff. In keeping with the 'no privacy' policy
there were no doors on the lavatories and in swimming lessons
we were told 'real men don't wear swimming trunks'. Everything
I valued and had taken for granted in my life thus far abruptly
stopped in that nightmare of a school.

The teachers hated teaching as much as they hated children.
I don't remember any of them ever smiling. One particular
master was the most horrific-looking person I've ever seen to

this day. He chain-smoked, had one brown suit that hung off
him; he was like a walking skeleton with a thin layer of skin
stretched over it. He permanently grimaced, showing really bad
teeth. He was fearsome. If any pupil's attention drifted away
in class he would walk to the back of the classroom, take aim
and throw the blackboard duster at his victim, infallibly hitting
them right behind the ear. The walking-wounded were then
sent off to see Matron. I was too petrified to let it happen
to me.

The teachers weren't there to educate pupils but to break
their spirit. This was the school's idea of preparing you for
life. Needless to say, music of any sort was discouraged and
nobody would've dared smuggle in a transistor. The rock 'n'
roll I'd recently discovered became a well-kept secret among a
few like-minded friends. I've a rare fond memory of three of us
huddled together on the radiator in one of the empty classrooms
after lessons, singing Lonnie Donegan and Buddy Holly songs
out loud.

I wasn't strong, and always on the thin side. School meals
were disgusting, usually a tasteless mush of over-boiled veg,
leathery meat and unidentifiable mince. It was a diet totally
lacking in nutrition. As a result I got weedier still and soon
became ill. I was tired all the time and suffered stomach pains
which I put down to the lousy food. I wondered if it was a psy-
chosomatic thing because I was so miserable. We all avoided
visits to Matron, who wasn't known for her compassion; her
answer to everything was a giant spoonful of cod liver oil or
an aspirin. Several times I was so poorly with my undiagnosed
illness that my dad had to drive to the school and take me home.
I felt very guilty, but I was so physically drained.

Not only were the meals revolting but you had to eat everything put in front of you. I became proficient at scooping food
into a hanky and disposing of it later. One Sunday I carefully

18

put the contents of that morning's fry-up into my pockets before compulsory church attendance. The school gave you a sixpence to put in the collection box. I could see the verger approaching and discreetly put the remnants of breakfast to one side on the pew while I rummaged in my pocket for the coin. After we filed out from the church, I realised I'd left my discarded bundle of greasy sausage and bacon behind.

Needless to say, the vicar found my leftovers and was outraged. He contacted the headmaster. Questions were asked and the answer came back that the culprit was Lauder. I was given a proper dressing down in the headmaster's study. This was during my third term there, by which time I'd had enough. Instead of being my usual passive and penitent self, I started telling him what I thought of his school. It all poured out, an endless list of everything I loathed about the place. The Head was so taken aback by my outburst that he called my parents and told them I'd had some sort of fit of madness and they'd better come fetch me. I left Corchester Boys Prep School that day.

The incident was never spoken about again. For the final weeks of term I had daily home tuition, but after two weeks I became ill again and was taken to hospital and given a blood test. It turned out I had glandular fever. I was prescribed some very large green pills to be taken three times a day, and for the next few weeks had to spend half an hour a day in front of an ultraviolet ray. I'd sit there wearing goggles, imagining I was W.E. Johns' Captain Biggles in the cockpit of his Sopwith Camel, while happily listening to Little Richard or Buddy Holly blasting out on my record player.

Next term my dad came up with a school in the Lake District. The Craig School was as good as the first one was bad. It had a friendly atmosphere and even encouraged interests outside of the school curriculum. I was there from winter term in 1959 to the end of summer 1961. The Craig was located on Lake Road, Windermere, and all the dorms were named after lakes. It was a beautiful place, up on a hill within walking distance of the lake. The first thing I noticed as we drove in was a soccer pitch, so that gave me hope. The grounds were spectacular, surrounded by wild woods. Cricket and football were keenly taught and played, and the boys had regular expeditions to the hills. Walks up Helvellyn to see the sunrise in the summer term were spectacular and we also enjoyed boating on the lakes and trips to Scafell, Harrison Stickle and Great Gable.

I still found it hard getting to sleep in the dorm, lying there to the sounds of sneezes, snuffles, farting and the odd cry in the night. At least the school had modern plumbing, but every morning you had to have an ice-cold bath, submerged up to your neck. In winter, if you were first, you had to break the ice. That aside, the Craig was a lot more fun and I made a lot of friends there and even acquired a nickname. I was known as Harry, after Sir Harry Lauder, the world's most famous Scottish entertainer. Ten years after his death he was still remembered for singing Scottish ballads, comic songs and an image defined by his kilt, tam-o'-shanter hat, and walking stick. I was able to tune in to Radio Luxembourg at night, so I no longer felt I was losing the plot about what was happening in music. I kept my tranny under the pillow, which of course we weren't supposed to do. I'm sure the dorm master turned a blind eye to this and our after-hours gatherings.

The Craig had a cricket coach called Mr Kitchen who tolerated me babbling on about cricket all the time. After two terms he was waiting for the season to start to see me play. I'd given the impression that I was a talented cricketer who'd transform the school team. When we went to the nets, I lived up to expectations by playing extremely stylish, technically perfect shots – except that I'd fail to connect with the ball every time.

20

He soon made his diagnosis and one day in his geography class wrote something at the top of the board and said, 'Lauder, please read what I've just written.' All I could see was a white squiggle. So I was marched off to see Matron, then off to Keswick for an eye test which revealed that I had one lazy eye, leaving the other one to do all the work. To correct the problem, I had to wear an eyepatch over the good eye so the muscles over my lazy left eye would have to compensate.

From then on I was mercilessly ribbed by everybody saying 'Where's your parrot?' and 'Aargh Jim lad', impersonating Robert Newton's pirate captain Long John Silver in *Treasure Island*. Not for the last time did my pop music knowledge came in handy. I was already a fan of Johnny Kidd and the Pirates, who'd had a minor hit with 'Please Don't Touch'. They followed it with 'Shakin' All Over', which is arguably the greatest British pre-Beatles rock 'n' roll single. On stage the band wore full pirate garb, but Kidd's gimmick was to wear a patch over his right eye. 'Shakin' All Over' topped the charts in June 1959 just as I was required to wear an eyepatch. Unusually, he'd co-written the song himself under his real name Fred Heath and when 'Shakin' All Over' went to No. 1 he was pictured on the front page of the *Daily Express*. I still had the piss taken out of me, but I'd respond by bringing out the cutting and saying: 'Look at this. Pretty soon you'll all want to wear an eyepatch.'

Despite his gimmicky appearance Johnny Kidd predated
the R&B boom

There was a young music teacher who taught appreciation of
classical music. He had a Pye Black Box record player and after
lessons on a Friday he'd play rock 'n' roll records for anyone who

wanted to stick around. He'd play Cliff Richard's early rock 'n'
roll singles such as 'Move It' and 'Mean Streak', which sounded
more authentically American than any other British attempts.
I bought the first Cliff album, simply called *Cliff*, where he was
backed by the Drifters. By 1960, Cliff's band was called the
Shadows and though I soon stopped buying Cliff's increasingly
slushy pop singles I bought most of the Shadows' singles for a
few more years, as well as a lot of other instrumental records.
I had a couple of Ventures LPs – they were 'the American
Shadows' – and three LPs by Johnny and the Hurricanes. They
had a very different organ-and-sax-based sound on hits like 'Red
River Rock' and 'Rockin' Goose'. I bought a lot of instrumental
45s by other British groups like the Cougars, the Eagles, the
Fentones and the Hunters. These groups recorded some of the
best British group music before the Beatles.

After seeing the Shadows on television playing their Fender
Stratocasters, I had to have a guitar. During the first summer
holidays at the Craig I went shopping with Mum and Dad in
Newcastle and saw my first Fender Stratocaster on display at J.G.
Windows, a music and record shop in the arcade that's still there
today. I stared in awe; it was red, and exactly like Hank Marvin's.
The Shads' guitarists Hank and Bruce Welch both came from
Newcastle, so it was a poignant moment. Priced at 160 guineas
it was way out of my price range. I got hold of some guitar
catalogues from a company called Bells in Surbiton. They had
Gibson and Fender catalogues but the nearest equivalent I could
afford was a Hofner Futurama 2, which was 25 guineas. It took
a few months to save up for it and make it part of my Christmas
present. Simon was working in London and picked it up for me
from Surbiton. And of course I needed an amp too, so he brought
both back when he came home for Christmas in 1960. I'd already
bought Bert Weedon's *Play in a Day* and Johnny Southern's *Skif-
Rok Guitar Tutor*, which boasted 'no musical knowledge required'.

I'd never wanted an acoustic guitar, sales of which went through the roof during the skiffle craze. The Shadows were making a similar impact with a new generation of kids who wanted to plug in. I vowed to learn how to play seriously but of course I was too impatient. I did at least manage to tune it and would put a record on and try to play along. It was mostly either the Shadows or the Ventures but it was great just to plug in a guitar, and make all the moves, oblivious to the terrible noise I was making. My dad must have rued the day he allowed me to have a guitar.

In the spring break I persuaded Dad to take me to see a live pop show. My first gig was seeing Jess Conrad with the Red Price Combo at the Hartlepool Empire. Jess Conrad was one of far too many insipid British rock 'n' rollers. When Jess walked out, he said, 'This is the first time I've played where there are more people on stage than in the audience.' He wasn't kidding. Dad liked the Red Price Combo but wasn't too impressed by Jess Conrad's half-hearted pouting; nor was I. Poor attendances weren't uncommon and later that year the Empire was turned into a bingo hall.

Much to my dad's disappointment, I failed the Common Entrance exam to get into Bradfield College, where he and my brothers had gone. The pass mark was 64 per cent. I asked him what my percentage was, and he said I'd got the right numbers but in the wrong order. Their second choice was Wellingborough, where thankfully I did pass. Again, I asked by what percentage, to which he replied 'enough'.

Wellingborough School was one of the oldest public schools in the country, founded in 1595 and situated between Northampton and Market Harborough. It was well regarded but not academically renowned, which probably accounted for my getting a place there. A lot of farmers and landowners around the Midlands packed their kids off to Wellingborough. Many boys arrived from overseas as well, from places like Singapore, Malaysia and Persia. There were also pupils like my future school band's bass player Kevin Laker. He wasn't stupid but could never apply himself to anything. He was the son of Freddie Laker (of Laker Airways fame, although it was then called British United Airways); a pioneer of cheap international air travel, Freddie was knighted in 1977. Kevin's dad was a very wealthy man and I figured money had exchanged hands with the school authorities.

I arrived at Wellingborough School in September 1961. It was a grand red-brick building and followed a typically Spartan approach. There were six houses in all and four were for boarders only: Garnes, Friars, Platts and Weymouth, where I ended up. There were also two houses for day boys. I was placed in Hatton Hall for one term before we were assigned our houses. I met Kevin there and another future bandmate, Simon Thirsk.

My elder brother Nigel married the daughter of the man who ran Blacketts, the biggest building company in Darlington. It wasn't a strategic decision; they are still happily together and at one point he was MD of both companies. Simon moved to London, where he drove a minicab for a while. These were the first minicabs – the famous red Renault Dauphines, a rear-engine economy car that broke the monopoly on traditional London black taxis. He later went into the travel business as a courier before settling in Menorca. With my brothers gone and me away at school, Mum and Dad moved into an old farmhouse known as the White House. It was in the middle of nowhere, though not far from the A19 which took you north to Sunderland and Newcastle. The nearest town was Castle Eden, where the Castle Eden Brewery used to be, one of the many North-Eastern breweries that have long since disappeared.

I was by this time fourteen years old and a seasoned boarder. One thing that boarding school does is to make you stand on your own two feet. I had no misgivings about going to Welling-borough, although I was fortunate that fagging was soon abol-ished; I only caught the tail end during my first year there. After that I was spared running round after prefects and carrying out menial tasks. I didn't enjoy being a lackey, but I never experi-enced any humiliation or unwanted advances at Wellingborough. There was only one ogre among the teachers, who I encountered towards the end of my time there. He was a barmy Welsh maths master who used to flog me with a leather belt. I never thought it was because of my admittedly poor algebraic skills but purely personal gratification on his part.

The rest of the teachers were fine, but one in particular stood out. John Elwick, the housemaster at Garnes, was in his early thirties, always supportive, very funny in a dry sort of way and sartorially different to any of the other teachers. They were generally scruffy, whereas John Elwick was a snazzy dresser in his tailored tweed suits and waistcoats; he always used a cigarette holder and wore a fob watch.

He knew me and my friends were into pop music and would invite us to his room to see the Beatles on television if it wasn't post curfew. When the Beatles did the Royal Command Perfor-mance, our housemaster also allowed a few of us up to his study to watch it. The Beatles had the same effect that skiffle had had in the fifties, so there were loads of boys learning to play guitar and there were three school groups. John Douglas was the lead singer of the Comanches, the best of the school beat groups. Not long after I arrived at Wellingborough, I saw them walking about with John Elwick; they'd returned after the break wearing tight, tapered trousers and pointy shoes. They even looked cool in the obligatory grey-suited school uniform. I never got to know them. That two- or three-year age difference at a boarding school is quite a chasm. Each year and each house would have a different day room and that was your particular world.

I had no idea there was a school group till Johnny and the Comanches played at a Christmas show in 1961. They played in the big hall, which usually staged Shakespeare plays and Gilbert & Sullivan operas. The Comanches had their own backdrop of Monument Valley, made popular in so many John Ford/John Wayne Westerns. They were well rehearsed and had good equipment – Vox and Fender amps and a Watkins Copicat echo unit. Their repertoire was mostly Shadows inspired, but with some Buddy Holly and the Crickets, and their own Western-themed instrumentals. They looked and sounded great, and the presentation was really slick. To cap it all they bussed in girls from Wellingborough Girls' School who screamed at them the whole time. They put Jess Conrad to shame.

Seeing them play opened up the possibility that I could have a beat group. I'd now been playing for two years within the four walls of my bedroom, but ahead of the first term in 1962 I set about forming a four-piece group called the Deacons with Simon Thirsk.* The Deacons comprised me and Simon, who was the better guitar player. He was the lead and I played rhythm – I was Bruce Welch to his Hank Marvin. Our drummer was Big Mick DeVetta, who was a year ahead of us. He was one of the school's great characters, a real bruiser on the rugby field and a dangerous fast bowler. I was never bullied but Mick was very protective of me and one day said, 'If anyone gives you any grief just let me know.' There was one boy called Lee from Singapore in our dorm who was like Cato in the *Pink Panther* films. He'd pounce on unsuspecting pupils or give you a Chinese burn, usually in the middle of the night. I mentioned he was becoming a real pain in the arse to Mick, who said, 'I'll have a word with him.' Lee never bothered me again.

---

* I found out years later that Quicksilver Messenger Service guitarist John Cipollina's first group was called the Swinging Deacons.

Mick and Simon were in Friars and I was in Weymouth; the two houses were a few hundred yards apart. We planned the group during that spring term. Mick had a drum kit in London and we'd bring our guitars next term. We needed a bass player and asked Kevin Laker, who was also in Friars, if he fancied joining. When he returned in the summer term, he had a Fender Precision bass and the biggest Selmer bass amp you could buy. Kevin had just gone to the local music shop and said, 'What's the best bass and what's the biggest amp you've got?' His dad bought them for him. The amp was enormous and took three of us to carry it. That was our line-up.

We started off rehearsing in a classroom till there were complaints about the noise. John Elwick said, 'I'll arrange for you to use the cricket pavilion. You can make as much noise as you want and no one will hear it.' It was a lovely building with a thatched roof and a front step that came from W.G. Grace's house in Gloucester. It was a hallowed place for our group to rehearse. We'd set up in the changing rooms and built up a set list dominated by Shadows instrumentals, some Ventures, some Outlaws and a bit of Buddy Holly. John Elwick was also our biology teacher. He knew that I had zero interest in biology and didn't have the stomach to dissect frogs. He'd say, 'Lauder, I think your time would be better spent on the guitar.'

We did have a spin-off group the following year that I like to think of as early country rock – several years ahead of Gram Parsons and the Byrds. We did Johnny Cash, Marty Robbins and Kingston Trio covers, such as 'I Walk the Line', 'El Paso' and 'Tom Dooley'. I found an old frame for a banjo back home which my dad had in India and got new parts for that; Simon played acoustic. We played our country-folk set as the Cumberland Four. Both our bands only ever played in school, usually at the Cat's Whiskers dances which John Douglas and his mates had established a few years earlier. There were a couple of other groups in school. The Aharis were led by a Persian student called Mehran Ahari. They were better than us, but square. Mehran Ahari later recorded a few singles for CBS and Decca with a group called the Two and a Half; Mehran was quite short, so he was 'the half'.

Along with my guitar, amp, and banjo, I'd arrive at the start of every term with two record carriers. I'd amassed about a hundred singles and EPs by then. I also took along my Bush portable record player. Playing records in the day room was my main contribution to school life and if anybody wanted to know anything about pop music, I was the person they asked. After the Beatles took off in early 1963 more and more kids got into music. Liverpool was an almost mythical place for me. The Beatles captured my imagination beyond the actual music. I read a story in *New Musical Express* about their first single 'Love Me Do' being released in October 1962. That was the first time I'd seen their name. It said their single was likely to chart just because they were so popular in Liverpool and on Merseyside. And within weeks 'Love Me Do' was at No. 27, purely based on local sales. That meant they had a 'new to the charts' profile which mentioned there was a scene there. I was fascinated. Why had all these groups sprung up in Liverpool?

I was adding to my record collection every week at school. You needed pocket money at boarding school, a kind of allowance which my parents gave me at the start of term; every so often you'd get a letter with a five-pound note in it or the proverbial postal order that Billy Bunter was always expecting. You had to have money for the tuck shop and for going into town. We were allowed to go into Wellingborough after lessons on Saturday – and before sports in the afternoon. We were required to wear straw boaters outside of the school perimeters, which made you a target for the townies. They'd try and knock your boater off; some car drivers would actually try to knock you off your bike.

I'd usually forgo Mars bars, crisps and fizzy drinks in the tuck shop to ensure I had a pound note at the end of every week when I went along to the record shop in Wellingborough. The price of singles used to fluctuate slightly but at that time they were 6 shillings and 8 pence, so a £1 note bought three singles. The shop seemed to order at least one copy of everything that was released. I'd take in a list of ten or so new singles I'd found out about that week, give it to the guy behind the counter, go into the booth on the other side of the shop and listen to them.

Having read about 'Love Me Do' I put it at the top of my list. I was so excited, but it sounded too much like a country and western song, so I passed on it. I did buy it eventually and learned to love it. It hung around the charts, almost till Christmas, without getting any higher than No. 17. Then I heard 'Please Please Me' and immediately thought 'Now I get it.' It didn't sound like an American record or like any British group either.

I was still in the fourth form in January 1963 when there was a knock on the day room door and I was told, 'Taylor's outside and he's looking for you.' Taylor was a prefect for another house and the bass player in the Comanches. He said: 'Lauder, we have reason to believe you have a copy of the new Beatles' single "Please Please Me" and we were wondering if we might borrow it in order to learn it.' It was a great honour – and I realised that my reputation as the boy who played the records in Weymouth had spread to another house.

After 'Please Please Me' I wanted to hear everything coming out of Liverpool. There were two compilations put together by John Schroeder for a small independent label called Oriole. He'd rounded up all the groups that hadn't yet been signed and recorded them at the Rialto Ballroom. They were eventually released across two volumes of *This Is Merseybeat*. Bill Harry, who brought out the *Mersey Beat* paper, had helped organise it. I loved those records because they were so raw and carefree. They were significant albums during my school days in 1963. I played the hell out of them – groups like Faron's Flamingos, Rory Storm and the Hurricanes, Sonny Webb and the Cascades or Earl Preston and the TTs. The simple strategy for each group was, 'It's your turn, plug in and play', just like they did on stage – warts and all. I loved the bum notes and rough vocals compared to the pristine Abbey Road recordings by Billy J. Kramer, Gerry and the Pacemakers and the Fourmost.

During the Easter holidays in 1963 our drummer Mick had seen a group called the Rolling Stones at the Railway Hotel in Richmond and he bumped into their manager Andrew Oldham who he knew from Wellingborough. Mick asked if I remembered Andrew, but the name meant nothing to me. He'd left the summer before I arrived. His final end-of-term report had said: 'Andrew may do well . . . but not here.' Mick said he was best mates with John Douglas, and he'd been one of the prime movers in setting up the Cat's Whiskers dances. Andrew Oldham was held in high esteem by the school's cool gang.

Andrew told Mick he was managing the Rolling Stones and how they weren't a beat group but played R&B music. Mick didn't know what that meant, but I knew from reading *Record Mirror*. They had a record contract with Decca and a single coming out in June. I bought 'Come On' without hearing it and thought it was great – all 1 minute 45 seconds of it. It was a Chuck Berry song I'd never heard before; the B-side 'I Want to Be Loved' was even better and written by Muddy Waters. I'd come across both names in *Record Mirror*, which ran a photo of the Rolling Stones when 'Come On' entered the charts. They looked as scruffy as their rough-and-ready sound suggested. The Rolling Stones' second single was 'I Wanna Be Your Man', a cover of a Lennon and McCartney song they'd yet to record. It was the song Ringo was given to sing on *With the Beatles*. So the Stones must know the Beatles! 'I Wanna Be Your Man' was released in mid-November 1963, and just missed out on the Top 10. In the space of a year, British pop music had undergone a dramatic upheaval. It felt like it was only the start of something significant, which was already becoming more important to me than anything else and that most definitely included continuing my education.

I left Wellingborough one term after I'd reached the fifth form at the end of that year. I'd taken one O level in English Literature, the sole measure of my academic achievement. I'd managed to persuade Mum and Dad to let me leave school, arriving back home in West Hartlepool in time for Christmas. In return, I promised to continue my studies at night school.

Following my departure, I was mentioned in the next issue of the school magazine, the *Old Wellingburian*. My name appeared at the end of a list of departing prefects and those who'd done something distinguished. It noted that, apart from taking five wickets in a match for Weymouth House, 'we're saying goodbye this term to Andy Lauder, the House's answer to the Beatles'. I'd made my mark.

Chapter 3
First Time I Met the Blues

I never thought it was a big deal for my parents that I left
school at sixteen. Neither of my brothers had pursued an
academic course; Nigel was already working in the timber yard
and gaining the experience to take over when Dad chose to step
down. Simon had gone to work in London without any definite
prospects. I already had a dream, however vague it might be:
I wanted to do something in 'the music business'. I'd already
hinted at that and made a point of saying it didn't require
exams or qualifications. I always brought up Andrew Oldham's
achievements in evidence. Despite leaving Wellingborough with
the same one O level as me, he was managing a group with a
record deal. And not just any group; it was the Rolling Stones,
soon to become the only real rivals to the Beatles.

I'd never met Andrew Oldham, never even set eyes on him.
My parents must have been sticking pins into an Andrew
Oldham doll during 1964 because I kept banging on about him.
The fact that he was only three years older than me was further
indication that 'it can be done'. I also knew that, whatever I was
going to do, it was only going to happen in London. Mum and
Dad weren't going to agree to me leaving home at only sixteen
years of age, but I needed to go before it was too late.

So I had to bide my time, telling my beleaguered parents how
well the Stones were doing at every possible opportunity. They

had their first big hit in February getting to No. 3 with 'Not Fade Away', a song I already knew by Buddy Holly. My argument was always 'I can do that – I can follow in Andrew's footsteps', and during 1964 my contention gathered momentum as 'It's All Over Now' and 'Little Red Rooster' both made No. 1 – and their debut album also made No. 1. Andrew Oldham's managerial success was at the forefront of my campaign to make it in the music business, although I had no idea how to go about it.

In order to leave school, I'd agreed to continue taking O levels at technical college. They'd kept their end of the bargain, but I didn't and never had any intention once I'd left school. I just sat in my room for several months listening to my records and playing my guitar until my dad eventually said, 'It's time you got a job.' I wasn't far off turning seventeen but I had very little experience of life. I hadn't been anywhere on my own apart from school. I'd led a sheltered life and was used to more or less getting what I wanted.

I hadn't kept in touch with any of my old friends from the big house by the park or at Rosebank High School. If I went out at all it was usually to go to the record shop in Hartlepool. Bruce Moore's was an electrical store that had a decent record counter. Even Binns had a record department. Buying records had been a major thing in my life for at least five years. I'd been given *With the Beatles* as a Christmas present in 1963 and they followed it with *A Hard Day's Night* in the summer, which had crafted a new sound dominated by George's twelve-string guitar. *A Hard Day's Night* was the first album where they'd written all the songs, effectively distancing themselves from the new crop of R&B groups, who were reliant on covers. The Beatles were still the frontrunners and in 1964 they went global. They conquered America and made headlines all over the world, which gave me further ammunition as to the power and potential of pop music on an almost unprecedented scale.

34

Since 'Please Please Me' I'd been trying to keep up with every beat group record that came out, but I was now getting more interested in R&B and blues music. I'd always preferred the rawer, less produced beat groups but the R&B groups coming through were rawer still. The tone had been set by the Rolling Stones, and particularly their self-titled debut album released on 16 April 1964. It was co-produced by none other than Andrew Loog Oldham. He even wrote some brief notes declaring 'The Rolling Stones are more than just a group – they are a way of life.'

The Rolling Stones was revelatory, and not least because nine of its tracks were covers. This wasn't in the least retrograde, though; they were championing blues and R&B while still making it their own. The album sent me on a quest to hear all the original blues men they'd drawn attention to on that album: Willie Dixon, Muddy Waters, Slim Harpo, Jimmy Reed, and Rufus Thomas, as well as the already familiar Chuck Berry and Bo Diddley. Pretty soon it was clear that all the more interesting groups emerging during 1964 were covering songs by the same American blues musicians. That certainly applied to the Kinks, the Animals, Manfred Mann, Them and the Pretty Things. 1964 was a significant year in my forging an enduring love of the blues. The Stones had exposed huge gaps in my knowledge. Their album was like gaining entry into a secret society. The music papers only went so far in covering blues and R&B, so I began subscribing to specialist monthlies: *Blues Unlimited*, co-founded by Mike Leadbitter and Simon Napier, and Mike Vernon's *R&B Monthly*, which was launched in February 1964. I also began ordering records from London that I read about and couldn't get over the counter locally.

I was never too purist in the way some of the blues magazine writers and readers were because I liked the British R&B group cover versions as much as the originals – often more so. They

weren't carbon copies, but they put their spin on it. I wasn't a
blues snob. It was a while before I understood the significance
of Cyril Davies or Alexis Korner in terms of people who came
through the ranks of their bands or how important Chris
Barber had been bringing over blues artists from America since
the fifties. In quick succession other R&B groups were coming
through – and none more important than the Animals, because
they were from Newcastle. They weren't exactly a local group,
but I was living just off the A19 that led there. The Animals
were a bunch of Geordies on the same wavelength as the Stones.
They followed the same path yet sounded totally different
because they included organist Alan Price, and Eric Burdon was
more a blues shouter than Mick Jagger. They came over as much
tougher despite their brand-new, smart but ill-fitting suits.

I bought more LPs than ever in 1964, mostly acoustic and
electric blues albums by the likes of Elmore James, Muddy
Walters, Howlin' Wolf, Little Walter, Big Joe Williams, Sonny
Boy Williamson, and John Lee Hooker. I read that Guy Stevens
– a name I recognised from reading about the blues – had put
a compilation together of the more rockin' Excello tracks. It
was called *Authentic R&B* and it came out on Stateside. That
became a big favourite; it had Lightning Slim, Lazy Lester
and Slim Harpo's original versions of 'I'm a King Bee' and 'I
Got Love if You Want It', which the Stones had covered. Most
of all though, I was drawn to a series of singles and EPs being
released by Pye International, which carried the legend 'R&B' in
the centre of its yellow-and-red label. They'd licensed records on
the Chess label by every major blues artist in Chicago, including Howling' Wolf, of course, who released the life-changing
'Smokestack Lightning'.

I firmly believed that 'Smokestack Lightning' was the greatest achievement of all time. It put everything else in the shade
– you could forget the discovery of penicillin, the Mona Lisa or

the Sistine Chapel. This was music from another planet and I tried to reproduce it on my tape machine in my room with my guitar. I dread to think what it sounded like, but it was the last straw for my dad. That's when he said, 'Since you've no intention of taking exams, you'd better get a job and contribute to your upkeep.' He was dead right and I needed to be reminded of this because the end result of trying to recreate 'Smokestack Lightning' and the Wolf's powerful, raucous, unearthly voice was that I couldn't actually speak for two weeks. I had to drink liquid out of a straw because I'd lacerated my vocal cords. My poor parents must have wondered what the bloody hell was going on. They'd given me all the comforts of home and an expensive education and here I was, up in my room howling.

Howlin' Wolf on *Ready Steady Go*, December 1964

Mum and Dad were celebrating their thirtieth anniversary that year and went away for the weekend in a posh country hotel. They had to take me along. I didn't want to miss *Juke Box Jury*, so Dad had to arrange for me to watch it in the TV room. Every week there'd be a mystery guest tucked away in a booth who, that week, was none other than Howlin' Wolf. He had to endure three of the four panellists being particularly rude and dismissive about 'Smokestack Lightning'. Ubiquitous television and radio personality Lady Saunders, aka Katie Boyle, patronisingly said it was an 'interesting noise'. It was voted a 'miss' and the Wolf, who was a big man, towered over them as he had to walk down the line to shake hands with them. He must have wondered what on earth he was doing there. I was in a positively bad mood the rest of the night. My long-suffering parents probably couldn't wait to pack me off to bed.

After months of me acting like a complete layabout it was decided that I'd better get a job at the timber yard, which had, after all, been paying for my upkeep. Not that it was any hardship. Dad would give me a lift to work and back every day. It was a very cushy arrangement. He asked one of the younger guys in the office to teach me how to order timber. If we'd won a contract, we had to supply the timber in specific lengths and in certain sizes, whether directly from a company in Sweden or from a shipping company. It was surprisingly complicated – and maths had never been my strongest subject at school. I never really learned how it worked. Nor was I overly interested; I was more fascinated by the concept than the reality of doing it. Needless to say, my dad never trusted me to handle an order and I ended up more a general dogsbody.

I was assigned to the foreman of the timber yard, who'd have me running around looking for people with orders for the saw-mill but usually getting lost among the acres of timber. I knew I was wasting time – my own as well as my dad's. He knew I was never going to be tempted to join the family business. I was very lazy and allowed to be so, yet still picking up a wage packet. I would give half of it to my mum and most of the rest went on records.

The music papers were still important and throughout 1964 they were the source for an elaborate series of graphs covering my bedroom wall. These detailed how all the different major record labels were faring week by week and mostly focusing on the four major labels – EMI, Decca, Philips, and Pye. There'd be the odd independent single too, if it made the charts. I'd add up the points from the Top 75 in *Record Mirror*, starting at one point for the record at No. 75 and 75 points for the No. 1. I did that over a year, separately itemising Parlophone, Columbia and HMV – all the EMI labels – then Fontana (Philips), Piccadilly (Pye) and so on. I loved the statistics of it; if only I'd applied myself the same way in ordering timber. I could see that aside from the Beatles and the Searchers, and Manchester's Hollies, the first wave of beat groups was petering out in the charts while the Stones, the Animals and Manfred Mann signalled the impact of R&B groups.

My father may not have understood what I wanted to do, but he was very caring and supportive even to the point that when we were driving back on a Thursday he'd pull in at the high street so I could buy the music papers. Some weeks I'd ask, 'What have we stopped for?' and he'd say, 'It's music papers day', so I could pick up my *Melody Maker*, *Record Mirror*, *New Musical Express*, *Disc* and *Music Weekly*. *Record Mirror* was my favourite because it had specialist charts as well as the most comprehensive pop charts. On Fridays he'd say, 'We'd better leave now or you'll miss *Ready Steady Go*.' He knew that's where my weekend started and how distressed I'd be to miss it.

I was infatuated with the Pretty Things, the latest R&B group off the rank and, from photos I'd seen, the roughest and hairiest of the lot. I decided I was going to grow my hair as long as singer Phil May's. The longer it grew, the more grief I got

39

from the blokes in the timber yard, jeering, 'Can I carry your handbag?' and giving me the odd wolf whistle. One week in particular, I read that the Pretty Things were making their debut on *Ready Steady Go* performing their first single – 'Rosalyn'. It was a frenetic take on the Bo Diddley riff, driven by maracas, a pulsing beat and with a snarling vocal. We always had afternoon tea when we got back and my dad was in his favourite chair in front of the television, reading the *Daily Telegraph*, while I was waiting excitedly for the Pretty Things to appear. Suddenly, there they were in all their dishevelled, long-haired splendour. Out of the corner of my eye I noticed Dad folding down the paper so he could look over the top and saying, 'What in God's name is that?' I said, 'That, Dad, is the Pretty Things.' Up went the paper in disgust and I could hear him tutting under his breath, 'God help us all.' I had to stop myself shouting, 'Yes! Fantastic!' It was a great moment. I loved him dearly, but such was my delight at his reaction. I felt totally vindicated because he couldn't stand the music I was into.

I didn't manage to grow my hair to Phil May's length, otherwise my routine remained the same. It was too easy to fall back into it every day and with no urgency on my part to follow my dream. As would often prove to be the case, fate played its hand. Sometime in November, I heard a forthcoming single on *Saturday Club* by a group called the Artwoods. 'Sweet Mary' was a Leadbelly song that had been on a Cyril Davis All Stars EP on Pye, and the Artwoods performed it in very much the same way. That weekend my parents were going shopping in Newcastle as usual and I asked Mum if she wouldn't mind buying me the Artwoods' single from J.G. Windows in the arcade. I wrote everything down – the name, the title, and catalogue number. Sure enough, she went in and they had it, and she recognised the boy behind the counter as somebody I'd been at school with in Windermere. It was a boy called Ian Sutherland who Mum remembered as a very nice, very polite boy. At the Craig, parents were allowed to visit at weekends and we'd taken Ian out during one of their visits. He was working at J.G. Windows before Christmas to save up some money because he was off to London in January. He had an apprenticeship at the Savoy. And my mother said, 'Andrew wants to go to London as well. Why don't you go together?'

So that's how it came to pass after me bleating on about wanting to go to London, which my parents had never showed any signs of agreeing to. Here was my mum turning it into a reality because of a chance meeting with Ian. Simon was coming home for Christmas and would be driving back to London a week later. It was perfect. He was charged with taking the two of us down in his mini-van and helping us find somewhere cheap to stay and making sure we settled in OK.

It seems inconceivable even now. I'd only been to London a handful of times, and always with Mum and Dad. If he had business in London, Mum would sometimes go with him and they'd take me. We always seemed to go to a Whitehall Farce with Brian Rix in the evening. I can only think that they assumed I would be back in a matter of weeks with my tail between my legs. It would get the ridiculous dream out of my head and I'd settle down to a normal job. Maybe I'd even complete my education. As it was, I hadn't exactly strategised my assault on the music business. It was more a conviction that because I wanted it badly enough then it would happen. I knew I had a decent knowledge about music, having scrupulously read the music papers for years. I knew I could write reasonably well and I thought that was my way in. I was going to turn up at the offices of each of the papers and offer them my services. Jotting down their addresses was the only preparation I made, and I didn't even get that right. 'What if I don't get a job?' was never on my agenda.

Chapter 4
Landing on My Feet in London

Simon drove Ian and me down to London on the first Sunday after the New Year, arriving around 7.30 in the evening. Everything I brought down with me fitted into two suitcases, so no records, record player or guitar. I had £33 in my pocket. I needed to find a job and get settled first. Simon had arranged rooms at the YMCA on Russell Street off Tottenham Court Road and even stayed there himself that first night.

Keen as mustard and dressed in my brand-new suit, I trotted off to the address I had for the *Melody Maker* offices, arriving at nine o'clock on the dot. I didn't even get through the door of the six-storey building on Fleet Street, whose entrances, front and rear, were manned by security men in uniforms and peaked caps in the belief they were still in the army. I got a brusque, 'Where do you think you're going, sonny?' from the doorman. 'You have to write in and make an appointment.' I pathetically pleaded that I'd come all the way down from West Hartlepool, but he was having none of that.

So I moved on to *Record Mirror*, a twenty-minute walk away on Shaftsbury Avenue. I was allowed in this time by a couple of friendly girls on reception. I said, 'I'm looking for a job', and they said, 'Well there's nobody here at the moment.' They said it might be a while because everybody had been to a party the night before celebrating Georgie Fame and the Blue Flames getting to No. 1 with 'Yeh Yeh'. This was exactly the kind of life I wanted to be part of. After half an hour watching me twiddle my thumbs, the girls suggested I come back later.

Last on my list was the *New Musical Express* and an address I had at No. 5 Denmark Street where a sign on the door read 'Moved to Longacre', wherever that was. I felt like I'd already had my three strikes. I was starting to think, 'What do I do now?' It was still only eleven o'clock and, somewhat befuddled, I wandered across the road and stood outside Southern Music's offices at No. 8. Either side of the door there were displays of Pretty Things sheet music. I remembered noticing them the night before when we went out for a walk. Thinking they'd know where the *New Musical Express* had moved to, I went inside. Next thing somebody was asking 'Can I help you?' and I pitifully blurted out, 'I'm looking for a job.' The voice – I soon found out it belonged to Peter Foss, who ran the trade department – then said, 'How did you know we've got one?' I stared at him blankly till he asked, 'Can you do invoicing?' I must have muttered something about working in the office at my dad's timber merchants, because he offered me a job straight away. I took it without having a clue what it entailed or what music publishers did. I'd unwittingly become an invoice clerk at Southern Music, earning seven pounds and ten shillings a week plus Luncheon Vouchers – whatever they were. It was strict office hours – nine to five with an hour for lunch.

I'd been in London for less than twenty-four hours, but here I was sitting at a desk in Denmark Street with an invoice book in front of me, noting down sheet music sales for two of my favourite groups, the Rolling Stones and the Pretty Things. Ordering timber was a hell of a lot more complicated than this. After about twenty minutes Peter Foss explained, 'The door behind you goes down to a basement where we have a small recording studio. When musicians come in you might have to move your chair and get out of the way or hold the door open while they carry their equipment down.' It was another wow moment that there was a studio beneath me.

Later that morning, I saw somebody struggling to get through the door with a drum kit. I held the door open and immediately recognised Clem Cattini. He'd been the drummer in the Pirates. His photo was on an EP I had. He'd actually played on 'Shakin' All Over' and was in the Tornadoes when they recorded 'Telstar' with producer Joe Meek. I was still getting my head round Clem Cattini coming in when Brian Locking pushed through the door carrying a string bass. Brian 'Liquorice' Locking had taken over from Jet Harris in the Shadows a couple of years before and played on some of their biggest hits like 'Dance On' and 'Foot Tapper'. They were both legendary figures to me.

Surely, I wondered, every day can't be like this? At which point the day went from the bizarre to the surreal. I noticed Terry Kennedy's name on a list of phone contacts on the adjacent desk. He was part of Ivor Productions, whose name appeared in the credits for the Artwoods' single 'Sweet Mary', which had obviously been recorded in Southern's studio. This was the single that had set off the chain of events that resulted in my being there. It was pretty mind-blowing and still is when I think back to the synchronicity of events. It was almost as if it was out of my hands.

When we met up in the evening, Simon couldn't believe what had happened either. We phoned the parents, who were also in disbelief. I got the impression they were relieved that I'd basically landed an office job. I'm sure it helped quell some of my mum's fears that I would soon be swept into the pop world's den of iniquity.

Our next task was to find somewhere for me and Ian to live. That too was easy. We found a bedsit in Notting Hill Gate through the *Evening Standard* and moved straight into 16 Horbury Crescent, a short walk from Notting Hill Gate tube. I remained there

for two years. I rarely saw Ian because as part of his training at
the Savoy he was working shifts till late and I was getting up
early to get to Southern. We only really caught up at weekends.

The job was ridiculously straightforward. All I had to do was
note down the orders for sheet music across a series of columns in
a large invoice book. If the title was a Southern Music copyright, I'd
put the order in the first column and so on across each column for
all the other companies we provided and sold the sheet music for.
Walking up one side of Denmark Street and down the other, it was
clear that almost every other office was another music publisher
and Southern Music provided the sheet music for most of them.

The biggest one was Essex Music. It was a huge buzz because
the Rolling Stones were part of Essex Music. They were a magnet
for so many other acts: the publishing for the Who's Fabulous
Music, the Moody Blues, Procul Harum, David Bowie and Marc
Bolan all eventually went through Essex Music. At the end of the
day I'd take the invoice book up to the accounts department on
the fourth floor and they'd apportion what they owed in royalties
on the sheet music. The invoice book would be back on my desk
the next morning. Every day was exactly the same.

Sometimes I'd also pick out the order, which might be ones or
twos of things but more often than not it might be for a distributor, so it could be fifty copies or more. There was a set way of doing
things going back decades; sheet music was packaged in units of
25 one way and then 25 the other way round. At Southern this
was always done by Mr Hart, who made up immaculate parcels
wrapped in brown paper and string. Mr Hart was a grumpy
oriental-looking chap who'd been there for years. He was a Mill-
wall supporter, which probably explained his glum outlook on life.

The trade department also had an office boy who did all
the running around. The 'trade boys' delivered the sheet music
packages to nearby shops and distributors around Soho and the
West End, and last thing made a trip to the post office lugging

45

a wooden railway porter's trolley behind. If the office boy didn't show up, was on holiday or off sick, it fell to me to do that job. Quite often Elton John – in those days Reg Dwight – who was in the trade department at Mills Music on the other side of the road would be racing alongside me to catch the last post.

The downstairs studio was always busy. Mike Vernon was a regular outside producer. He worked at Decca, where he went on to produce the classic Eric Clapton and Peter Green albums with John Mayall's Bluesbreakers and later founded the Blue Horizon label. Mike was producing the Artwoods' debut album in the basement. When I introduced myself he remembered my name as a subscriber to *R&B Monthly*; he used to address and post the envelopes himself. I chatted to several of the Artwoods, particularly Art Wood, drummer Keef Hartley, formerly with Rory Storm and the Hurricanes, and guitarist Derek Griffiths, who always arrived on a bike and we'd have to find somewhere to stash it.

I took my lunch break between 2 and 3 p.m. and was left manning the office while everybody else took theirs an hour earlier. About a month after I'd started at Southern a boyish-looking lad walked in wearing a jean jacket, blue jeans and denim cap. He introduced himself as Donovan and asked if Peter Eden, his manager, had been in. I said I'd not seen him yet, so Donovan hung around and we got chatting. He had a very softly spoken Scottish accent and almost self-consciously said, 'I've got a record coming out soon.' It was 'Catch the Wind', which he'd recorded in the basement. Only a couple of weeks later he made a huge impact appearing on *Ready Steady Go* and was invited back over three consecutive weeks. 'Catch the Wind' made it to No. 4 in the charts a few weeks later. I gave him a copy of a Woodie Guthrie book we sold, and we became quite matey for a while. He'd drop by with Gypsy Dave and a harmonica player called Mox, who had the longest bright orange hair I'd ever seen. It was longer even than Phil May's. We'd usually go next door to the Giaconda coffee bar.

Southern was on a bit of a high, first with Donovan, then the Ivy League. They had the first in a handful of hits with 'Funny How Love Can Be' and later 'Tossin' and Turning' – both Top 10. The group was built around session singers John Carter (nee Shakespeare) and Ken Lewis (Hawker), writers on Southern Music's books, who'd arrived in London from Birmingham in 1959. They were always lurking around the offices and penned countless hits during the 1960s. Denmark Street had been established as Britain's Tin Pan Alley in the 1950s and, even though groups were now encouraged to write their own songs, the street was still a hub for seasoned songwriters such as Tony Hatch, Barry Mason, Phil Coulter, Geoff Stephens, Ken Howard, Alan Blaikley and Les Reed. They were still in demand, providing songs for the likes of Cliff Richard, Sandie Shaw, Cilla Black, Tom Jones and Petula Clark.

By 1965, the new and the old worlds of British popular music were coming together in Denmark Street. The old was still represented by the likes of Lawrence Wright and theatrical and show tune publishers Noel Gay. Lawrence Wright was the first composer and publisher to set up his office in the street in 1911 in the same basement as our studio. His motto was 'You can't go wrong with the Wright songs'.* Box and Cox were next to us at No. 7. They were best known for publishing 'I've Got a Lovely Bunch of Coconuts'. It was run by two gents called Elton Box and Desmond 'Sonny' Cox – straight out of P.G. Wodehouse's *The Delayed Exit of Claude and Eustace*. I took some brass band arrangements to their office; it was just one room with a coal fire burning all day and probably all year round. One day Peter Foss was excitedly chatting with two very old ladies who I assumed were his aunties until he told me they were Elsie and Doris Waters, music hall comics and singers who'd created the Cockney characters Gert

---

* The other main studio was Central Sound, above the Giaconda. Years later, Lemmy told me that his Blackpool beat group the Rockin' Vicars recorded there.

47

and Daisy, a hugely popular wartime radio show. I told my mum, who was far more impressed by that than me meeting Donovan or seeing the Stones outside in the street.

During the 1960s a number of recording studios opened on Denmark Street. The best known was Regent Sound, at No. 4, where the Rolling Stones recorded 'Not Fade Away' and the whole of their debut album. So many other 1960s groups and artists recorded demos or singles there, including Tom Jones, Sandie Shaw, the Yardbirds, the Easybeats and the Bee Gees. The Kinks recorded many of their early demos there, including 'You Really Got Me'. The Kinks had a complicated management set-up; one of their managers was Larry Page, who ran Denmark Productions with publisher Eddie Krassner whose office was situated at No. 25. Page's other major success story came with the Troggs and 'Wild Thing', also demoed at Regent Sound.*

There were agencies in the street too. Jimmy Duncan and Bryan Morrison's management agency was actually on Charing Cross Road on the corner. They managed the Pretty Things and the Fairies. Roy Tempest's agency was renowned for booking tours for American groups where there'd often be only one founder member to be found, like the Original Drifters, the Fabulous Temptations or the Dynamic Isley Brothers. Elton John's early group Bluesology did quite a few tours backing such groups. The street was full of characters. Even the guy who ran the newspaper stall had a story to tell. Jimmy Logie won two First Division titles with Arsenal and played in their 1950 FA Cup victory. After sixteen years with Arsenal he backed a few too many wrong horses from the racing pages of the papers he was now selling.

---

* Wright also started *Melody Maker* in 1926, while promoter Maurice Kinn founded the *New Musical Express* in 1952 across the road at No. 5. They compiled the UK's first singles chart based on record sales, which eventually replaced sheet music sales.

It wasn't till the rock era in the 1970s that music shops, particularly guitar shops, dominated Denmark Street. In 1965, most of them were either in Shaftsbury Avenue or in New Oxford Street at one end of Denmark Street and Charing Cross Road at the other. Ronnie Wood used to spend days in Joe and Lou Macari's guitar shop. It was one of the first to open in Denmark Street at No. 22. Pete Townshend said it was where he first discovered the original Tone Bender fuzz boxes.

Denmark Street was a magnet for musicians congregating in the Giaconda or one of the two pubs at either end – The Crown (on new Oxford Street) and the Royal George (on Charing Cross Road). In the Giaconda, next door to Southern, one Luncheon Voucher would get you shepherd's pie and beans or spaghetti bolognese with change for a coffee or a Coca Cola. I remember excitedly sitting near Keith, Bill and Charlie from the Rolling Stones, probably recording at Regent Sound. There were regulars hanging out there most days, hoping something might turn up. That's what happened to Mitch Mitchell and Noel Redding. Mitch was very chatty. I knew he'd been in Georgie Fame's Blue Flames and was now in the Riot Squad. Mitch told me he'd just auditioned for a trio with an unknown American guitarist called Jimi Hendrix.

There can't have been a more perfect place to have landed on my feet – aged seventeen and totally naive about the music business. It didn't really matter that my job was mundane because I was getting such an insight into how the music business functioned. I made so many friends and even more connections with people who'd play a part in my life further down the line. I'd often go into a meeting and it would be, 'Oh, I remember you from Denmark Street.'

I certainly didn't have a lot of money for buying clothes but in the summer of 1965 I did buy myself a very mod, red-and-black-striped corduroy jacket that I was extremely proud of. I thought I looked the part and was stopped in the street to do an

49

interview for *Disc Weekly*. Next to a photo of me in my favourite jacket was a reasonably honest series of answers, although the fact that I liked shoes 'and spent about 4 or 5 guineas per pair' doesn't ring true. I could have bought three LPs for that.

Andrew the mod stopped on the street by *Disc Weekly*,
7 August 1965

I met Wayne Bardell on my second day at Southern Music during my lunch break. I wandered into Francis, Day & Hunter's store round the corner on Charing Cross Road. Half the basement space was a record counter on the right-hand side with the publishing company above. They also carried musical instruments and sheet music. Wayne's domain was the record counter and we got chatting. He asked what I was into and I said, 'The blues – you know, Howlin' Wolf, Sonny Boy William-son, Muddy Waters . . .' So he started playing records and that was how we became friends. I'd go in there every day and hear all the new releases. They stocked early Elektra albums on import and that's where I first heard the Paul Butterfield Blues Band and the first Love album. We were amazed the first time we saw full colour on both the front and rear sleeve of Love's self-titled debut. After a while I noticed that art director Bill Harvey's name appeared on every Elektra sleeve. No other pop label credited the art director, and almost every Elektra sleeve stood out in the racks. The impact that great artwork and graphics made was something I never forgot.

Wayne had been working at Francis, Day & Hunter for over a year and he filled me in on the people I'd see walking around Denmark Street and the key shops, pubs and venues stretching into nearby Soho and the West End. He seemed to know every-body too. Wayne was friendly with David Bowie dating back to when he was recording as Davy Jones with the Mannish Boys. I met Bowie a few times through Wayne, usually at the Royal George. I didn't take to him at all and tended to chat with his guitarist, who went by the name Teacup. I formed an opinion pretty quickly that unless you were going to further David Bowie's career, he wasn't particularly interested in talking to you. One day he told Wayne: 'You know that when I get famous I won't want to know you any more.' I thought that was a bit off, but Wayne said, 'Well, I can see what he means.' A few years

51

later Wayne was at a reception and he went up to say hello but was totally blanked. I thought, 'What a tosser', but Wayne was much more forgiving than me. What was clear, even in 1965, was that David Bowie was going to make it eventually and that you probably needed that kind of ruthless streak.

Andrew Oldham would come into Southern Music from time to time and speak to Peter Foss. I wasn't about to barge in just to say, 'Hello, and by the way we went to the same school.' One day Andrew came in during the lunch hour when I was there on my own. I was able to answer his questions and we chatted a while. Eventually I did mention I went to Wellingborough, and it got the reply I expected, along the lines of 'poor you' or 'never mind'. He was never going to say 'They were the best years of my life', but he writes about his school experiences in the first part of his brilliant autobiography *Stoned* with a fair amount of affection and in much the same way I enjoyed my time there.

Andrew went back to the school on speech day in 1964. Old boys were encouraged to attend open days or a sporting event. Andrew turned up with Keith Richards in an impressive blue Chevrolet Impala. He was still only twenty and already well known in his own right as a manager. Next time Andrew arrived in a Rolls-Royce with Reg King, his chauffeur-cum-bodyguard. It caused quite a stir with the boys while cocking a snook at some of the masters.

Our old drummer Mick had now left Wellingborough and we hatched a plan to hire a Rolls-Royce with a chauffeur in a kind of homage to Andrew. Mick said, 'My dad can sort that easily', so we drove up to the old school. It was a Saturday in late November 1965. There was a record player in the boot of the Rolls which had six slots for playing singles – we only had the one record and that was 'My Generation' which had just come out. We played it non-stop, singing along while glugging down cheap champagne. The words were never more meaningful. When we got to Wellingborough we were surprised to see Andrew and

Reg parked by the football pitch in the Rolls again. Mick went over to speak to him but I kept my distance. We had a great day watching the football and hanging out. When Andrew next came into Southern he snorted and said, 'Yes . . . very funny.'

What I never expected was that a few days later Reg King turned up and said, 'I've got to go to Wellingborough this Friday on a bit of business, do you wanna come with me when you get off work?' He was good looking, and very trendily dressed. I figured he must be OK because he worked with Andrew. He said, 'I'll come by at five to pick you up. Andrew's lending me the Roller.' So come Friday, there was Reg parked up outside. Two hours later we'd only got as far as the Finchley Road, caught up in a typical Friday-night traffic jam. I asked what time the meeting was, since I figured we wouldn't get there till at least nine o'clock. He said, 'It doesn't matter, it's kind of loose', which got me wondering what I'd got myself into. When we arrived, he asked where Hatton Hall was. I said it was a building about a mile away from the school itself. So this was where his 'meeting' was and why he wanted me along as a guide. We drove on and I pointed out the building. That's when things got even more fishy, because he chose not to drive right up to the hall entrance.

It was after lights out and the place was in darkness. He asked the whereabouts of one of the dormitories, which I said was on the first floor round the back. We crept round across the noisy gravel surface that made loud crunching noises in the silence of the night. I pointed out the window, whereupon Reg picked up a handful of gravel and tossed it up. A boy came to the window and opened it, but before any words were exchanged all the lights went on and a loud voice bellowed, 'I know you're out there and the police have been called.' Reg reacted like lightning and said, 'Right, into the bushes!' and we scampered off. I had no idea what was going on. There was a high wall around the building with bits of glass set in the bricks at the top. Reg barked, 'Give me your coat', and threw it over the wall. Very agilely he shinned up a tree and hauled me over, landing in an area of allotments and garden sheds. Reg looked around, pointing to one of the sheds, grabbed something lying on the ground and began levering off the lock. 'Get inside and down on the floor and keep quiet,' he commanded.

We could hear police car warning bells and could see the afterglow of rotating blue lights in the night sky through the filthy shed window. Silently crouched on the floor, I was terrified. It wasn't long till we could hear voices and the heavy footsteps of people prowling around. One of the voices said, 'I think they went up that way.' Once the voices hushed, Reg whispered, 'We'll stay here for another half hour.' I'd not uttered a word as time ticked slowly by. 'Can we go now?' I half pleaded. 'Not yet,' he said, 'let's wait another half an hour to be sure.'

I was now freezing cold and feeling numb from crouching down. At last Reg said, 'OK, let's get out of here.' So we made our way back to the Rolls, clambering over fences. I had visions of the Silver Cloud Rolls-Royce – which wasn't exactly incon-spicuous – being surrounded by police. I had no idea what Reg's bit of business had been, but clearly nothing legal. I just kept thinking, 'I'm going to end up in custody', which would cost me my job, and 'What on earth will my parents think?' It was my mum's worst fear.

We drove back to London in silence and arrived well after midnight. I was too scared to ask what he'd been up to, and he didn't volunteer anything. I'd known nothing about Reg or his reputation, but Wayne did and was aghast. He said, 'You went alone with Reg King! You must be mad.' I'd been so naive. As years went by, I heard plenty of outrageous stories about him. I never encountered Reg again. Whether he was there supplying drugs, or his accomplice at the window had stolen a load of silver trophies, I had no idea.

A few years later I heard Pete Townshend talking about Reg in a documentary where he described him as a complete thug. He was nicknamed Reg 'The Butcher'. Once, he and Andrew barged into a newspaper office and dangled a journalist out of a high window. Another time, when a record company employee leaked the title of the next Stones single, the pair supposedly threw him in a car and threatened to drop him in the Thames. There were so many rumours about him, although Marianne Faithfull described him as a sweetheart and said it was all an act. After the incident, I'd still see Andrew at Southern but nothing was ever said about what Reg had been up to that night, if he even knew. Reg had dropped me off outside my bedsit and for months afterwards I'd wake in a cold sweat thinking, 'He knows where I live.'

Chapter 5
Anyway Anyhow Anywhere

Wayne was far more confident than I was and knew his way
around. He'd talk to anyone where I would have held back.
There were places I probably wouldn't have risked going to
without a more outgoing mate to tag along with. I went to my
first gig in London with Wayne to see Long John Baldry and
the Hoochie Coochie Men at the Marquee early in February. I'd
bought Baldry's first single in 1964; 'You'll Be Mine' was a cover
of a Willie Dixon song. Despite a long history singing folk blues
in the 1950s, as a member of Alexis Korner's Blues Incorporated
and with Cyril Davies' breakaway All Stars, the R&B boom had
left Long John Baldry behind. The Rolling Stones provided the
basic model for most R&B groups, all now beginning to wean
themselves away from R&B covers and making the pop charts.
The likes of the Yardbirds, the Pretty Things, Them and Manfred
Mann all featured a lead singer who played harmonica and
shook maracas; some added a keyboard, otherwise it was only
the length of hair and the differing degrees of sneering vocals
that set them apart. The lanky, well-dressed Long John Baldry's
genteel approach had dated but that didn't stop me enjoying it
immensely, along with the thrill of being at the Marquee in its
most celebrated location at 90 Wardour Street. And the band
had some top musicians in bassist Cliff Barton and pianist Ian
Armit, both highly rated on the scene.

I didn't know that Rod Stewart had parted company with
Baldry a few months earlier and he was now supporting him,
backed by a decent Southampton R&B band called the Soul
Agents. Rod already had the rep as 'Rod the Mod' and as we
arrived at the Marquee he was sitting at the ticket desk kicking
his legs out so we had to ask him to let us through. He was
checking out the girls coming in. Rod had the familiar mod
haircut and a tight-fitting suit. He got up on stage and sang a
few numbers with the Hoochie Coochie Men which really loos-
ened them up. It was the only time I ever saw Rod Stewart play.
There was a kerfuffle – people running around shouting – at the
end of the night. We were hanging around and Wayne went to
see what was going on. He came back and said it was just Long
John chasing Rod, who'd locked himself in the toilets at the
back to get away from him. I remember asking Wayne, 'What,
is Long John a homosexual?' and he said, 'Didn't you know?' It
was apparently common knowledge but, despite having been to
boarding school, I was pretty naive and it never occurred to me.
He was a real character and supposedly recruited Rod into the
band after hearing him singing on Twickenham railway station.

Three weeks later I was back at the Marquee for 'An Evening
with the Blues' with Long John Baldry again, on a bill with
Chris Barber, but headlined by Buddy Guy. It was the only time
I ever saw Chris Barber play; this was his 'Jazz and Blues Band'
with a really good but unheralded electric guitarist called John
Slaughter. It was Buddy Guy I was there to see though. He
was one of the younger generation of Chicago bluesmen. I had
bought a few of his singles on Chess and loved 'First Time I Met
the Blues', so this was a must. Buddy Guy was mind-blowing
and his performance still ranks as one of the best things I've
ever seen in my life. He was young and good-looking and dressed
in a smart suit. He played a biting, penetrating Fender Strat
that was totally exhilarating in itself, but he also delved into a

57

full bag of tricks for good measure; playing with his teeth, with the guitar behind his back and while gyrating on the floor – everyone there had their mouths open. It was mental. There was no doubting that you could see where Jimi Hendrix got some of his stage moves and tricks. Twenty-five years later I spent time with Buddy Guy and he said he'd got them from Guitar Slim in Louisiana. It was all part of a tradition where each new player added their own unique brand of showmanship.

My third gig at the Marquee on 8 March was historic; it was Jeff Beck's first London gig with the Yardbirds. He'd come into Southern the week before and excitedly told me, 'Eric's left the Yardbirds and I've just joined.' Incredibly, he'd been in the group for less than a week. Clapton had played his final gig with them on 3 March. The papers didn't even carry the story till the following week. Diehard fans would have spotted the change but there were no shouts of 'Where's Eric?' and the set list hadn't changed since *Five Live Yardbirds*. It was great hearing 'I'm a Man', 'Good Morning Little Schoolgirl' and 'Smokestack Lightning', even though Jeff Beck was months away from injecting the more experimental sounds and effects and Eastern influences he brought to the Yardbirds.

Towards the end of March I braved the more intimidating experience of my first Flamingo all-nighter. The Flamingo was very popular with West Indians and American airmen stationed just outside London on weekend leave. The air force tried to ban them attending as too many GIs arrived back in their Oxford barracks barely fit for duty. It was also a favourite club with mods and hipper young white kids who were soul music fans first. Rik Gunnell, who ran the Flamingo, described the Marquee as a 'kiddie's club'. He had a point. The Flamingo, located at 33 Wardour Street, was pretty scary. It didn't have a drinks licence, but you could see heavies dealing drugs quite openly outside. Wayne had to stop me from gawping. Pill-popping was not so much tolerated as essential at the Flamingo; everybody was simultaneously chewing pills and gum.

Larry Williams and Johnny Guitar Watson played there on 27 March. Larry Williams used the same band that played with Little Richard. The Stormsville Shakers were the backing band at the Flamingo, one of many outfits who benefited from a Musicians' Union ruling whereby US acts couldn't bring their own bands over. I'd bought a couple of Larry Williams singles in the late 1950s; 'Bony Maronie' and 'Dizzy Miss Lizzy' were beat group staples. Larry Williams didn't disappoint but Johnny Guitar Watson was a revelation. He was the band leader and another outrageous showman. Larry usually began each song pounding on the piano and then Johnny took over, playing at breakneck speed and doing wild impromptu solos while the band somehow managed to keep pace. Larry went through his hits as well as 'Long Tall Sally', 'Slow Down' and 'Whole Lotta Shakin''. He came over as part Little Richard and part Jerry Lee. No complaints about that. It was a fantastic night.*

My second Flamingo gig was seeing Sugar Pie DeSanto sometime in April. She was signed to Chess, and 'Soulful Dress' was a real mods' favourite. Her name is never mentioned without adding the adjective 'diminutive'. She was four foot eleven inches tall and her act was non-stop action, complete with crazy dancing and even back flips. She was a kind of female James Brown and had been part of his famous revue. Every night she would pick somebody out from the audience and call them up on stage at the end of her set. The night I was there this young black guy got the treatment and was shamelessly mauled by

---

* Mike Vernon made a record with them for Decca – *The Larry Williams Show featuring Johnny Guitar Watson* – and Guy Stevens made another album on Sue – *Larry Williams on Stage*. Both were actually recorded in studios during those UK dates.

her on stage. I began co-managing a group called C-Jam Blues at the end of that year. I got talking to Cess, their singer, about seeing Sugar Pie DeSanto that night and he said, 'Tell me about it – that was me.'

I saw the Animals at the Flamingo, not a typical Flamingo group but they totally let rip with Alan Price's driving organ sound offset by Eric Burdon's belting voice. He had an incredible presence and they had a brilliantly eclectic repertoire. Guitarist Hilton Valentine was always criminally overlooked. Over the coming months I also saw Zoot Money's Big Roll, Georgie Fame and the Blue Flames, Geno Washington and the Ram Jam Band, John Lee Hooker with Tony McPhee (in John Lee's Groundhogs) and Chris Farlowe and the Thunderbirds with Albert Lee on guitar. He was another familiar face from working at Selmers Music Shop on Charing Cross Road. The Flamingo groups – aside from Georgie Fame – didn't have regular hits, if at all; most fell into a loose black Flamingo style based on cool repertoires mixing soul, ska and jazz.

I heard about the Who through John Carter and Ken Lewis. They'd recently done a session for Shel Talmy doing backing vocals on the Who's first single. That single was 'I Can't Explain', released on 15 January. They told me the Who had a residency at the Marquee and were amazing. The Tuesday night residency had begun in November and would run till 27 April. It was the brainchild of managers Kit Lambert and Chris Stamp, securing a block of dates on a Tuesday, always the hardest night for any club to sell. A couple of weeks after 'I Can't Explain' was released the Who appeared on *Ready Steady Go*, after which everybody was talking about them.

I didn't get along to see them till the first Tuesday in March and they completely blew my socks off. 'I Can't Explain' was slow out of the traps and had taken weeks to chart. They were absolutely stunning. The dates were touted as 'Maximum R&B'

but the Who's take on R&B was like nothing else I'd witnessed. Their set was almost all covers from James Brown to Muddy Waters, but best of all was a new song of their own being played for the first time. 'Anyway Anyhow Anywhere' was totally wild and totally captured the Who's musical violence and prowling aggression on stage – all, that is, aside from statuesque bass player John Entwistle. Till seeing the Who I'd thought the Pretty Things embodied the sound of disrespectful youth, but the Who upped the ante.

I went to see them three more times. The last time it took a good half hour to inch our way into the hall. People at the front were fainting and being carried out above the heads in the crowd. The condensation was like a steady drizzle dripping down and it was too crushed to even lift your arm high enough to swig your drink. I was soaked by the end. It was an event just being there and I knew it was something important. 'Anyway Anyhow Anywhere' came out a month later, much shorter than they played it live but still one of the most innovatory singles ever. Nothing was going to change my love of records, but live music was something else. It was about the now – about a moment in time nobody could ever take away from you. After three months of gig-going, seeing the Who and Buddy Guy had me hooked for life. Just as well, since going to endless gigs would soon become an occupational necessity.

Ian Sutherland left Horbury Crescent after about six months because he wanted somewhere nearer the Savoy. I couldn't afford to pay the full five guineas a week, so I moved to a smaller single bedsit in the same house where the rent was an affordable 2 pounds and 5 shillings a week. My meagre Southern Music pay packet didn't stretch too far but I was very good about keeping the rent money back and my Luncheon Vouchers ensured I had one square meal a day, usually at the Giaconda. What few records I bought were mostly singles because a

61

32-shilling LP was a fifth of what I took home. With the thrill of live music eating into my budget, I learned to nurse drinks as long as possible and I walked everywhere I could.

There were so many memorable gigs during my first year in London, although I never got to see the Pretty Things. I did get to see the Small Faces around the time 'Sha-La-La-La-Lee' was a massive hit in February 1966. Ian McLagan had just joined the band when I saw them at Tiles; they were shambolic sound-wise but got away with it by sheer force of personality. Tiles was on Oxford Street opposite the 100 Club. It was a bizarre set-up; the owners tried to create a mini shopping mall for the in-crowd with record and clothes shops, beauty salons and a soft drinks bar. Resident DJs included Kenny Everett, Jeff Dexter and even John Peel.

It wasn't until early summer 1966 that I went to Klooks Kleek, upstairs at the Railway Hotel on West End Lane. I'd been told that if the band playing there had a Hammond organ – and usually a hefty Leslie amp to go with it – you could ingratiate yourself by offering to help drag the heavy gear upstairs. Bands came with just a driver and a humper at best. The first time I tried it was when John Mayall's Bluesbreakers were playing there not long before Eric Clapton left. The ploy worked and I was allowed to stay till it opened. The venue was like a large living room; there was no stage and it was fully carpeted with thick red velvet curtains and flock wallpaper all around. Seeing any band there was totally up close and personal. I hadn't heard a lot by John Mayall. I'd bought a couple of singles, his debut 'Crawlin' Up a Hill' and 'I'm Your Witchdoctor', his sole Imme-diate single, which featured an amazingly ferocious solo by Eric Clapton. They played mostly familiar blues and R&B songs such as 'Stormy Monday', 'All Your Love' and the fiery instrumental 'Steppin' Out'. The famous *Beano* album wasn't released till after Clapton had jumped ship. What stayed with me was his intensity and passionate soloing, which more than lived up to his godlike reputation. The memory of that night grew in significance once everybody began talking about Cream.

I'd seen the Graham Bond Organisation play at the 100 Club in 1965. The first LP I bought in London was their seething *The Sound of 65*. They looked and sounded like no other R&B group I'd heard. All four members had started out as jazz musicians. Significantly they had no guitarist once John McLaughlin left and was replaced by saxophonist Dick Heckstall-Smith. They were so powerful on record and even more so on stage, where Graham Bond's Hammond organ and Ginger Baker's drumming were both equally explosive. It was hard to tear your eyes off Ginger. He had such a physical presence, but Jack Bruce stood his ground, stepping up with his wailing harmonica piece 'Train Time', which carried into Cream's repertoire. I saw Cream soon enough at the Fishmonger's Arms in Wood Green under somewhat different circumstances, as the co-manager of a group called C-Jam Blues who were supporting them.

Chapter 6
C-Jam Blues and the Long Lost Weekend

Peter Austin worked upstairs at Southern for the publishing company. His job was to try and place songs or look for potential covers. He was a little older than me and we got talking and decided we wanted to find a group we could manage together.* Peter had met a couple of girls who told him about a band called C-Jam Blues who had a Sunday residency at the Witches Cauldron in Belsize Park. The venue alternated between folk nights,

---

* I was itching to find something more exciting than filling in an invoice book every day. At the beginning of 1966 Wayne and I came up with a plan that at the very least would get free records sent over from America. There were so many singles I read about in *Billboard* that weren't getting a UK release. Under the name Andrew Lauder Enterprises we fired off letters to small labels offering a deal for a potential UK release. The first response came from a tiny break-out label called Black Hawk Records out of Jamaica in New York, which sent a package containing two copies of Roy C's 'Shotgun Wedding'. The enclosed letter said, 'Please make your best offer', but we had no money or any way of putting it out. I thought we should tell Guy Stevens about it. He'd been taken on at Island as a freewheeling A&R man. He was already on it and Roy C's 'Shotgun Wedding' duly came out in April '66 and was Island's first Top 10 record since Millie's 'My Boy Lollipop'. An obscure Texas label sent us two copies of a weird polka instrumental single which we didn't follow up. That was it for Andrew Lauder Enterprises.

folk blues and R&B bands. C-Jam Blues – after the Duke Elling-
ton track – were more a soul band. We went to see them the
next available Sunday. The Witches Cauldron was a cellar dive
with a small stage in a setting of arty posters and tables with
candles in wine bottles. C-Jam Blues had a black singer called
Cecil James, known as Cess, and three white guys. The bass
player and drummer worked in a garage in Acton. Mel Buckley,
the guitar player, drove a taxi and was the main organiser for
the band. Cess looked good and had a decent enough voice for
the kind of songs they did – Marvin Gaye, Impressions, James
Brown, Sam & Dave. They had none of their own songs, but all
their soul covers were well chosen.

C-Jam Blues – learning the highs and lows of managing a
band

We had a chat with them and said we were working in the music business and would like to manage them. It wasn't much of a pitch but they weren't getting any other offers so they said, 'OK – see what you can do.' I mentioned the group to John Merritt at Burlington Music, the Decca group's publishing arm, who came into the Southern's office regularly and with whom I'd become quite friendly. He said he could get them an audition at Decca if they could get there one lunchtime to play in the canteen at Decca Records on the Embankment. He also arranged for Ivor Raymonde to come by; I knew the name from Dusty Springfield and Walker Brothers records he'd arranged. He liked the group and wanted to go ahead. The way it worked at Decca was that you had to record four tracks in a couple of hours in their studios in West Hampstead – next to the Railway Hotel. Gus Dudgeon was the engineer, already an up-and-coming producer. Once they had the tracks, they'd be assessed at the next A&R meeting.

We didn't put a lot of thought into it. Even I came away thinking it had none of the vibe they had playing live. I wasn't surprised when Decca turned them down. I'd go to the Witches Cauldron every Sunday and a few weeks later we were approached by Sean Blake, who announced himself as working in A&R for EMI Records. He had the most over-the-top plummy accent I'd ever heard, until he introduced us to his friend Tim Rice. Sean offered us a shot at making a record.

I'd been trying to find them more obscure songs and came up with a single on Stax by the Astors – called 'Candy', co-written by Steve Cropper. Sean thought it was a great choice, but it featured the Memphis Horns and we needed more of an arrangement than we could carry off as a four-piece. Tim suggested we meet his friend Andrew Lloyd Webber, who invited us round to his parents' swish apartment overlooking Hyde Park. I'm sure it was his first arrangement for a record company. We sat round his grand piano, where he came up with various ideas we

66

thought would work. Andrew then produced one or two bottles of fine wine and it was a very pleasant evening. We recorded 'Candy' a month later, but Andrew Lloyd Webber's arrangement made the Memphis Horns sound too much like Herb Alpert's Tijuana Brass. We got the nod from EMI anyway. Now we had a long wait to hear about scheduling the single.

Peter found an agent for the band. George Webb was a one-man operator, which was perfect for us. He was a former jazz pianist whose Dixielanders had been at the forefront of the post-war trad jazz revival. Having a single in the pipeline was enough to put pressure on George to get more gigs. I was the one usually tasked with going along with the band. It's fair to say that most of C-Jam Blues' gigs outside of the Witches Cauldron were eventful, to say the least. The first one George came up with was just off Brick Lane at the All-Star Club. As we walked in the first thing I noticed was a sign saying *Please leave all knives and weapons at the desk*. It was an almost entirely Jamaican crowd and all that was being played was bluebeat and ska. The stage itself was caged and you had to lock yourself in. I was left on the outside. It was an intimidating experience. Nobody announced the band. We were told to go on when the music stopped, at which point the dancehall completely cleared and everybody went to the bar round the back. After a while four or five blokes came back out, stood in front of the stage with their arms folded, and just stared up at the band. When they finished there was no applause. Nothing. We were due to play two sets but decided just to get the hell out of there.

The next weekend was the El Partido in Lewisham, which also played mostly Jamaican music. I'd never been south of the river and the band said they'd drop me off back home after the gig. I had just about enough money to get me there. I found my way to the El Partido and announced myself to the two bruisers on the door and said, 'I'm the manager of the C-Jam Blues.' They said,

'You are, are you? So where's your fucking band? They were due here an hour ago.' I went out looking for a phone box and phoned Mel, hoping he wouldn't pick up. He did and said, 'The van's broken down so we can't get there.' I don't know why they hadn't phoned the club, but I didn't fancy going back there myself to face the two heavies. There I was in Lewisham, it was pissing with rain by now and I had no money to get home. I trudged on back to Notting Hill and arrived home like a drowned rat.

We went back to George Webb and explained that he wasn't booking us in the right places. I said, 'We should be in the Rikki Tik in Hounslow, or the Manor House. They're the Mod hang-outs and they'll get the band.' He said he'd take that on board but then came up with a Sunday night at the Leeds International Club Festival. I'd got some money from my dad for some British Gas shares he'd bought for me when I was born. I was able to cash some in and put in fifty quid towards a new van. The guys in the garage found a Commer Van and assured me it would get us there and back. Halfway there, the brake went and was scraping across the tarmac. They patched it up, but we knew we'd have to stay in Leeds, find a garage and get the van fixed on the Monday. One of them had friends at Leeds University so we could crash there.

When we got to Leeds Town Hall we found there were three stages set up. George had told us there were multiple bands playing, but not that the other fourteen were steel drum bands. It was another disaster playing to an audience of middle-aged parents with kids at what was more a Caribbean festival. The organisers totally ignored me backstage and Cess had to sort out getting paid. It was unlikely to cover the garage bills plus my return trip to London next morning on a milk train. I arrived at work just on time. Managing C-Jam Blues was beginning to conflict with my job.

George wasn't delivering so Peter managed to arrange an appointment with Don Arden's Galaxy Entertainment agency during our lunch break. Their offices were just a short walk away in Soho, so it was doable. Unfortunately, it was the same day that *Top of the Pops* was being filmed and the Small Faces were on that night. Don had given them money to go buy new clothes. We sat in reception watching the clock tick by while they were larking around with Don. I didn't know about Don Arden's reputation, and he had another guy in with him. This was Pat Meehan, covered in tattoos and looking positively evil, standing behind Don not saying a word. 'So what's this group all about then?' was Don's brusque opening question. We told him about the single and how we weren't being booked into the right clubs. By now we were due back in ten minutes so it was a relief when he said, 'Give us a list of your dates and we'll come and see 'em.' We were happy to get out of there. We never got back to Don; we realised that if he liked the band, we'd be history. The whole set-up in his office with Pat there looking deliberately menacing was very much 'Don't waste my fucking time'.

Wayne and I knew John Gee and Jack Barrie at the Marquee because we were there so often and I told them about C-Jam Blues, how they were London-based and could cover at short notice. John put us on a reserve list and in the last week of July I got a call from George saying, 'Can you get hold of the boys tonight?' The Carlisle-based VIPs couldn't make it, so I said, 'OK, I'll round them up.' It was rash of me, but we'd be doing the Marquee a favour. Cess wasn't on the phone so Mel had to track him down. The others were at the garage, so that was fine. I wasn't supposed to use the phone at work for personal calls but had to keep calling Mel, who wasn't able to track Cess down. All the calls were going through the switchboard upstairs and our managing director Bob Kingston got wind of what was going on. The calls were easily tracked back to me and Peter. To cap it all, we ended up letting the Marquee down.

We were called in to explain ourselves to Mr Kingston. From

69

his point of view, we were using the company's time to manage
a group that they didn't even have the publishing for – not that
there was anything to publish. Peter was contrite and rightly
so – he had a lot more to lose; I should have just apologised, but
I was too hot-headed and besides, I was confident something was
happening with C-Jam Blues and I could foresee that clashing
with the job even more. I didn't take to being given an ultima-
tum of, 'Either you focus on your job here – give up the management idea – or you go.' So I said, 'I'll leave then.' It was a really
stupid thing to do. I was going home that weekend anyway; it
was the famous weekend of 30 July 1966 when England played
Germany in the World Cup Final. I left it till the next day to
break the news that I was out of a job.

'Candy' by C-Jam Blues was eventually released by Columbia
on 18 November. It was during the heyday of pirate radio. Peter
found out that if you wrote the B-side and gave the publishing
to a company called Pall Mall Music, they had an arrangement
with Radio London. If you agreed, your single would automatically go onto Radio London's schedule as a 'Radio London
Climber'. They even told us where it would land in their charts
over the next two weeks. After that we'd have to provide sales
information through EMI. Depending on the figures, they'd
either stick with it or drop the single.

So we had to write a B-side. Mel wrote the music and I came
up with the lyrics; the only ever Buckley/Lauder masterpiece
was called 'Stay at Home Girl'. It did the trick and we gave it to
Pall Mall Music and, sure enough, when 'Candy' came out they
played it about eight times a day, seven days a week. It sounded
good on the radio and went on their chart the next week and
went up the week after. I was convinced the record just might
take off. We also did a Radio Luxembourg interview with Alan
Freeman on a show with Lee Dorsey and we played a Radio
Caroline night miming to 'Candy' on a bill with Gerry Dorsey,

before he changed his name to Engelbert Humperdinck. By week three I was able to get the official sales figures from EMI to give to Radio London; 'Candy' had sold 735 copies. It wasn't enough.

Peter was still co-managing the band but obviously keeping his head down at work. C-Jam Blues were offered a coming-out party down in Kent. They played outside on a terrace and were really on it that night. Peter had a new Mini Cooper and we'd driven down together. It was a Sunday night and there wasn't much traffic on the way back, but Peter must have dozed off and the car drifted into the metal barrier in the centre of the motorway. I was nodding off too and we both came to with a start. Peter tried to drive across to the hard shoulder but came to a dead stop in the middle lane. We started to push the car to the side but in the distance we could see a large articulated lorry heading towards us in the same lane. He slammed his brakes on and steered the cab away to avoid us, but the back was swinging like a baseball bat across all three lanes. We ran like mad out of the way just as it swatted Peter's Mini Cooper a hundred yards down the road. We weren't injured at all, but I have no memory of how we got home. His car was a write-off and after that he cooled off on the band.

The last time I saw C-Jam Blues was at the Fishmonger's Arms in Wood Green, where they had a support slot for Cream. This wasn't long before Cream's first album, which was easily my most played album the rest of that year. Both bands played two sets. Mel was beside himself to be playing on a bill with his hero Eric Clapton. C-Jam Blues went down really well for their first set. Then Cream came on and were amazing – and very loud. The set was more or less everything from the first album. When C-Jam Blues came out again, Mel just froze. It was a tough ask following Cream and Mel had lost it so badly that he was mostly just aimlessly strumming. They got away with it because the audience was so stunned by Cream that they didn't much care anyway. It was something to have supported Cream, but too many of the gigs had been one calamity after another. Something always seemed to go wrong.

I was still going to gigs with Wayne most weeks. In late November Wayne heard about a fiery American guitar player who had just arrived in London. I didn't twig that he was the guitarist Mitch Mitchell mentioned in the Giaconda. Wayne had a way of getting into gigs and that's how we went to see Jimi Hendrix at the Bag O'Nails for what was his first performance in this country. He didn't come on stage for ages, by which time I'd had far too many vodka and Cokes on an empty stomach. Suddenly, Hendrix strolled on looking almost sheepish until he started to play. It was overwhelming. The Bag O'Nails was a small cellar dive and the band was so unbelievably loud that it's nothing but a blur. It's embarrassing but I remember very little about the gig.

I saw Hendrix at the Flamingo on 4 February though, and that was rammed. I got there early because 'Hey Joe' had gone Top 10 that week. This time I took it all in and it was incredible. The band looked great too, the familiar flamboyant image and the wild haircuts were in place, and it did make me think of Buddy Guy in terms of Jimi's showmanship, but Hendrix brought something new. He was using a lot of effects and creating sounds that nobody before had ever conjured up. He was still playing the blues but not as anyone knew it, transformed into something which was vivid and expressionistic and still ferociously loud. I even got to see him a third time at the Saville Theatre, one of only two occasions I went there; the other was to see Cream. We knew what to expect from Hendrix by then, but it was no less amazing. I'm sure no two performances were ever the same and I feel privileged to have seen him three times in those early months.

After I left Southern Music I wasn't able to get another job during the rest of the year. In all honesty, I didn't try that hard.

I cashed in more British Gas shares for a couple of hundred quid which more than covered what I would have earned at Southern. I wrote to all the major record companies and got the standard polite brush-off. I became very lazy. One day I woke up and there were sixty-five milk bottles stacked up around the bedsit – they'd accumulated in every corner, some of them still had the rancid dregs of milk in them. It was so unlike me to be such a slob but typical of my five-month-long Lost Weekend.

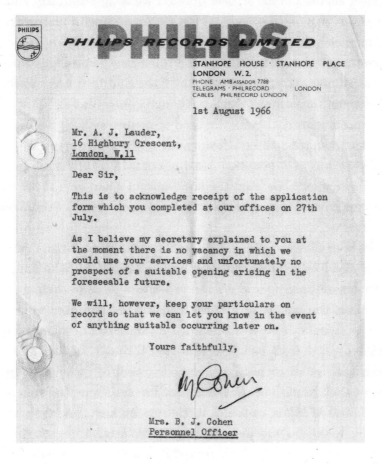

All four major record labels rejected Andrew's services

I'd get up late every day, go to various record shops where I couldn't risk buying anything then meet Wayne at lunchtime. If we didn't go to a gig after he'd finished work I'd hang out with the girls who'd first turned us on to C-Jam Blues. I used to go round to their bedsit, smoke a lot of dope and listen to records and then shuffle off to their local, the Devonshire Arms on Marloes Road, Kensington, opposite St Mary Abbot's Hospital where Jimi Hendrix died.

After seeing photos of Eric Clapton wearing a military jacket, one of the girls – Rosemary Watson – came up with an idea to try and get hold of some old military jackets, tart them up to make them more colourful and sell them down Portobello Road. We heard about a warehouse in the East End that had hundreds of these old uniforms. Rosemary thought we could turn this into a business venture. It was the kind of money-making madness that sounded great after a few drinks, but we all agreed it wasn't as daft as it sounded. Having nothing better to do, I said I'd help out. We filled the back seat of a car with these old uniforms from the warehouse which I fronted some of the money for.

Rosemary began creating these hot new fashion items. She was chatted up by a journalist from the *Daily Mail* who had overheard us talking and offered to write a piece in the paper. I had one of the first jackets she'd transformed and used to wear it round London. I always thought I looked pretty cool, although I did get abuse from people who'd lived through the war and thought it was disrespectful. They borrowed my jacket for the photo to run alongside the feature and asked Tom McGuinness from Manfred Mann to model it. He was bulkier than me and in order to do the buttons up at the front they had to cut the jacket down the back, which ruined it. I was a bit pissed off with that and then, once the paper appeared, it focused on how it was illegal to deface military uniforms – or even to wear them. In the New Year Jimi Hendrix popularised military jackets even more – and we were months ahead of *Sgt Pepper* – but we'd all lost interest by then.

I went home for Christmas and knew that I couldn't carry on doing nothing when I came back to London at the beginning of 1967. Everyone's enthusiasm for C-Jam Blues had waned. Once the single flopped, EMI had no interest in making another, so we went in different directions and I made my way to the Job Centre. They asked what I wanted to do and I said, 'Anything to do with music.' The girl at the desk flicked through a card index and said there was a vacancy at the Performing Rights Society for a filing clerk. Even after a year and a half as an invoice clerk this really was the most boring job in the world, sitting facing a wall of filing cabinets, mindlessly registering musical compositions by an endless stream of complete unknowns. There was no redeeming feature other than getting paid. At least the office was in Berners Street, only a five-minute stroll to Denmark Street where I'd meet up with Wayne. Since I'd left Southern, I'd kept my hopes alive that something would turn up and most likely through somebody in Denmark Street. That's exactly what happened, and it was thanks to the first friend I'd made there – Wayne Bardell. Fate was working for me again.

PART TWO
Sideways Through Time, 1967–1977

Chapter 7
Liberty Records – Living the Dream

I'd gone to Francis, Day & Hunter as usual to meet Wayne at lunchtime and he said an American guy had come in earlier and it was Bob Reisdorff. Fortunately for me, Wayne was such a record fan that he knew who he was and they got talking. Bob told him he was in London to set up a UK office for Liberty Records and had left his number. I was too excited to leave it another day. I phoned Bob straight away from the office behind the counter. Wayne knew how much I wanted to get a job at a record company. I had no idea how lucky I was that Liberty Records was that record company.

Bob picked up straight away and I just blathered down the phone to try and impress him with my knowledge about what he'd done and what I knew about Liberty Records. I knew it had put out the Ventures records in the early 1960s; plus there was Eddie Cochran, Jan & Dean, and the Crickets after Buddy Holly's death. I'd started learning guitar to the Ventures and had bought 'Walk Don't Run' and 'Perfidia' and other early instrumental hits which Bob produced for Dolton. That was his label, which he later sold to Liberty. Our first meeting went well and he said to come round to his flat in Knightsbridge. We had a couple of dinners and talked about everything under the sun, not simply music. He could obviously tell I was keen and knowledgeable for someone my age.

Bob had a very subdued American accent, almost Anglicised, and was by no means the clichéd blustering, cigar-chewing American Record Man. He was tempted to come back to England where he'd lived after the war, had made friends here and relished the challenge of setting up a UK office. After those meetings, he said, 'I'd really like you to join us but I don't know what you're going to do – we'll just figure it out.' I started working there in early May and was paid 18 guineas a week, substantially more than I'd been getting at Southern.

Liberty Records had been founded in 1955 but it was incoming president Al Bennett who turned the company round a few years later, and he was still running the label in the States. The breakthrough came with Julie London's 'Cry Me a River' in 1958, but it was teen pop and novelty records that Liberty soon became known for, notably a succession of hits by the Chipmunks who took on the names of the chief Liberty executives Simon, Theodore and Alvin – the latter after Al Bennett. The pop acts that sustained them as well as the Ventures included Johnny Burnette, Gary Lewis and the Playboys, Jan & Dean and Bobby Vee, who was easily Liberty's biggest selling act in the UK. Their only true rocker was Eddie Cochran, who, like Gene Vincent, had bigger hits in Britain than in America with 'Summertime Blues', 'Somethin' Else' and 'C'mon Everybody'. They'd all first come out on London Records here, marketed by Decca.

Al Bennett had sold Liberty to electronics company Avnet in 1962 and bought the label back two years later for two thirds of what he'd sold it for. Liberty by then included the Imperial and Minit labels. I knew about both: Imperial for releasing Fats Domino and Ricky Nelson records; Minit was a New Orleans label with a roster including Allen Toussaint, Irma Thomas and Aaron Neville. Al Bennett also brought Pacific Jazz and World Pacific and Blue Note under the Liberty umbrella. This was an incredibly broad catalogue base available for release in the UK.

80

So much of it was totally up my street, and the more I discovered, the more excited I became.

I met Al Bennett soon enough. He was a big man, and a really ebullient character. He was born in Joiner in Mississippi County into a farming family and still had a farm in Arkansas. He once told me his ambition was to become governor of the state. When Al was in London he'd always stay at the Dorchester. I used to drop things off to him in the morning and he'd usually be there in his dressing gown, having been out wining, dining and gambling the night away. And it was always 'Great to see ya, Andy, how ya doing?' Nobody called me Andy, but I wasn't about to put him right.

Britain had become a hunting ground for new talent since the Beatles and the 'English Invasion' of America. That's what prompted Liberty to open an office here once their five-year deal with EMI had ended. That was another cause for excitement because Liberty was definitely looking to sign UK acts and had a completely clean slate. We started working at Metric Music, Liberty Records' publishing arm, operating out of Chappell Music's offices on Maddox Street. In June Liberty's new UK division moved into offices at 11 Albemarle Street in Mayfair. Bob was already building a team. The first person he brought in was a promotion man called Ronnie Bell, who I soon learned was a total legend among his peers. He'd also already hired an International Manager – a really good guy called Frank Davies – and Alan Keen, the former Head of Radio Luxembourg, looked after Metric Music. Alan in turn later took on Mike Batt as an in-house writer, arranger and producer. Bob very much wanted people that he liked around him. He trusted his instincts and it was only after we'd moved to Albemarle Street that I met Ray Williams, who'd been appointed as head of A&R.

Ray was a partner in his own Mayfair publicity company and was working with the Hollies, among others. Bob had a hunch

about this streetwise, good-looking young mod with a good reputation. Only after we'd got to know each other did Ray mention
he'd worked in Denmark Street in Noel Gay's office, representing
the likes of the Kinks, Sonny and Cher, and Tommy Roe. Roe's
management then hired him to work for their company in
Atlanta. Ray was incredibly experienced but didn't think he was
qualified for a job as an A&R man. Bob didn't complicate A&R
as anything more than 'Go out and find some acts and sell some
records.' You can't really argue with that. Ray was only a little
older than me and was brought up in the East End of London.
He introduced me to hip clubs like Blaises and the Speakeasy.
We got on really well and he wanted to move to somewhere more
central, so we decided to share a flat in Drayton Gardens in
South Kensington.

The Albemarle Street office was very smart and tastefully
furnished. It was above a Lloyds Bank on the corner. You came
in and up the stairs to reception on the first floor. That's where
Ronnie and I had our office. It was called the Exploitation Department, which makes it sound a lot more pernicious than it
was. Bob soon hired a production manager, Alan Whaley, who'd
come over from CBS. He never really engaged with the rest of us
and always seemed eager to get home of an evening.

My first task at Liberty couldn't have suited me any better. I
was handed a printout of what was available through the EMI
deal, plus all the sales figures, and Bob asked me to make a list
of what I thought we should put out. I identified around fifty
albums to give us an initial catalogue. I felt I'd been given an
extraordinary amount of responsibility. I had to be guided by the
figures, whatever I might be into personally. I was amazed that
country crooner Slim Whitman always sold so many records. As
did the lush orchestral MOR sounds of Tommy Garrett and his
50 Guitars. *Fats Domino's Greatest Hits* and the *Eddie Cochran
Memorial* album were also high on the list. Anything EMI had

previously released we just gave a new numbering system. My first week we hired a van to go to EMI and retrieve all the master tapes, records and files. I was in my element, clearing out the cupboards and shelves and then starting a new master file of the tapes I'd suggested. We did a deal with Philips for manufacturing, sales and distribution, so it was a completely new start. Liberty UK adopted a new label design, new house bags, new everything.

Ronnie Bell needed an assistant and that was another role I took on. So I became a promotions man, which was the last thing I expected. That was more daunting but still a thrill to be going into the BBC. It was hallowed ground. Ronnie Bell knew every-body and everybody liked him. He had the most conspicuous toupee I'd ever seen but, respectfully, nobody ever mentioned it. We got on famously even though he was in his early fifties when he joined Liberty. He'd started out at EMI in the classical divi-sion after the war before moving into light entertainment, where he witnessed the transition and rise of the LP in the 1950s and the switch from 78s to 45s. He'd worked for a succession of companies: EMI, MGM, Top Rank, Oriole, Pye and now Liberty.

There was nobody better to show me the ropes, basically telling me 'Do this or don't do that', and make friends with the secretaries at the BBC. They were the ones you'd always see – not the producers or the DJs. He did mention one or two I'd do best to avoid getting in a lift with. Ronnie would say, 'Just make sure our records are at the top of the pile on everybody's desk.' I'd discreetly fish through them and put ours on top. I'm sure every plugger did the same. I was also dealing with the remaining pirate stations, and Radio Luxembourg, which had been hit hard by the pirates; mostly I was just mailing records out to them.

The first album the new UK label released was something Bob picked up before we really got started; it was an LP by the Band of the Coldstream Guards. We released it in a bright, colourful gatefold sleeve and it sold surprisingly well. It never took up much of my day. More significantly, Liberty had an early hit with a record by Vicky Carr called 'It Must Be Him', which Ronnie thought was a cert to get airplay. She was a Texas-born nightclub singer who'd had a much-publicised relationship with Elvis Presley. It was hardly up my street, but I wasn't about to question Ronnie's judgement. It was perfect for request programmes and particularly the long-running *Two Way Family Favourites*. The producer agreed but said, 'I need a request before we can schedule it.' So we went back to the office and wrote a dozen postcards along the lines of 'Please play "It Must Be Him" by Vicky Carr for my husband at BFPO 49 in Germany.' And sure enough, a couple of weeks later there it was on *Two Way Family Favourites* and by mid-June it reached No. 2, selling over a million singles.

Easy-listening group the Johnny Mann Singers gave Liberty its second Top 10 hit by the end of the summer with their cover of 'Up Up and Away'. Liberty had started a label with Johnny Rivers called Soul City. Rivers churned out hit after hit in America, usually creating a good-time party atmosphere. Soul City had not only signed the Fifth Dimension but Jimmy Webb was signed to Rivers' publishing company, writing and arranging most of the songs on the first two Fifth Dimension albums, including their original hit version of 'Up Up and Away'. I did stick my oar in to say that the Fifth Dimension's original was much better, although I wasn't about to question why Ronnie had taken the Johnny Mann version to the BBC. It was a fantastic start for a new label to have two Top 10 hits within a couple of months, but I was itching to work on something that was more me.

Staple acts like the Ventures, Johnny Rivers and Bobby Vee were still releasing albums regularly and they'd usually be given

84

a UK release. There were enough instrumental fans out there to make it worthwhile to continue releasing Ventures albums. I was more interested in Jackie de Shannon, who'd initially been signed purely as a writer to Metric Music. She'd written so many great songs, not least 'Needles and Pins', but Liberty in the UK never promoted her as an artist. We brought her over when she had a Top 10 hit in the US with 'Put a Little Love in Your Heart'. I was introduced and said 'hello'. Her friend and co-writer Sharon Sheeley came with her.* She got friendly with Ray Williams and stayed overnight at our flat. About two in the morning I could hear them having a bit of a tiff and she stormed off and came into my room. She climbed into bed beside me, and I froze. All I could think was 'Eddie Cochran's ex-fiancée is in my bed.'

World Pacific and Pacific Jazz were intriguing labels both run by Dick Bock and I released four Ravi Shankar albums over the next couple of years which found a wider audience thanks to George Harrison. Just for the heck of it, I even scheduled a 'Best of' by hip, eccentric American comedian Lord Buckley. Blue Note we figured wasn't worth pressing here because jazz fans always wanted the American original; we imported them mostly for mail order and specialist shops. My immediate impression was that Liberty and Imperial were still living in the past and despite being based on the West Coast failed to pick up on what was happening on their doorstep. The charts were full of timeless hits being churned out by studios in Los Angeles during 1966 and '67 by the likes of the Byrds, the Beach Boys, the Mamas and the Papas, and the Turtles. The A&R guys at Liberty spent

---

* Sharon Sheeley was one of the few women to break into the male-dominated rock 'n' roll era in the 1950s. She wrote songs for Ricky Nelson ('Poor Little Fool'). Richie Valens and, with his brother Bob, co-wrote 'Somethin' Else' for her fiancé Eddie Cochran. She sustained serious injuries in the car crash that killed him. She wrote hits with Jackie DeShannon, and for Irma Thomas, the Crickets and Duane Eddy, among others.

more time on the golf course than checking out new groups and saw the new 'hippy thing' in San Francisco as just a passing fad.

I became fanatical about the San Francisco scene during the summer of 1966. Not long before leaving Southern, John Merritt from Burlington Music had brought in a copy of *Jefferson Airplane Takes Off* which wasn't released here. Their name alone sparked my interest and musically there were touches of folk, blues and a distinctive Byrds-like jangle with a very distinctive vocal sound and harmonies. I'd chanced upon a group that was at the centre of a growing underground subculture in San Francisco. I'd heard and read enough to make me want to find out more about the scene there. I already had the first two Beau Brummels albums that were on a small San Francisco label called Autumn Records; something was happening there.

At the same time I discovered a bunch of extraordinary posters in a bookshop off Kensington Church Street. They had an arrangement with City Lights in San Francisco and imported these incredible psychedelic posters with luminescent colours and amazing graphics that melted and flowed like the waves of an acid trip. They were for various bills in San Francisco venues such as the Avalon Ballroom, the Matrix, and soon the Fillmore Auditorium. I was intrigued by the names of bands such as Quicksilver Messenger Service, the Grateful Dead, Country Joe and the Fish, which were often billed alongside blues giants such as Bo Diddley, Junior Wells, Muddy Waters, and Chicago's Paul Butterfield Blues Band. San Francisco was the Mecca of the poster art movement led by Rick Griffin and Victor Moscoso. The posters were tantalising because in 1966 none of these weird-sounding bands had records out. If they lived up to their names, then I wanted to hear them. By the beginning of 1967 the San Francisco scene was on its way to becoming a media phenomenon that was being written about in *Newsweek*, the *New York Times*, *Life Magazine*, culminating in *Time Magazine* in July 1967. The photos of the bands in *Time* were something else; they all looked like they came from another planet.

Jefferson Airplane raised the profile of the scene to another level. They were the first San Francisco band to really break through commercially with their wonderfully evocative singles 'Somebody to Love' and 'White Rabbit' from their second album, *Surrealistic Pillow*. Both made the US Top 10 in June and July 1967 and were written by the incoming Grace Slick, who'd replaced original singer Signe Anderson. She had a powerful, soaring voice that blended distinctively with that of pop singer turned folkie Marty Balin. She also had photogenic looks; Grace Slick didn't look like she was from another planet.

Most of the other Bay Area bands I'd read about released fabulous debut albums in 1967, including the Grateful Dead, Big Brother and the Holding Company, Moby Grape and Country Joe and the Fish. I was particularly taken with a band called the Charlatans. They had peaked too early, been horribly screwed on a lousy deal and split up. The Charlatans had been there before it all began, playing a residency in the summer of 1965 at the Red Dog Saloon in the old mining town of Virginia City, Nevada. A poster designed by founder member George Hunter and drawn by piano player Mike Ferguson is generally acknowledged as the first example of psychedelic art. My passion for the San Francisco scene never ceased and for years to come it almost defined me as a 'man on a mission' to spread the word about the bands coming out of the city.

So it was galling to be sitting in my office, the UK outpost of a Los Angeles-based record label that was too slow off the mark as well as lacking the judgement to sign anything of merit. Imperial signed a light psychedelic group called The Moon and had sunshine pop groups like the Sunshine Company and the Love Generation. We did release some of these albums here, but they were no match for the Turtles or the Association. Liberty eventually signed a mediocre Los Angeles group called T.I.M.E. (which stood for Trust In Men Everywhere) which I put out, and more promisingly they signed Hour Glass, an early group with the then unknown Gregg and Duane Allman. I'd seen the group's name on various posters, but my expectations were deflated; their first album was dreadful, mostly songs that had been foisted on them. I did release the second one, *Power of Love*, which was far better but barely hinted at the potential of the Allman Brothers.

The advert that brought Elton John and Bernie Taupin together

It wasn't till October that the first UK signings started to come through. They had all come about after Ray Williams placed an advert in the 17 June 1967 edition of the *New Musical Express*. On page four of the paper, a large ad proclaimed LIBERTY WANTS TALENT. It was completely Ray's idea and it paid off when a sea of packages flooded into his office. It was from that announcement that the Idle Race, Family, and the Bonzo Dog Doo-Dah Band all came to his attention, and all were signed to Liberty in the autumn. The ad's gone down in history because two of the others who contacted Ray were Reg Dwight and Bernie Taupin. Reg recorded demos for Liberty at Regent Sound but neither Bob Reisdorff nor Alan King were impressed enough to sign him. Ray, however, remembered a letter from Bernie Taupin saying he wrote lyrics but couldn't write music – while Reg wrote music and could sing but couldn't write lyrics. The lightbulb went on for Ray, who was responsible for pairing them.

The Idle Race were the first signing to the UK division of Liberty Records; they also accepted a management deal from Ray. It's the kind of opportunism you could still get away with. The Idle Race evolved out of Birmingham beat groups Mike Sheridan and the Nightriders and Mike Sheridan's Lot, contemporaries of the Move, eventually becoming the Idle Race soon after Jeff Lynne replaced Sheridan. It was Lynne who contributed most of their original songs; he both wrote and shaped them with a flair for melody and a lyrical invention and humour that he carried into all his later work. The first single was a Jeff Lynne song called 'Imposters of Life's Magazine' which was very much inspired by *Sgt Pepper*'s studio innovations. Ray did most of the running with the Idle Race, but I was still involved in handling radio promotion.

Ronnie Bell (standing) and Bob Reisdorff, signing the Idle Race

Radio One had launched in September and 'Imposters of Life's Magazine' was the first record I could take to John Peel and his producer Bernie Andrews with any degree of confidence. Peel was now firmly installed as Radio One's key underground DJ and the Idle Race became firm Peel favourites. Everybody at the BBC seemed to love the band. Kenny Everett went as far as describing them as second only to the Beatles. We got a lot of airplay and they did numerous daytime and evening sessions for the BBC.

Yet 'Imposters of Life's Magazine' was never a hit, nor were the three singles that followed during 1968, all equally well received. Their debut album *The Birthday Party* met with the almost inevitable plaudits throughout the music press and on radio. It was Ray's idea to give the LP a lavish gatefold sleeve. Its inner gatefold spread was a photo that looked like a birthday party held in a school refectory. The finishing touch was to put an array of important people's heads on the bodies of those sat

round the tables. These included just about everybody from
Radio One. Even my face is superimposed on somebody's body –
I'm seated next to Alf Garnett actor Warren Mitchell.

Not long after the first Idle Race single I arrived at the office
one Monday morning to find that production manager Alan
Whaley was gone. I took over the desk he'd vacated and began
opening all the packages coming in, including all the singles and
albums being released in America. Nobody raised any objection
to me more or less taking over his duties. So I just carried on.
The following week Bob saw me sitting at the desk and as he
walked by said, 'You seem to have started doing this job, so you'd
better carry on.' He walked on by, turned around, smiled and
said, 'And there'll be a pay rise too.' It wasn't long before my job
as a plugger was phased out.

This happened just as we released the first and only single on
Liberty by Family. The gentle, haunting 'Scene Through the Eye of
a Lens' is rightly regarded as one of the great British psychedelic
singles. Ray and I were now going to a lot of gigs together. We
were considering two particular groups, but both were playing
the same night. Ray went off to see Ten Years After (who we
passed on) and I went to the Marquee to see Family. They had a
following in their hometown of Leicester and in the Midlands and
were now making inroads in London. They were still shedding the
hallmarks of an earlier R&B style but had something different
about them, not least cadaverous singer Roger Chapman's bleating, rasping vocals. I said we should sign Family and in the first
instance we agreed to release their debut single, produced by
Jimmy Miller. Miller was hot property, having remixed the Spencer Davis Group's powerhouse 'I'm a Man' single and then the
debut album by Traffic, the more cosmic and experimental group
which nineteen-year-old Stevie Winwood formed in 1967.

Family were managed by John Gilbert, an up-and-coming film
producer who was the son of the director Lewis Gilbert (whose

recent credits were *Alfie*, and *You Only Live Twice*, his first in a
number of James Bond films). Family were already recording an
album which Dave Mason was producing. He'd left Traffic – only
to return six months later before leaving again – in between he'd
released a solo single for Island, 'Just for You', on which he'd
been backed by Family. Mason had taken over because Jimmy
Miller was now recording the Rolling Stones' *Beggar's Banquet*.
John Gilbert arranged a champagne launch party around the
single at Sybilas which over 200 people turned up to, including
John and George with their wives Cynthia and Patti, and Brian
Jones. Family's transformation was complete by then, wearing
brightly coloured kaftans and sprouting fashionable facial hair.
They'd also adapted their instrumentation to include Jim King's
atmospheric flute and bass player Ric Grech doubling on violin.

Gilbert already had his sights set on the American market
and arranged to meet the American company in Los Angeles.
I was immediately concerned because I knew how square they
were. I couldn't see them getting their heads round Family's
strange brand of English psychedelia. While there he also met
with Warner Reprise, who'd already signed the Grateful Dead,
the Beau Brummels, Ry Cooder and Randy Newman, among
others. They wanted Family for the world, so we couldn't compete. I'd already done all the label copy for the album and the
artwork was also finished. The extraordinary *Music in a Doll's
House* was all but ready to go when the deal with us was pulled.
I was utterly dejected, even more so when it was released six
months later and became a major cult album overnight.

Ray was already set on signing the Bonzo Dog Doo-Dah
Band. Until I heard the album I'd more or less written them
off because they had a couple of singles on Parlophone in 1966
which were very much in the jokey trad band style of the New
Vaudeville Band. They'd had a huge hit in September that year

with 'Winchester Cathedral'. It even made No. 1 in America.* I'd
tarred the Bonzos with the same revivalist brush. The Bonzos
were actually an unruly bunch of art students who'd all attended
different art schools in London: Viv Stanshall and Legs Larry
Smith attended Central School of Art; Neil Innes, Goldsmiths;
Roger Ruskin Sear, Ealing; and Rodney Slater, St Martin's.
Stylistically they played some jazz age dance band oddities but
were far more anarchic and risqué, which blew all comparisons
with the staid New Vaudeville Band out of the water. Appropriately, they'd originally been called the Bonzo Dog Dada Band.

Having approached Ray, their manager Gerry Bron played us
their album *Gorilla* which he'd produced. Gerry Bron was a very
straight business guy and both the group's manager and booking
agent. I was more impressed that he was actress and satirist
Eleanor Bron's brother. We both thought the album was fantastic
and not at all what we expected. There were only a couple of
jazz age novelty songs, but both 'Jollity Farm' and 'Mickey's Son
and Daughter' were brilliantly tailored for the Bonzos' reimagin-
ing. They discovered the songs from rooting around piles of old
78s in junk shops. The rest of the album was made up of original
songs written by Viv Stanshall and Neil Innes, including soon-to-
be-classics 'Death Cab for Cutie' and 'The Intro and the Outro'.

I went to see them with Ray at Blaises in Queensgate a short
walk from our flat. Their live act was hysterical, and some of the
routines seemed completely unrehearsed. The stage was littered
with recycled props and domestic appliances and assorted instruments. Some of what became trademark Bonzo features were

---

* The New Vaudeville Band was initially made up of studio musicians put
together by Geoff Stephens, who I knew as a songwriter and co-manager of
Donovan. He needed a band to take out on tour and approached the Bonzo Dog
Doo-Dah Band. All bar one declined the offer. John Carter is the 'megaphoned'
singer on 'Winchester Cathedral'.

already in place – running gags, quick costume-change sketches, explosions and Roger Ruskin Spear's mad boffin exploits. I just remember being in pain from laughing so much. They had yet to add any kind of rock element but nothing about them or the album seemed dated or unlikely to appeal to rock audiences.

We did a launch at Raymond's Review Bar in October 1967 where the band played a half-hour set that got the press and radio onside immediately. Kenny Everett got behind them as he had with the Idle Race – and John Peel too; he would have a long association with the group and Viv in particular. You had to see the Bonzos play live for the full experience. It was probably like hearing *The Goon Show* on the radio for the first time in the 1950s. Gerry Bron worked them hard and once *Gorilla* was released they soon became favourites on the underground club, university and college circuits. Pretty soon they'd become one of the highest-paid bands in the country without a hit single.

The Beatles had already asked them to make a cameo appearance in their film *Magical Mystery Tour*. They performed 'Death Cab for Cutie', part American pulp novel pastiche, part Viv's exaggerated, speciality Elvis impersonation. They had so much going for them and nobody was going to rein them in. At the end of the year they also recorded the pilot for children's television's *Do Not Adjust Your Set*. It was an instant cult success; it wasn't just kids who watched every week mostly to see the Bonzo Dog Doo-Dah Band amid sketches by then unknowns Terry Jones, Michael Palin and Eric Idle.

The first Hapshash and the Coloured Coat album was released in November 1967. That was a different kind of anarchy. I heard that Guy Stevens wanted to come in and talk about an album he'd recorded with ultra-hip underground artists Nigel Weymouth and Michael English. Along with Australian ex-pat Martin Sharp they were responsible for so many of the vibrant psychedelic designs that identified the London underground,

including posters for the UFO and Middle Earth clubs. Nigel
had also opened the famous Granny Takes a Trip boutique on
Kings Road with his girlfriend in 1966.

I jumped at the chance of meeting Guy Stevens, although I
hoped he wouldn't remember how much I used to pester him to
come and see C-Jam Blues even though he never got back to me. I
first came across Guy as an enthusiastic writer about blues whose
passion for soul and R&B and his record collection, full of rare,
imported 45s, was legendary. He was a real mover and shaker
in that mod in-crowd. Chris Blackwell brought him in to take
charge of the cool Sue Records catalogue in 1964 for the fledgling
Island Records where he soon became an A&R man and producer.
The recording he brought in to Liberty was nothing less than a
psychedelic, bongo freak-out jam under the name Hapshash and
the Coloured Coat featuring the Human Host and the Heavy
Metal Kids – the first ever use of the term 'heavy metal' that I
can recall. The latter were members of the group Art (formerly
the VIPs) that Guy had signed to Island and soon became Spooky
Tooth under his guidance.* The *Hapshash* album was recorded
at Pye Studios, where 'the Heavy Metal Kids' laid down a series
of piano and rhythm tracks which provided the foundation for
a drugged and disorderly jam session dominated by various
percussion instruments and impromptu chanting led by Guy,
Mike and Nigel. They'd invited a load of their friends to a party

---

* Guy's credits as a producer at Island included Free's debut album *Tons of
Sobs*. He signed Art/Spooky Tooth and was fundamental in bringing Mott the
Hoople together, naming them, and producing their first two albums. After an
erratic period where he struggled with alcoholism and drugs, the Clash openly
acknowledged his past importance by asking him to produce *London Calling*,
where, as unconventionally as ever, he generated loads of energy. He died in 1981
from a prescription drug overdose. I last saw him when he came to the Radar
offices just before Christmas 1980. He was broke and in a bad state. I gave him
some money, ostensibly to get him to wherever he was going to spend Christmas.

at the studio where everyone dropped acid before being handed assorted hand drums, tambourines and whistles. The words were nonsensical and totally loopy. It was the sort of free-for-all that I imagined Ken Kesey's 'acid trips' must have sounded like and which I assumed Island Records had turned down.

Rather than release it on Liberty, we had just cleared the Minit label, so I suggested releasing the LP on Minit and on red vinyl. Michael and Nigel gave it a full-colour, psychedelic cover and a black and silver insert. It looked stunning. I knew it was important to seize the moment and it sold really well through the underground press because of the credibility of the three main protagonists. It also did well in France and Holland and, to my surprise, Imperial went for it in America. Looking back, I now find it hard to believe that nobody ever questioned me releasing it.

American blues band Canned Heat became a *cause célèbre* for Andrew

In much the same spirit of adventure I went outside the Liberty group and tried to license the first 13th Floor Elevators album from International Artists. I'd heard 'You're Gonna Miss Me', which I thought was totally out there on its own and had seen the group's name on various posters. The Elevators were from Texas but played some of the San Francisco ballrooms. I bought the album at One Stop Records on South Molton Street, which specialised in the best American imports. International Artists was a small independent label that nobody knew much about – nor was there any buzz about the band here. They wanted an advance that was too expensive for me to commit to making an offer. It was going too far out on a limb to license an album by a totally unknown band.

The most important act I picked up on in those early months as a product manager was Canned Heat. Liberty's American A&R department had at last come up with something which really excited me. The band had taken their name from an obscure late 1920s song by Tommy Johnson called 'Canned Heat Blues' about a drink brewed in the prohibition era from a household product called Sterno, a kind of jellied alcohol in a can used for cooking fuel. *Canned Heat* was a straight blues album, bordering on a heavier blues rock sound at times, and they were the first white American blues band to make an impact in the USA. They came after the Paul Butterfield Blues Band, which was a mixed-race band. *Canned Heat* was released in America soon after they played at the Monterey Pop Festival in June. I scheduled the album as soon as I could a few months later.

Bob Reisdorff said at the start that he expected Liberty UK to take at least two years to build any success, but so much had already been achieved in less than eight months. Brenton Wood's 'Gimme Little Sign' had even given Liberty Records UK its third Top 10 hit at the end of 1967 to put the seal on the label's broader and hipper achievements. I was twenty years old and definitely beginning to live the dream I'd had of being in the music business.

Chapter 8
Can Blue Men Sing the Whites?

I was taking something into Bob Reisdorff's office and recognised Bryan Morrison in the chair opposite him. Bryan remembered me from Denmark Street and Bob said, 'Since you two know each other, why don't you sit in on the meeting.' Bryan had two albums he'd made through his Bam-Bam production company, one by Alexis Korner, the other by Aynsley Dunbar's Retaliation. I said, 'That's fantastic', or something equally effusive. Korner was such a seminal figure through various incarnations of Blues Incorporated, which at different times featured Mick Jagger, Charlie Watts, Graham Bond, Jack Bruce and Ginger Baker. Wider recognition in his own right had eluded him. The album Morrison was touting was pretty much a solo album called *A New Generation of Blues*.

I knew that Aynsley Dunbar's Retaliation had released the second single for Mike Vernon's label Blue Horizon – the first having been by Peter Green's Fleetwood Mac, now at the fore-front of the second British blues boom. Aynsley had also served time in John Mayall's Bluesbreakers. Bob was keen to add more British records to the catalogue and my enthusiasm was such that he said, 'We'd better do a deal with Bryan for both albums.'

A New Generation of Blues sold poorly. Bob had trusted my instincts, which were based on Korner's reputation, but he was now playing mostly in folk clubs. It was an acoustic album featuring Alexis's own compositions, which was out of sync with the current blues boom. We went on to release four albums by Aynsley's group; each one sold well enough to warrant another release but only that first one did particularly well.* The Retaliation were never more than a popular band on the club and college circuit. Victor Brox was a distinctive singer and guitarist. John Moorshead was excellent but overlooked. It was only drummer Aynsley Dunbar who got wider recognition, next with the Jeff Beck Group, and then playing with Frank Zappa.

We'd done the deals with Bryan Morrison in April but before the albums were released in June, Bob Reisdorff received the bombshell news that Liberty Records had been taken over by a huge American holding company called the Transamerica Corporation which owned Budget Rent a Car and had recently taken over United Artists, the publishing company, the film company and the record company. Liberty was to be amalgamated with United Artists. The two labels would retain their own identity and Al Bennett had agreed to remain in charge of both labels, but Bob was gutted. He'd set up the UK office little more than a year ago. It was doing well but he knew that the team he'd put together would be pulled to pieces and his own autonomy would be eroded in the shake-up. So within a few weeks of the announcement he left and returned to America.

None of us knew what to expect in the future. After Bob left, Frank Davies, our international export manager, began planning a move to Canada. Ray knew his position at Liberty was no longer secure and opportunities outside of Liberty were more

---

* Both albums were designed by the team known as Hipgnosis, who had just designed their first ever album cover: Pink Floyd's *A Saucerful of Secrets*. The Retaliation's front cover was a darkly atmospheric photo of the group reflected in a pond on Hampstead Heath. It had no writing at all on the front cover. I thought that had been really cool when the Stones did it.

appealing. He stuck around for the rest of 1968 to see Idle Race's *The Birthday Party* released and to see the Bonzos get their only hit single with 'I'm the Urban Spaceman'. It was released in November and peaked at No. 5 in the New Year. Gerry Bron was very territorial about his role as producer and positively draconian about wasting time – and therefore money – in the studio. Everyone had agreed that 'I'm the Urban Spaceman' was the obvious single and of course Gerry wanted to produce it. It was written by Neil Innes, who had other ideas, but Gerry would only step aside if they could find somebody better. When Neil was able to say, 'Well, it just so happens that Paul McCartney wants to produce it', Gerry backed down. We couldn't name McCartney for contractual reasons, so his credit was Apollo C. Vermouth. The two sides of the single highlighted the contrast between what Neil and Viv brought to the band. With the surreal but commercial 'I'm the Urban Spaceman' in the bag, Viv pulled out all the stops on the B-side. 'Canyons of Your Mind' brilliantly sent up pretentious pop lyrics (specifically Bob Lind's recent hit 'Elusive Butterfly'). It was always a riot live. Viv would come on stage in a silver lamé jacket and wriggle suggestively as he delivered ridiculous pay-off lines with perfect deadpan timing.

The Bonzos' second album, *The Doughnut in Granny's Greenhouse*, was made up of completely self-written material, all down to Viv and Neil aside from one of the group's all-time classics, 'The Trouser Press', written by Roger Ruskin Spear. *The Doughnut in Granny's Greenhouse* was much more a rock album than *Gorilla*. They now had an electric bass player, Neil was standing up playing electric guitar as well as piano, and Legs Larry had switched from tuba to drums. They were dubbed Britain's equivalent to the Mothers of Invention, which never rang true even though Neil was a big Frank Zappa fan. There were deliberate rock references such as 'We are normal and we want our freedom' from Love's *Forever Changes* but Arthur Lee didn't rhyme it with 'and we like

100

Bert Weedon'. They also dropped the Doo-Dah from their name, along with Gerry Bron as their manager.

Since Ray Williams had been responsible for bringing Elton John and Bernie Taupin together, Dick James hired him to look after Elton's day-to-day management. With Elton, as with Bowie, you knew he was going to make it but he was still working in Musicland record shop on Berwick Street. I used to go there on the day all the imports came in and Elton would pull out the stuff he knew I liked. Next thing he was telling me he was going to Los Angeles to play at the Troubadour – with Ray in tow looking after everything. That was in August 1970; Elton's career took off spectacularly in America after those shows.

I took on Ray Williams' A&R responsibilities when he left. With half the team at Liberty leaving during 1968, I thought, 'We're still a record company so we'd better keep putting records out.' I didn't have to worry about the business side of things; the day-to-day running of the company, including copywriting and accounts was run by a guy called Brian Alderman. His department had been set up by Bob Reisdorff and he was very good. He was one of the few – along with myself and Ronnie Bell – who eventually transferred from Liberty to United Artists.

Having released their first album, I was keeping an eye out for *Boogie with Canned Heat* on the American release schedule and hustled for an advance white label. As soon as I heard 'On the Road Again' I knew it had to be a single, and it took off straight away, first as a turntable hit. People just liked it. 'On the Road Again' was wonderfully concise and had such a strong melody, but it was Al Wilson's lovely high-pitched falsetto vocal that hit home. Al undertook multiple roles on the track – responsible for the three tamboura parts that gave it such a memorable intro, harmonica, vocal, and guitar, all recorded at different times. They came good with a surprise Top 10 hit in July. Then as the single climbed the charts *Boogie with Canned Heat* took off and was a Top 5 album.

He's a big noise in the disc world

THERE must be many a young Tees-sider who sits and dreams of fame and fortune amidst the glamour of the £1m-a-year hit parade.

But not many are prepared to gamble their lives in this glittering world. And still fewer manage to scramble aboard the cut-throat bandwagon along-side the men who put the power into flowers and freakouts into motion.

Not many . . . but we did just manage to find one young Teessider who, at the tender age of 20, has already lifted his head among the giants. Our reporter found him sipping a whisky in an expensive drinking house, just of Piccadilly in London.

He is Andrew Lauder, an executive of Liberty Records Ltd.,—one of the big five American firms that have just opened up in this country. And his home is at The White House, near Wolviston.

"I left Teesside two-and-a-half years ago for the fame and fortune of the pop - world," he smiled

PICTURED at his London desk, Teessider Andrew Lauder prepares for another day which will bring him in close touch with the latest chart-busters of the pop-record world.

Local boy makes good – from the *Hartlepool Mail*

Canned Heat became my *cause célèbre*. We brought them over while 'On the Road Again' was still current and I went with Ronnie to meet them at Heathrow. Back then you could arrange to meet passengers as they came down the steps off the plane on the tarmac. As they descended, the first thing I noticed was that guitarist Henry Vestine was clutching a box of 45s. This contained all his favourite records that he insisted on keeping with him during the flight. I was already drawn to them because I knew they were all such blues record fanatics. Bob Hite had an almost legendary collection of 78s. He'd started gathering 78s and 45s at a very young age, buying old jukebox records.

Al Wilson already had plenty of credibility from having produced and played harmonica and guitar on the Son House album *Father of Folk Blues* for Columbia Records in 1965. Son House had been 'rediscovered' in 1964 by Wilson, John Fahey and others, but had forgotten most of his old songs. Al played Son House's old recordings to him and re-taught him the songs. Al was a really quiet, sweet guy and was passionately interested in ecology and nature. Canned Heat stayed at the Royal Garden Hotel in Kensington and he wanted to explore the park. I knew Kensington Gardens and Hyde Park because I used to walk through them every morning on my way from Notting Hill to Denmark Street. We spent the afternoon exploring trees and plant life. It was frustrating; that was all he wanted to talk about and I just wanted to know more about Son House.

Ron Kass was the Los Angeles-based head of international for Liberty who spent a lot of his time over here. He too was leaving, having had an offer to set up and run Apple Records for the Beatles in 1968. He took me aside and said he thought Liberty in the UK was going to fall to bits without Bob, and would I like to come and work at Apple. I wasn't about to say no, although he never outlined what I might do there. I was already worried that I'd probably be passed over in the merger with United Artists. The possibility of a job at Apple only lasted about ten days once Al Bennett came to London and warned Ron off from poaching me. He also gave me a pep talk, saying how important I was to the company. I felt a little more secure about the future. Ron's position at Apple lasted less than two years. His other main claim to fame was that in 1972 he became Joan Collins' third husband after she divorced Anthony Newley; Kass and Collins were divorced in 1983.

I was making the most of my remaining time at Liberty in Albemarle Street, which I figured would at least last out the remainder of 1968. It was a totally unreal situation because there was nobody at the head of the company. Nor did anybody from United Artists come over or explain how the merger was going to work out. So I decided to keep on putting records out. I knew I could release whatever I wanted if it didn't involve a lot of money. I decided to do a couple of compilations. The Nitty Gritty Dirt Band records were a mixture of blues, jug band music, bluegrass and the odd contemporary songs, but none of their albums had been released in the UK. I chose my favourite tracks from their first two albums, wrote some liner notes, and called it *Pure Dirt*.

We'd done nothing with the Minit catalogue, so I put together a compilation called *33 Minits of Blues and Soul* with Irma Thomas, early Bobby Womack, Jimmy McCracklin, Homer Banks and Clydie King, among others, mostly independent soul productions. That was my first-ever compilation, the first of many as it would turn out. I released a whole slew of blues and R&B titles on Minit over the next year, including another compilation along the lines of the first one called *Soul Food*.

It was a crazy situation, I was twenty years old and more or less running a successful record label while almost everybody around me was jumping ship. After Ron Kass left, his job went to an English guy living in California called Lee Mendell. He had a long Mexican moustache and used to cruise round Los Angeles in an old Rolls-Royce. He made the most of a certain cachet in America from having a British accent. He was always very helpful to me and rang one day after a meeting with Bob Krasnow, who'd most recently been vice president of Kama Sutra Records, and then Buddah Records. Krasnow was starting his own label called Blue Thumb. He said Liberty could have the label for the rest of the world outside the US.

Lee thought the most appealing release was an Ike & Tina Turner album called *Outta Season*, but there were a couple of other albums I had to agree to put out in order to do the deal.

One was a W.C. Fields album, so I wasn't expecting too much about the third one. Lee didn't exactly give it the big build-up but the name alone was enough to almost give me heart palpitations when he said it was by Captain Beefheart and His Magic Band. I blurted out, 'What – are you serious?' I'd first come across the name Captain Beefheart on a couple of Avalon Ballroom posters long before his debut album *Safe as Milk*, which I thought was amazing and had been released by Buddah. I hadn't made the connection with Krasnow. Beefheart, aka Don Van Vliet, was the only voice I ever heard to rival Howlin' Wolf's. I couldn't believe my luck. Beefheart was so cool in Britain as a result of John Peel's tireless championing. So Lee did the deal and very soon after Ike Turner did a separate deal with Liberty that continued till 1976.

The new Captain Beefheart album, *Strictly Personal*, was released in America a month earlier, where critical reaction and sales were disappointing. I wasn't at all let down and nor were the more loyal British fans. The cover alone was amazing with a gloomy, ominous black-and-white photo on the inner side of the gatefold where the Magic Band look like aliens from another world. *Strictly Personal* was still very Delta blues based but stretched into a more avant-garde, psychedelic style; lyrically, it was more abstract too, hinting at the wordplay and surrealist images of *Trout Mask Replica*. The greatest disappointment for me was that I had no contact with the great man, who didn't promote the album here at all.

If you rang Liberty Records about most things – aside from accounts and copyright queries – the calls came through to me. I was looking after the press, meeting with managers, and because we had no art department, I was seeing designers and photographers, which is why Roy Fisher came in. He'd acquired a video studio and had this facility to make videos or short films. I said I'd keep it in mind but as we were chatting away he said he had an unreleased single by John Lee's Groundhogs from when he managed them and was I interested?* They'd been frontrunners as a blues band as early as 1963 but ceased playing live at the end of 1965. The single had come about through a recommendation by John Lee Hooker; he thought the Groundhogs were the best British band to have backed him and he particularly praised bottle-neck guitarist Tony McPhee. Apparently, Tony was now working for the GPO as a telephone engineer and playing regular gigs with the John Dummer's Blues Band. I couldn't release the single but said if he could put together a new Groundhogs line-up, I'd sign them. A couple of weeks later Roy rang and said, 'OK then – Tony's reformed the band.'

It was Tony, the original bass player Pete Cruickshank, a new drummer, Ken Pustelnik, plus harmonica player Steve Rye who was well known on the blues circuit. So the Groundhogs were my first bona fide British signing and quite a bargain at £52. What was effectively a second blues boom was gathering pace so we needed to strike quickly and get a record out. I asked our staff writer/arranger Mike Batt if he'd produce it. We booked the Marquee Studio and recorded the album in two four-hour sessions over consecutive Sundays, mixed it the next day and rushed it out in November. *Scratching the Surface* was a pure British blues album, but the Groundhogs were already heavier than most of the others around and added a few twists to the expected twelve-bar format; the standout was a fierce cover of Muddy Waters' 'Still a Fool'. I was further encouraged when Dick

---

* Roy handed me a copy of the John Lee's Groundhogs single 'Shake It'/'Rock Me Baby' – and wrote his phone number on the bag. It was on a label called Interphon and had been recorded in England and produced by Calvin Carter, whose sister Vivian co-founded Vee-Jay Records in America, which was the parent label. It was far better than the only other John Lee's Groundhogs single released on Planet in January 1966, by which time they'd turned into more of a soul band.

Bock at World Pacific picked up on it straight away and released it in America. It was a decent calling card and I even credited myself as executive producer.

The lunch hours were always the busiest for people making appointments. I never minded too much except on one particular day, 30 January 1969. Wayne Bardell was now working for Apple Publishing in the Savile Row Building. His office was on the top floor and was the only access to the roof. Wayne rang and said, 'The Beatles are going to be filmed playing on the rooftop at lunchtime. I can sneak you in, but you'll need to get here early.' Every time I see those familiar rooftop images, I wonder why on earth I hadn't just asked the girl on reception to make my apologies to anyone I had a meeting with that lunchtime.

Chapter 9
An Underground Eruption

A lot of the labels that Decca represented in the UK, which included Stax Volt, Brunswick and the San Francisco label Fantasy, came through Burlington Music, but not everything was given a release. Sometime around early summer 1966, John Merritt of Burlington called to tell me they were having a clear-out and if I was interested he'd fill a large suitcase with singles that I could have for fifty quid. There were loads of gems – London American 45s, A-Label Test Pressings of the Small Faces, Them, even the Who's 'My Generation', some American labels including GNP Crescendo (which had the Seeds) and Scorpio Records, which was administered by Fantasy Records in Berkeley, California. It had a bright yellow label and included a couple of singles by a band with the godawful name of the Golliwogs. Before I dismissively put them in the reject pile, I thought I should give them a listen; all four sides of the two singles were a brand of terrific, basic, garage rock but with good tunes and with a distinctive lead singer.

The Golliwogs split up when singer and guitarist John Fogerty and drummer Doug Clifford were drafted and placed in the reserve force. By late 1967, they'd completed their army stints and Fogerty was actually working in the mailing department at Fantasy. The label had recently been bought by Saul Zaentz, who had joined Fantasy as a salesman in 1955, assembled a group of investors in 1967 and purchased the label from its original owners. The Golliwogs had started working again and Zaentz really liked the group's return to 1950s rock 'n' roll values. He knew they wouldn't get anywhere as the Golliwogs and suggested a name change; they became Creedence Clearwater Revival, who released one single, 'Porterville', on Scorpio before shifting to Fantasy itself where they began recording an album.

In September 1968 Creedence Clearwater Revival had a No. 11 *Billboard* hit with a cover of Dale Hawkins' 'Susie Q', the standout track on their self-titled debut album. They were playing places like Winterland and Fillmore West, usually third or fourth on the bill on some of the posters I was still collecting. Zaentz had immediately recognised the potential of a local rock 'n' roll group which had very little in common with the groups that had emerged in San Francisco in 1966. As soon as I heard 'Susie Q' I recognised the singer from the Golliwogs, but musically they'd moved on; this was an eight-minute track spread across the two sides of the 45. It was powered by a relentless groove punctuated by lengthy guitar solos and with a hint of trademark San Francisco psychedelia.

I rang John Merritt and asked if there was a spare copy of *Creedence Clearwater Revival* he could send me. The next day a package arrived by courier with a note from John saying, 'Call me when you get this.' He said the album wasn't coming out in the UK because Fantasy's deal with Decca had run out. So Creedence Clearwater Revival was unsigned in the UK. He said, 'If you're quick you might be able to get the rights to it.' I rang Lee Mendell and twenty-four hours later he called back to say that he'd not only got me the rights for Creedence but also the rights to the entire Fantasy label for the whole of Europe apart from Germany. I knew Fantasy had a lot of jazz releases – Dave Brubeck, Gerry Mulligan, Chet Baker, Charlie Mingus, as well as Lenny Bruce and various beat poets, including Allen Ginsberg.

The prospect of having the label was mouth-watering, but I was only a kind of caretaker manager at Liberty and couldn't commit to a $25,000 advance. Lee said: 'Don't worry, we'll front it and sort it out through the International Department.' He'd already ordered parts for the album plus a white label of the band's next single from their as yet unfinished second album.

The package arrived the following week, including an untitled test pressing. I played it and it was a song that could only have been called 'Proud Mary'. I was totally bowled over by its inspired mix of styles with elements of something Sun Records or Stax might have released. It also had a belting vocal and the most amazing lyrical hook of a chorus – all in a little over three minutes. 'Proud Mary' simply sounded like a smash hit, not just in America but here too. I was so excited that I wanted everyone in the office to hear it. I ran round the building but Liberty Records was so depleted at this stage, there was no one else to play it to aside from the girl on the switchboard.

We got the parts through for the first album but the second one followed very quickly and that was *Bayou Country*. I was so certain that 'Proud Mary' was a hit that I held back from releasing the first album or 'Susie Q'. I knew nothing would have the impact 'Proud Mary' was going to make. This was all coming together just as we were finally about to move out of Albemarle Street so, reluctantly, I held the release back until we'd completed our move to the new offices in Mortimer Street in March 1969. By then 'Proud Mary' had just peaked in America where it reached No. 2 and the buzz was already building here. Three months later 'Proud Mary' reached No. 8 in the UK, by which time 'Bad Moon Rising' – also from *Bayou Country* – was No. 2 again in America. There was clearly no stopping this band.

I delayed releasing *Creedence Clearwater Revival* and *Bayou Country* until the summer just before releasing 'Bad Moon Rising' which became my first ever No. 1 single. We took a long time catching up with the American schedule, but it never seemed to matter that we were always two or three months behind. I'd signed the most prolific singles and albums band in America and knew it was through a combination of luck and judgement sparked by the record collector in me. In 1969 alone, Creedence Clearwater Revival released three major albums – *Bayou Country*, *Green River*, and *Willy and the Poor Boys*, the last of which we predictably didn't put out here till the following March. Those albums gave Liberty in the UK four Top 10 singles.

Having been responsible for bringing Creedence to Liberty, I knew I was in a healthy position when we finally moved in with United Artists. There'd also been a second hit for Canned Heat. It was another Al Wilson fronted single from a half-live double LP called *Living the Blues* released three months earlier. 'Goin' Up the Country' once again highlighted Al's falsetto voice. He rewrote the original lyric to give the song a back-to-nature refrain in keeping with the times and his own beliefs. It didn't quite have the hooks that propelled 'On the Road Again', but it still reached No. 19. I was in a bizarre situation. Here I was, the acting A&R man/product manager for Liberty Records, with all that recent success behind me, and I was finally about to meet people at United Artists. I was introduced to Noel Rogers, who was the chairman of the United Artists Group, and it was the same all over again. Just as Bob Reisdorff had said when I joined his Liberty team, Noel said, 'I'm not sure what you're going to do.'

United Artists was a label I'd never thought about too much. It had been founded at much the same time as Liberty and was best known for its soundtracks, some of which were big sellers in the 1960s; the Connery Bond films with music by John Barry, *The Magnificent Seven* and Ennio Morricone's music for *The Good the Bad and the Ugly* and through the Bond connection Shirley Bassey was now signed to them, which wasn't about to win me round. More recently the record company in America had enjoyed a run of mainstream pop hits by Bobby Goldsboro and vocal group Jay and the Americans that had done nothing in the UK. The best artist on the label was folk singer and songwriter Gordon Lightfoot, who was about to move to Reprise.

United Artists in the UK signed the post-Stevie Winwood Spencer Davis Group, which had a couple of minor hits including 'Time Seller', a great pop psyche single that they never bettered. They also signed Australian band the Easybeats and immediately had a Top 10 hit with the 'Friday on My Mind' produced by Shel Talmy. People identified with its theme of the grind of the working week highlighted by catchy guitar and a rousing chorus. Once they split with Talmy they never found the same level of success again.

All Long John Baldry's recordings between 1964 and '66 had been for United Artists and were mostly produced by United Artists' staff producer Martin Davis. He was now general manager of the label in the UK and my new boss. Martin had already hired Noel Walker, who'd been at Decca as Head of A&R, and he'd hired an experienced label manager in Alan Warner, who had been at EMI. So where did I fit in? For a while at least, Liberty and United Artists each retained their existing manufacturing, sales and distribution deals (with EMI and Philips) so, thankfully, common sense prevailed to have two separate label managers. I continued to look after the things I'd brought over from Liberty and the Liberty catalogue,* while

---

* The Liberty catalogue included *Thoughts and Words*, an album by the duo Bob Ponton and Martin Curtis, former members of the Pandas, a group from Gravesend who had asked me to manage them early in 1967. They released three singles for CBS as Pandemonium, the best of which, 'No Presents for Me' is a staple of British pop-psyche compilations. I had little to do with *Thoughts and Words* beyond putting it out in 1969 just as the move to the new offices was happening. Produced by Mike Batt, it's now becoming increasingly collectable. Their folk rock–sunshine pop style is reflected in the album's title, taken from a Byrds song. 'Morning Sky' was a strong single but did nothing.

Alan Warner would stick with United Artists. What made it easily workable was that Alan was so good at his job and we quickly became close friends. There was never any conflict or competition between us – the opposite, in fact; we worked really well together and complemented one another.

The Groundhogs had been building steadily since their return from exile, but Tony McPhee never wanted to paint himself into the corner that bands such as Chicken Shack or the Savoy Brown Blues Band inhabited as just another blues band. He'd seen how Peter Green successfully shifted Fleetwood Mac into a completely new direction after two formulaic blues albums. Tony knew you could only re-hash the blues so much and following on from what Cream and Hendrix had already done with louder, heavier interpretations, he wanted the Groundhogs' second album to break the shackles of the format.

Musically, *Blues Obituary* – released in July – was only a step in the right direction. Steve Rye had left months before, so they were now a solid trio with the focus completely on Tony's guitar playing. He's always been underrated compared to Clapton, Peter Green, and Hendrix. His amalgam of styles drew particularly from John Lee Hooker and Buddy Guy, who Tony would always say was the first to really instigate feedback. We'd often talk about Herbert Sumlin, who played with Howlin' Wolf, and was another big influence on his playing. *Blues Obituary* also marked the first use of what became Tony's trademark slightly slurred vocals. The Groundhogs always drew good live crowds. Outside of Tony's acoustic blues slot, the Groundhogs became more abrasive, definitely much louder, darker or more free form. They were a real fan's band, but Tony was prepared to risk losing some of the blues diehards in favour of picking up new fans along the way. *Blues Obituary* was a way of saying, 'That's enough of that, we're moving on.'

I began talking to Tony about involving him in more blues releases, so we devised a logo and started a Groundhog Series in 1969. We began with an anthology of British blues players, pretty much all his mates like Jo Ann Kelly, Dave Kelly, Andy Fernbach, Steve Rye and Tony himself. We went into the Marquee Studios with Mike Batt again and that was released as *Me and the Devil*. It was a snapshot of the end of an era of the British acoustic blues scene. We did a follow-up a year later called *I Asked for Water, She Gave Me Gasoline*.

We were both fans of Big Joe Williams. He had such an unusual sound because he played a nine-string guitar of his own making. He was best known for 'Baby Please Don't Go', which Van Morrison and Them had their first hit with. Big Joe was in the UK with one of Lippman and Rau's American Folk Blues Festival packages and Tony was able to track him down. We dangled 200 quid and a bottle of whisky in front of him and recorded an album in a day. We called it *Hand Me Down My Old Walking Stick*. I'd never spent any time with a genuine blues legend before. It was a real thrill, especially when Big Joe showed us the famous nine-string guitar: we looked at it in disbelief. It was literally held together with sticky tape. I still think our album stands up really well against his other later recordings.

The blues albums I was doing were never going to bother the charts, but they were selling a more than respectable few thousand copies and we were getting released in America, either by Imperial or by Dick Bock at World Pacific. They were very cheap to make, and nobody was coming to me saying that's enough of that. In fact, blues enthusiasts were seeking me out because it was unusual for an established label to be releasing such a specialist genre. I'd become friendly with *Blues Unlimited* founder Mike Leadbitter, and he compiled an album of Lightning Hopkins' recordings made between 1946

and '48. We called it *King of Dowling Street* and released that
on Liberty as well. I spent quite a lot of time with Mike and
learned an awful lot from him. He was already ill and died a
few years later.

I also came to the attention of the National Blues Federa-
tion. They'd been bringing original blues artists over for years
and they'd made an Arthur 'Big Boy' Crudup album – with
British musicians such as Hughie Flint and Tom McGuiness.
So I stuck my hand up for that and put it out as *Roebuck
Man*. We actually released it on United Artists. I followed
it with albums by a young country blues stylist, Juke Boy
Bonner, and *Son House Live at the 100 Club*, one of his last
recordings. Alan and I were delving in the catalogue we
owned; I continued releasing albums through Minit while Alan
released a compilation of the red-and-yellow Sue Records label,
one of the first cult soul/R&B labels of the 1960s; we also
put out a New Orleans based album to coincide with Charlie
Gillett's ground-breaking *Sounds of the City* book. I was even
able to sneak out a Cajun compilation. Budget sampler albums
had become popular since CBS had released *The Rock Machine
Turns You On* and most major labels followed suit. From our
blues and underground catalogue, I created two very successful budget albums – *Gutbucket* and *Son of Gutbucket*. On
Gutbuket we were even cheeky enough to include the Bonzo
Dog Band's 'Can Blue Men Sing the Whites' which cleverly
mocked the blues boom.

Andrew was earning a reputation for releasing blues
albums

I was following my love of the blues that had begun with
the first Rolling Stones album, but I didn't want it becoming
a straitjacket. It was time for me to move on. *Hapshash and
the Coloured* had worked because it was a timely artefact of
the British underground in 1967. The underground was now
almost all-encompassing; just about every genre including blues
came under its broad umbrella. The Hapshash album sold

116

well in America and Imperial kept asking for a second one. I thought, 'You can't possibly do a follow-up', but I approached Mike Batt and gave him a free hand to pull something together. Guy Stevens had been the prime mover but wasn't involved; I think it was when he was detained by Her Majesty following a drugs bust. Mike Batt gave the album a structure and distinct arrangements that the first album certainly didn't have. It had none of its cacophony. The songs on *Western Flier* fell into recognisable genres – pop psychedelia, folk and blues. Mike put a band together for it and it has some great slide guitar from Tony McPhee. Mike wasn't around much longer after the move to Mortimer Street. He'd recorded a number of quite curious singles for Liberty that went nowhere. Perhaps his best work for us was arranging the strings and brass on Family's *Music in a Doll's House*, but his credit was left off the final artwork. Three years later he was writing, arranging and producing the Wombles.

When I first moved over to United Artists, I could never figure out what Pierre Tubbs' role was. He'd been at different times a singer-songwriter, guitarist, producer, but had most success as a songwriter. J.J. Jackson recorded 'But It's Alright', which he'd co-written and was a No. 1 hit in America. Pierre eventually took on the role of art director at UA, but in 1968 he definitely had a foot in the folk scene. He'd already released folk guitarist Wizz Jones's debut album in 1968 and brought in the Famous Jug Band during my early days of Mortimer Street. I put both their albums out, the first of which, *Sunshine Possibilities*, included Clive Palmer from the original line-up of the Incredible String Band. Pierre's folk releases sat well alongside our blues titles, especially *Stereo Death Breakdown* by Ian Anderson's Country Blues Band. Pierre was also friendly with Roy Harper, although our releasing his breakthrough album *Folkjokeopus* actually came about through America. Shel Talmy had produced it and taken it to World Pacific, so we inherited it back.

Pierre was doing his thing and I was doing mine, and the head of A&R, Noel Walker, wasn't doing much at all. I got on well with Martin Davis from the start. He just let me get on with things without interference.* I never kept Noel in the picture at all. I tried to keep it friendly with him, but he was never interested in what I was doing while he was trying to make pop records. He actually took over the second Idle Race album which had some lovely songs, especially 'Please No More Sad Songs'. It was the same story as before though, plenty of interest but they weren't going anywhere. Jeff Lynne left to join the Move soon after its release. Noel produced a couple more singles with them, but we let them go soon after.

Noel's office was just across from mine, which was another bone of contention with him. This was the first of my two offices. It was very communal. If Canned Heat's manager Skip Taylor was over or when Seymour Stein was in town, they'd use the office. There was also a guy who used to work with Bob Cohen, the sound man at the Avalon Ballroom, and he came over with reel-to-reel tapes of Quicksilver Messenger Service, Big Brother and Moby Grape. He took to hanging round the office and doing everybody's star charts. The office was totally covered from floor to ceiling with psychedelic posters and I encouraged musicians, managers, journalists and DJs to drop by for a beer or a smoke

---

* Martin and I never locked horns over anything. Before I was made head of A&R Martin asked what I thought about taking on John Peel's new label. I decided pretty quickly that I wasn't interested and partly for selfish reasons. I thought we didn't need somebody who was hip to bring acts to the label because that's what I was doing. Martin didn't push it. Dandelion went to CBS and John released a lot of things I didn't really care for that reflected some of the quirkier aspects of his taste. Dandelion was never a success financially and even John admitted he was indulgent.

and a few free records. It just added to the fun. There was no hidden agenda. Martin came in after a few weeks and said you'd better put some smoke extractors in because the dope fumes are wafting down the corridor.

I'd made sure I inherited the Bonzos once Ray had moved on. I was the label contact and that was mostly working with Neil and Viv. *Tadpoles* was the first album I was directly involved with, although it was only getting the intricate artwork together and organising the tapes and mastering. *Tadpoles* rounded up the songs they performed on *Do Not Adjust Your Set*, recorded throughout a very busy 1969 that included two American trips and the Isle of Wight Festival. By the end of the year they'd also recorded *Keynsham*, their third album proper of entirely new material.

They'd snatched bass player Dennis Cowan from *The Rocky Horror Show* and he became an integral part of a more roadworthy, more rock-based band. He was on board before their first American tour in April. Promoter Bill Graham was a fan and put them on at the Fillmore several times. He loved their rock 'n' roll parodies and zany antics, but others in America weren't ready for Legs Larry Smith's cross-dressed tap-dancing routine, or Roger playing a theremin shaped like a leg. It was too camp and unorthodox for Imperial, even though they released all their albums in America. The band came back complaining they had very little support at times. Their second US tour six months later proved too much and that ended early. Most of them were married and they'd scarcely been home or seen their wives and kids during 1968 and '69.

Keynsham was a more serious and introspective record by Bonzo's standards, despite Viv's wonderful jazz age pastiche 'Mr Slater's Parrot'. Elsewhere there was a more serious undercurrent about what they were doing and why. And Viv's 'Sport (The Odd Boy)' was positively disturbing. For anybody of my generation *Keynsham* was a great title; we all remembered Horace Batchelor advertising his 'infradraw' method of doing the football pools. The address was always delivered in a rich monotone spelling out K-E-Y-N-S-H-A-M. It was a scam; if you won on the pools, Horace got a percentage, if you lost you paid him anyway. It definitely puzzled the Americans.

Viv was drinking more and had been prescribed tranquillisers which he became rather reliant upon, so there was something of a frisson developing between him and Neil. Viv was admitted to Colney Hatch Hospital after a mental breakdown not long after *Keynsham* was released in January 1970. The group were still mischievous. We did a launch at the Open Space Theatre in Tottenham Court Road and we laid on a decent spread of food but before the doors opened the band removed all plates, cutlery and napkins.

They'd reached a point where they all wanted different things and any feeling of unity from the early days was disappearing. The chemistry of the band was always greater than any one person; without Legs Larry, Roger Ruskin Spear and Rodney Slater, it wouldn't have been the Bonzo Dog Band. On stage they still played their part but on record they were increasingly sidelined. I got the feeling they were on the verge of breaking up and they announced it from the stage during a Christmas show at the Lyceum. They called it a day at Loughborough University on 14 March following a pre-booked college tour.

Before the end of 1969 I released albums by High Tide and Amon Düül II, both of which were totally underground in every respect. High Tide were managed by Wayne Bardell and were my first signing at Mortimer Street during the summer. The guitarist Tony Hill used to be in the Misunderstood, a volatile California band initially managed by John Peel. They'd followed him to London in 1966. They could never maintain a settled line-up, so Tony Hill (from South Shields) was recruited. He

120

co-wrote their two Fontana singles, including the remarkable 'I Can Take You to the Sun', so his name grabbed my attention. High Tide was built around Tony and classically trained violinist Simon House.

Wayne played me some tapes which High Tide recorded at Apple's studios. It was deranged-sounding music, featuring lengthy jams which gelled enough to keep me interested. Guitar-heavy rock was prevalent, most of it blues-based, but High Tide sounded a lot freer with its idiosyncratic combination of Tony's liquid intensity and Simon's flowing violin. The songs were merely jumping-off points for them to do their thing. Being able to work with Wayne clinched it. We made the album quickly and Paul Whitehead, a commercial artist I used regularly, did the sleeve. The album was called *Sea Shanties* and released in October.* It was reviewed well in the underground press, including John Peel in *International Times*, but the *Melody Maker* review predictably slagged them off as monotonous and ended by saying 'High Tide – low ebb'. Low tide or not, the album did well enough and was released throughout Europe and by Liberty in America.

Wayne had become a part of Clearwater Productions, a management and booking agency based in Notting Hill. He teamed up with Doug Smith, who managed much-fancied folk rock band Trees, and Richard Thomas, who managed jazz-blues outfit Skin Alley; both were signed to CBS. Clearwater was based in Westmoreland Mews in a neighbourhood around Notting Hill Gate, criss-crossed by Portobello Road, the Westway and Ladbroke

---

* I found an illustration of a sailing ship in a book from an antiques shop off Kensington Church Street called the Lacquer Chest. I regularly pillaged the shop for odd Victorian furniture and source material for artwork from old books, posters, annuals and postcards. The *Sea Shanties* cover is still one of my favourites. Paul Whitehead went on to design the surrealistic covers for Charisma's early Genesis and Van Der Graaf Generator albums.

Grove, that had become the headquarters of the counter-culture in the mid-sixties.

Clearwater had offices below Doug's attic room living space with a bedroom up in the eaves. I spent much of that summer hanging out at Doug's place. We'd listen to records all night, drinking wine, smoking pot and making grand plans. Clearwater ran gigs at nearby All Saints Hall, which was the perfect community-based venue; 200 to 250 people would pack it out. All Saints Hall was where Pink Floyd first evolved from R&B to more spacey rock against a backdrop of projected coloured slides. Clearwater's shows followed in a tradition of underground bands playing there, such as Mighty Baby, the Edgar Broughton Band, Quintessence, the Deviants and Pink Fairies, who all lived nearby.

I was drawn to another band on Clearwater's books called Cochise. They were one of a number of bands formed from the remnants of 1960s outfits that never made it. Cochise was usually lumped in with other so-called British country rock bands such as Bronco or Head Hands and Feet, largely because their line-up included leading pedal steel guitarist B.J. Cole.[*] As a Clearwater act, Cochise had that safety net of the underground and they weren't really a country rock band. B.J. Cole was no ordinary steel guitarist. He was very much into experimental composers like John Cage, and he loved Frank Zappa. He had already started to make a name for himself as a session player, notably on Elton John's albums.

Doug then happened upon another local band of musicians and misfits who turned up on 29 August when High Tide were

---

[*] They all had a back story. Their rhythm section of Rick Wills and Willie Wilson had been in Cambridge group Jokers Wild (where Pink Floyd poached Dave Gilmour); singer Stuart Brown had been in Bluesology with Elton, and guitarist Mick Grabham had been in one-hit wonders Plastic Penny.

headlining at All Saints Hall. Doug was there in the afternoon and approached by guitarist Dave Brock about his band playing a short set at the end of the night. They didn't even have a name, so Brock suggested Group X. Doug admits that he wasn't exactly convinced by the one long song they played later that night – a twenty-minute jam on the main riff in the Byrds' 'Eight Miles High'. John Peel was there though, checking out High Tide, and caught Group X. As he left, he accosted Doug and said something along the lines of, 'You should get involved with them, they'll be a big group.'

Doug thought Peel might just be right. Group X spent the rest of the year rehearsing in a basement in Great Western Road and getting gigs – mostly playing for free – wherever they could. I saw them a few weeks later. Their relentless jams, mixing free jazz sax, persistent choppy guitar riffs and feedback from Brock and fellow guitarist Mick Slattery, were hard to resist. To the side of the stage, almost hidden, somebody was creating intermittent whirring electronic noises that made them even more interesting.

Next time I saw them they'd acquired some ex-military strobe lights that were more like a weapon than a lighting effect when aimed directly at the audience. Dave Brock gleefully told me how the electronic frequencies they used combined with the strobe lights could actually make people physically sick – adding they could have a similar effect on the bowels. Their fans were even weirder than the band and included a couple of would-be wizards and cult science fantasy writer Michael Moorcock and his acolytes. The free shows they played helped to build up a sense of loyalty, fast becoming the Ladbroke Grove community's house band by the end of the year.

As well as Cochise, Doug's latest find was something I didn't want to miss out on. Dave Brock organised some demos – recorded at EMI's Abbey Road Studios. The first acetate Doug gave me had two names crossed out – Group X, Hawkwind Zoo and then just Hawkwind. That demo included 'Hurry on Sundown', a surprisingly catchy, folk blues protest song which became Hawkwind's first single.

Clearwater managed three of Andrew's early signings, including Hawkwind

Liberty Records had started up offices in France and Germany at the same time as in the UK; there was never anything of interest that the French label in Paris was putting out. Al Bennett hired Siegfried Loch to run the Munich-based label with a brief to target both the home market and abroad. I knew the name Siggy Loch from record sleeves. He'd been asked to head up the Star Club record label when he was working at Philips. Star Club released records by a lot of the lesser-known Liverpool beat groups. I had a live album combining the Searchers (before they signed to Pye) and the Rattles, the only German beat group that had any kind of recognition in Britain. I also knew Siggy's name from a series of American Folk Blues Festival albums released by Fontana, featuring artists from the annual Lippman and Rau concert promotions.

In 1969 Siggy hired Gerhard Augustin to front the A&R department. Gerhard had co-created *Beat Club*, Germany's first pop music programme on television that ran from September 1965 till well into the '70s; he even presented the first half dozen shows. Gerhard had lived and worked in New York in the early '60s and lived in San Francisco in 1968 where he became friends with such key figures as Bill Graham, DJ Tom Donahue and Bay Area journalist Ralph Gleason. He then took a job working for United Artists in Los Angeles, from where Siggy poached him. Once I got to know Gerhard it was obvious that we were not only in parallel jobs but loved the same music. It was Gerhard who sent me Amon Düül II's debut album *Phallus Dei*.

My immediate reaction was, 'What the hell is this?' I got it straight away because it was very guitar-based, very psychedelic and improvisational in the way San Francisco groups were. The band had recorded it live over two days in Munich. It was how I imagined early Pink Floyd must have sounded. The free-flowing title track took over the whole of side one, and that was a statement of intent in itself. They weren't playing by the usual rules. As soon as I heard it, I thought, 'Let's just put this out.'

I released *Phallus Dei* in October 1969 and it totally complemented High Tide and probable signings Hawkwind. It was made for that same underground coterie and would definitely appeal to the underground press. Of all the groups that eventually came under the krautrock umbrella, Amon Düül II was the most psychedelic and most shambolic. It had a commonality of sound and vision with everything I was signing. I've always believed that Amon Düül II was the group which broke the taboo about German music. *Phallus Dei* flagged up a new breed of German bands who defied the dependency on British and American pop and there was no doubting that Amon Düül II presented an indomitable alternative to 'Schlager', the usual German fare of sentimental ballads and mawkish folk music.

I had no idea who was in Amon Düül II or how many there were in the band. I'd half expected *Phallus Dei* to be a one-off. It was only later that I found out they had an English bass player called Dave Anderson. Later still I discovered that he had been a roadie for pop group Kippington Lodge, had fallen in with the Amon Düül commune when the group played in Germany and ended up staying there.

When Gerhard sent me *Phallus Dei* it reinforced a feeling I had that there were underlying musical forces influencing my decision-making; there certainly wasn't any kind of masterplan. Can weren't even in the picture for me at this time. They'd released their debut album *Monster Movie* in August on a small independent label called Music Factory, and Siggy Loch had helped with distribution. He was in talks about signing them, but I didn't have any conversations with Siggy or Gerhard about Can till the New Year.

I'd already made up my mind to sign Cochise and Hawkwind, but Doug and I were planning a three-week holiday in America in February. We decided to do deals for both groups in January and hold off from announcing the signings till we got back. I'd

126

been talking and corresponding with a lot of people in America ahead of my forthcoming holiday. Word had spread about me in San Francisco as somebody to 'look up if you're in London'. That suited me fine and Dave Cohen from Country Joe and the Fish was over and he told me that the band's former bass player Bruce Barthol had a new band called Formerly Fat Harry. They were playing at the Country Club in Hampstead before Christmas. Stuart Lyons, who ran the Country Club, said, 'You must catch the support group, Brinsley Schwarz.' I caught the second half of their set, which I enjoyed, and came away thinking this was a group to keep an eye on. Stuart said some of them had been in Kippington Lodge, a pop group I only knew by name. They'd released a few singles on Columbia that never troubled the charts.

Stuart told Brinsley Schwarz's manager Dave Robinson that I'd liked the band and he called me the next day wanting to arrange a meeting. I already had an awful lot mounting up in January and put him off till I came back from America, by which time whether to sign Brinsley Schwarz or not became a much more pressing matter.

Chapter 10

A Pilgrimage to San Francisco and a Fiasco in New York

Doug and I set off for New York midweek on 11 February; a week later we flew to Los Angeles for a week before spending five days in San Francisco. I wanted to visit the United Artists and Liberty offices in New York and Los Angeles, but it was the pilgrimage to San Francisco that excited me the most. There certainly wasn't much in the United Artists office that was of great interest to any current music fan or, frankly, to me but I'd got to know Stu Greenberg and Maureen O'Donnell. Stu and Maureen were real record fans. We'd exchange underground magazines and records and used to chat regularly. Maureen had worked for the notorious Morris Levy at Roulette Records and with Florence Greenberg, the one-time New Jersey housewife who founded Scepter Records. She was friendly with Juggy Murray Jones from Sue Records too, so I was very impressed. They were the only ones at United Artists interested in what I was doing and what was going on in Britain.

We'd arranged to stay at Maureen's parents' place in New Jersey and she and Stu met us at the airport, but we never expected they'd arrive in a huge stretch limo. It was an amazing way to drive into New York and see the famous skyline for the first time. Maureen gave us each a package of all the latest magazines and on top was the new *Rolling Stone*, which was totally dominated by the Charlatans. She knew I was rather taken with them. There was a five-page story and Dan Hicks was on the cover when it folded out. He'd taken on the Charlatans' mantle with his group Dan Hicks and His Hot Licks performing his own smart, witty songs to a gentle mix of folk, blues, country and western swing. All that was mind-blowing enough before Maureen said, 'There's a concert you might fancy at the weekend.' I asked who was playing and she said, 'The Grateful Dead at the Fillmore East.' It got better by the minute when Maureen said they would be supported by Love and the Allman Brothers. The Allman Brothers' first album wasn't long out and they already had a reputation as a killer live band.

On the Friday we went to see a United Artists' band, Boffalongo, at a short-lived venue called the Electric Circus. I released their second album *Beyond Your Head* later that year. They were OK, but it was impossible not to be counting down the hours to seeing the Dead the next day, 14 February. The Valentine's Day shows have become renowned by Dead fans as among the best ever. To have been there was an incredible experience. The Allmans were even better than I imagined, although Love was a major let-down. It was Arthur Lee's post-*Forever Changes* line-up, just ahead of their first ever UK tour. Coincidentally, they were part of the Musicians' Union exchange arrangement which enabled Brinlsey Schwarz to be able to play in New York six weeks later. The bands were all doing two shows a night and we were booked into the midnight show. Everything I'd read about the Dead's live shows now made total sense. It was a charged atmosphere of seamless music that the records could never quite convey. They were still playing acoustic blues and songs like 'Black Peter' from *Workingman's Dead* before plugging in. Hearing Pigpen playing harmonica and growling and howling through

129

'Smokestack Lightning' was incredible.

We came out about five in the morning completely unaware there'd been a blizzard. Trying to find the car involved scraping snow off a series of massive white, car-shaped blobs to get to the number plates, identify the car and then free up the doors. It was a magical first weekend in New York, where we saw one of the most legendary Dead gigs ever.

On the Monday I went into the office with Stu and Maureen. It was good to put faces to names and they weren't all as unwelcoming as vice president and promotion director Bob Skaff. He looked like a character out of *The Sopranos* in a fitted mohair suit. I played him High Tide, Hawkwind and the Groundhogs. I say 'played' – he took each one off after about twenty seconds, he was so disinterested, and proceeded to play me Little Anthony and the Imperials whose highly arranged ballads had long since dated. We got to explore New York, of course, nothing too touristy but visiting loads of great record shops and restaurants round Greenwich Village and Washington Square.

A few days later we flew to Los Angeles. We'd booked into the Roosevelt Hotel in Hollywood opposite Gorman's Chinese Theatre. The Roosevelt was a great old-fashioned Hollywood hotel with a room by the pool. It was a beautiful California day when we arrived, with blue skies and bright sunshine. It was the perfect antidote to the hurly-burly of New York.

One person I'd met before that trip was Greg Lewerke. His father Jack was the biggest independent record distributor in Los Angeles, handling Motown and Atlantic and most of the West Coast jazz labels, including Fantasy. Jack also owned Vault Records; I'd licensed an album by Seattle band Floating Bridge from Vault. Jack had two sons, the youngest of whom was Greg, so when I expressed interest in being the British end of Vault, he sent Greg over to London. Greg's first job at sixteen had been packing up Buffalo Springfield records in his dad's warehouse.

We were the same age, and liked the same music. Greg was a
big surfer, and used to hang out with the Challengers, a major
local surf band signed to Vault. He also knew Rick Griffin, who
was another surfer whose first album artwork had been for
the Challengers' *Go Sidewalk Surfin* in 1964. Greg took us all
around town and seemed to know everybody when we went to
the Troubadour where singer-songwriter Hoyt Axton was playing. Greg and I have been great friends ever since. We'd always
hang out if I went to Los Angeles and our paths kept crossing
down the years; he even played his part in the Stone Roses saga
some twenty years later.

On our first morning I walked to Liberty Records, down
Sunset Boulevard to Hollywood Boulevard opposite Hollywood
High School. I'd got to know a lot more people at Liberty over
the years, including Dan Bourgoise from when he was in
London with Del Shannon, and Lee Mendell who introduced
me to everybody in the office. I also arranged a meeting with Al
Bennett, who immediately said, 'Anything I can do for you while
you're here . . .' I mentioned the odd meeting I'd had with Bob
Skaff, and how he was pretty dismissive. To my horror, he flicked
down a switch on the intercom and said to his secretary, 'Get me
Bob Skaff', and tore him off a strip. I thought next time I go to
New York I'm going to end up at the bottom of the East River.

It was great seeing him again as well as Bob Reisdorff, who
was no longer in the music business. Bob insisted we stay at his
house rather than spend our money on the hotel. He lived in the
Hollywood Hills and treated us royally; he'd take us places we'd
never have found on our own, though I spent more time with
Greg than anybody else. We were halfway through our trip when
his dad found out we were already pretty skint. We didn't have
credit cards, so he lent us money and made sure we had funds
for the rest of our trip.

Next stop was San Francisco, where we'd booked a holiday

131

hotel on North Beach. The one Liberty Records office there
was run by a promo guy in the Bay Area. He took us to Tower
Records. They were just beginning to open up stores across
America. The one in San Francisco was huge – it seemed like
heaven. The Charlatans inevitably came up in conversation and
he said he knew Eric Jacobsen who had produced the Charlatans early on. So we went to lunch with him. Eric was on a high;
he had done a production deal with Warners, which included
Norman Greenbaum's 'Spirit in the Sky'. It was a massive
worldwide hit and by the time we returned home it topped the
charts in the UK too. Eric was happy to talk about the people
he'd produced, including Tim Hardin, the Lovin' Spoonful and
the Charlatans. He'd recorded the Charlatans' only single for
Kapp Records and said they were too far out and crazy and the
nine tracks he recorded remained unfinished. They have since
been released.

The Liberty Records promo guy then mentioned a gig that
was happening at the Winterland Ballroom he could get tickets
for. It was a benefit for the Grateful Dead, who'd been busted
in New Orleans a few days after the Fillmore East shows. The
line-up was almost too good to be true: Jefferson Airplane,
Quicksilver Messenger Service, Santana, It's a Beautiful Day
and Dan Hicks and his Hot Licks. I was totally overcome; the
place was jam-packed and it was almost unbelievable to see the
Airplane and Quicksilver in one of the city's most fabled venues.
I hadn't dreamt I might see so many of my absolute favourite
bands on the trip, even though it was no longer the twin-guitar
Quicksilver that recorded the classic *Happy Trails*. Santana
were the hottest band around after making such an impact at
Woodstock, and of course I was thrilled to see Dan Hicks.

The day after Winterland I met up with Peter Abram, one
of the co-owners (originally with Marty Balin from Jefferson
Airplane) of the Matrix, a nightclub that opened in 1965 out of a

renovated pizza shop. Peter had recorded almost every band that played there. His recording of the Great Society featuring Grace Slick before joining the Airplane had recently been released by Columbia. He had a little studio set up with a glass screen separating the stage from the recording desk. The night I went along, raga guitarist Sandy Bull was playing. There was hardly anybody there. While we were talking, I said to Peter, 'He seems to have stopped playing.' Peter looked across and said, 'He's nodded off again', and nudged him awake. A couple of months later I received a letter from Richard Olsen, clarinet player, music major and bass player in the Charlatans. He was managing Pacific High Recording Studios a few blocks away from the Fillmore West. Peter had told him about me. Later that summer I was able to get back to San Francisco and Richard drove me round on a rock 'n' roll sightseeing tour. He also took me along to see pianist Mike Ferguson, another founder member of the band and, like George Hunter, now a designer. He was working on the artwork for the debut album by Dead spin-off group New Riders of the Purple Sage, which was laid out on his desk.

The biggest band of the day in San Francisco was Creedence Clearwater Revival. I took a long taxi ride out to the Fantasy offices where I met Saul Zaentz. It was a funky little office in El Cerrito, between Oakland and Berkeley. It was no great shakes, just a small warehouse, a backroom studio and an office. Saul was really pleasant and welcoming. He'd been key to the transformation of Fantasy through his part in the success of Creedence. He asked if I wanted anything and clambered up the rickety old shelving to fish out copies of all the old Scorpio singles. He gave me a copy of an early Fantasy single I was missing by the Golliwogs as well as the first Creedence single on Scorpio. I left a very happy man. Saul was already talking about building a new office and studio complex for Fantasy; I saw the results of that a year later.

That first trip to San Francisco was among the most memorable of my life. I made so many friends and met so many people I worked with in some capacity or other in the future. Rarely a year went by after that where I didn't find a way to get back to San Francisco. The city and its music never lost its attraction for me. We went back to stay with Bob in Los Angeles before flying back to New York. I owed Bob so much but sadly never saw him again, something I've always regretted.

We returned to New York for a couple of days before flying home. I'd got on brilliantly with Maureen from the start. We were both such music fans. She gave me a lovely handwritten note just as I was about to get on the plane back. I wasn't going out with anybody and it was on the flight back I thought how much I really liked her. I was straight on the phone as soon as I arrived home saying, 'You've got to come over.' Before the year was out she joined the UK company as my assistant and we lived together for the next seven years. Doug also met his first wife on that trip. Ellie worked for Columbia and soon came to London to work in press at CBS.

Almost immediately after arriving home I was being presented with the Brinsley Schwarz dilemma. Dave Robinson phoned as I'd asked him to do on my first day back. He must have had it marked on the calendar. He said, 'I need to fill you in on what's happened.' The crux of it was that the band I'd seen at the Country Club before Christmas had been booked to make their debut at the Fillmore East supporting Quicksilver Messenger Service and Van Morrison in early April and he urgently needed a deal to release their first album at the same time.

Dave Robinson had been a tour manager for Jimi Hendrix, and manager of Irish band Eire Apparent whose only album Hendrix had produced. He'd been on the lookout for a new band to manage and placed an ad in *Melody Maker* in mid-October which the former Kippington Lodge spotted. They were already

moving towards a more American harmony rock sound that
Crosby Stills & Nash epitomised. They'd also decided to rename
the band after their guitarist Brinsley Schwarz. About seventy
bands auditioned but Dave knew this was the one he was after;
they played well, wrote their own songs, and knew what they
were about.

Having signed the band to Famepushers, his management
company, Dave teamed up with two guys, Steve Warwick, who he
already knew, and his partner Eddie Molton. They were a pair
of chancers who were juggling a number of small companies.
Warwick's background was in films, but they wanted to get into
the music business and had been looking to find a band to start
their own management company. That same month Molton
and Warwick were in talks with *Friends* magazine following the
collapse of the English edition of *Rolling Stone*. It was renamed
Friends of Rolling Stone, then *Friends* and later *Frendz*. It was
an underground magazine alongside the likes *of Oz*, *IT* and *Time
Out*. The pair didn't take an active part in the paper but shared
office space with them on Portobello Road. One of their other
enterprises was a graphic design company set up specifically for
genius designer Colin Fulcher, better known as Barney Bubbles,
who also became the art director for *Friends*.

Molton and Warwick were originally making a film about actor
Omar Sharif's Bridge Circus in London until the documentary
was abandoned through lack of finances. They immediately
shifted their focus onto a new film project that hinged around
Brinsley Schwarz playing the Fillmore East. It had been Dave
Robinson's idea; the gist of it was 'unknown English group from
Tunbridge Wells to make their debut at Bill Graham's Fillmore
East'. It was an outrageous plan but one that might just work
if only for its sheer audacity. Dave contacted Graham, who said
no at first but later relented and agreed to listen to tapes of the
band. And that settled it. Brinsley Schwarz were added to the bill,

below Quicksilver Messenger Service and Van Morrison, scheduled to take place Friday and Saturday – 4 and 5 April; they'd all
play two sets each night; the second for a midnight show.

Publicist Ricky Blears was added to the team, fronting
Message Makers who would handle the PR for the whole affair.
Ricky and Dave worked closely on ways to maximise the press
coverage, although it was Dave who ran with it. When he came
in to see me in early March most of the plot was in place, including the confirmed Fillmore East gig. I'm not sure anybody else
could have pulled it off. Talk about the gift of the gab or Irish
blarney, but Dave had them in spades. The group had almost
finished an album which he was producing, and they had a deal
in the offing in the US with Capitol Records, but he needed
one for the rest of the world. Barney Bubbles had designed the
artwork for a gatefold sleeve and had printed flats with a space
to add a logo and catalogue number on the rear sleeve and
spine. Dave had arranged for Aer Lingus to provide the flights
for the press junket and for Head Limousines to provide a fleet
of limos to meet them in New York. Things had really moved on.

The plan did smell of disaster and was perilously open to
negative consequences. That's why I was trying to push it onto
somebody else at United Artists to make the decision. After all, I
was still only a label manager. It wasn't really my responsibility,
so I let Martin Davis know, and sales manager Dennis Knowles,
and said, 'Are we interested?' I didn't want it to be my call. We
had tapes of rough mixes of the album recorded in Olympic
Studios in Barnes and I went along to hear the tracks and meet
the band. Brinsley was pretty quiet; Nick Lowe, on the other
hand, was full of energy; they'd known each other since school
days, and keyboardist Bob Andrews had been recruited the year
before. American-born drummer Billy Rankin had joined just
after they switched names. There was nothing that made me feel
any less interested, but I felt guilty about wanting to go back

to New York having met Maureen. We'd talked every day since the trip with Doug. I felt compromised about recommending this potentially disastrous scheme as a way to see my new girlfriend.

As it was, everybody liked the album and couldn't ignore the publicity that would surround the Fillmore gig. The fact that the whole thing was being filmed for a documentary was another plus point. We didn't have too many English bands either, having recently lost the Bonzos and let the Idle Race go – and Aynsley Dunbar's Retaliation were on the verge of breaking up. Everybody decided we should do it, at which point I felt comfortable saying, 'I think so too.' We managed to get all the parts sorted in time for the release to follow the trip. We also decided to put *Brinsley Schwarz* out on United Artists rather than Liberty.

I did meet Messrs Molton and Warwick a couple of times since they were investing in the project, although who actually got paid, I couldn't say. Most of my dealings were with Dave. Other than agreeing to a production deal to release the album, the rest was out of our control. I had nothing to do with the arrangements for the trip at all, which, almost overnight, went down in history as one of the greatest hypes of all time in the music business and one of its most ill-advised follies.

The trip to New York was only for an overnight stay which meant the margin for error was always tight and over the next twenty-four hours just about everything that could go wrong did go wrong. The UK posse was going over for the second night at the Fillmore. I was the only person from United Artists that went, and I was staggered by how many other people made the flight. I couldn't believe there were nearly 140 people on the plane, and it was only the music papers, underground press and various Fleet Street journalists who were likely to cover it. At most that counted for about 25 people. The rest may have included some people that today we'd call 'influencers' but the majority were freeloaders.

Everybody met up by Harrods on Brompton Road at 8.30
in the morning to board a coach to Heathrow for a 10.30 flight
on a Boeing 707. The plane was meant to land in New York
in the afternoon in plenty of time for the fleet of limousines
to take everybody to the hotel – the Royal Manhattan on 8th
Avenue – before leisurely heading to the Fillmore East in the
Bowery district. Having arrived at Heathrow on time, it all
began to unravel. Three hours were lost in London because Aer
Lingus had to fly their plane across from Dublin. Then we were
forced to make an emergency landing at Shannon Airport in the
Republic of Ireland, to replace 36 gallons of brake fluid that had
drained out during the flight. All we were told was that there
was a technical problem, but landing at Shannon and seeing a
bunch of fire trucks and ambulances racing towards the plane
was frightening in itself. Looking out of the window was even
more alarming since the pilot seemed to be skidding towards
the end of the runway and it felt like forever before the reverse
thrusters kicked in.

There was a lot of free in-flight booze so plenty of the passengers were already well-oiled. Nor was there any disguising the
sweet-smelling dope fumes coming from the back of the plane.
Aer Lingus then opened the bar at Shannon and started handing out more free drinks. It's always stuck in my mind that the
gift shop was doing great business in glow-in-the-dark, plastic
Jesus figures. Perhaps it was because of that near-death landing.
The delay at Shannon was another two hours, which meant
there'd be no time to stop off at the hotel. We'd be heading
straight to the gig on arrival in New York.

What I didn't know was that the group's trip over was equally
fraught. Brinsley Schwarz were due to fly out on the Tuesday
morning and have three days of rehearsal before the first gig on
the Friday. The first hitch came when Bob Andrews and Nick
Lowe couldn't get visas before departure because they'd recently

been busted for drugs. So they all flew to Toronto to try and sort it out through the US embassy there. Only Billy Rankin, the film and road crews arrived in New York according to the planned schedule. The band spent a couple of days in Toronto while Dave had attorneys in New York working on visas which finally came through on Friday. Following a hair-raising flight on a private plane that landed just inside the border at Buffalo, the group were driven to New York, arriving sometime mid-afternoon. They went straight to the Fillmore.

The delays in our flight meant we arrived in perfect time for the rush of New Yorkers driving into the city for a Saturday night out. We must have gone through immigration and customs, although I have no memory of this other than getting on a bus that stopped at a fence – this was still in the airport – and being herded through a gap in the wire fencing which had been cut and pulled back. From there we made our way to a car park just outside where twenty-five black Cadillac limos drew up to drive us to the early show at 8 p.m. There was something a bit dodgy about it though, and by then it was already gone 7 p.m. so we were up against it time-wise. Head Limousines had managed to arrange a police motorcycle escort to speed us along the way. Even then some of the limos were stuck in traffic and arrived too late.

I knew very few of the people being ferried to the Fillmore; possibly only Charlie Gillett, writing for *Record Mirror*, Pete Frame from *Zigzag*, Jonathan Green from *Friends*, and Mark Williams from *IT*, but I at least knew the names of the other music journalists – Keith Altham from *NME*, Richard Williams and Roy Eldridge from *Melody Maker*, and Richard Neville from *OZ*. There were journalists from the *Guardian*, *Evening Standard*, *Daily Mail*, and the *Mirror* there too, plus five *Melody Maker* competition winners with their plus-ones. Others on board were more puzzling – including journalists from the

Jewish Chronicle and trashy weekly tabloid rag *Reveille*, best remembered for its glamour model pin-ups. Others included Jenny Fabian and Johnny Byrne, the co-writers of *Groupie*, Jonathan Demme, then a London-based stringer for Boston's *Fusion* magazine, the original rock 'n' roll doctor, Sam Hutt (aka Hank Wangford), and former *Candid Camera* prankster Jonathan Routh.

A lot of people were there purely for the ride and if they had ever intended going to the gig, by now they'd made up their minds not to bother. Everybody was knackered from what was effectively a fifteen-hour journey, made worse by prolonged drinking and the effects of various illegal substances. Some didn't make it to the Fillmore on time, others claimed they couldn't get in because the Fillmore security turned them away. The traffic build-up was horrendous and at near 8 p.m., I asked our driver if we could get out a couple of blocks away. He said, 'Sure – turn left, then right at the next block, you can't miss it', and we made a mad dash. We then had to collect our tickets outside the venue, where I finally met up with Maureen. We found the first available seats because we could hear the band on stage. This was around 8.15, but they were only playing their first song in a thirty-five-minute set. The London contingent had arrived so late that the front three rows reserved for them had filled up with regular punters. It was every man and woman for themselves.

I thought the band was pretty good, under the circumstances. The core press gang hung around after the Brinsley Schwarz set to witness a dazzling performance from Van Morrison, featuring the same musicians and most of the songs from the recently released *Moondance*. I enjoyed Quicksilver Messenger Service more than I had in San Francisco while still bemoaning that the band had been hijacked by singer Dino Valenti. I stayed for the entire second show, though only Pete Frame toughed it out as well. You could hardly blame anybody for taking to their beds or preferring to experience New York after hours. It was a shame because the band was so much better at the midnight show, louder for one thing, more relaxed and much tighter. They went down well – earning a genuinely warm response and calls for an encore they weren't allowed to come back for.

Poor Ricky Blears was on a hiding to nothing. Whoever thought it was a great idea to bring over so many people needed their head examining. Even without the delays, it was always going to be a free-for-all. Later that night, back at the hotel, Ricky was threatening to jump out of the window because he was getting blamed for just about everything. His job had grown more and more impossible as the hours ticked by. There was a lot of shouting and finger-pointing and some heated conversations. I stayed out of it. I could take comfort knowing that it had nothing to do with me or United Artists. We'd done our bit because the album was ready to ship in a couple of weeks. I had no qualms about slipping away to spend some time with Maureen.

The next day as I was checking out, somebody must have put me forward as the man from the record company because I was kidnapped by the swarthy-looking boss of the limo company. They hadn't been paid – Dave, Ricky and the rest of the Fame-pushers team were nowhere to be seen. Eddie Molton hadn't even made the trip. I said, 'It's nothing to do with me', and told them that I was from the English company and it was Capitol Records they were signed to in America. They weren't having it. I was the one there and it was 'pay the bill or else'. They were refusing to drive everybody back to the airport. Fortunately, I had a business card I'd been given by Roy Ayers from United Artists; he was an Englishman I'd met on my recent trip. He'd scrawled his home number on the card, so I rang him and told him the story. I said, 'Famepushers have all buggered off and the limo company won't let me leave the hotel.' Roy knew the hire company and took care of it. I never asked if the New York office was reimbursed or by whom.

The flight back was quiet and uneventful. Everybody was hungover or just plain exhausted because it had all been such a whirlwind. The band was on the same flight, seated at the back and trying to remain as inconspicuous as possible. It wasn't difficult, since half the people on the flight had never seen them before and certainly not on stage at the Fillmore.

When it ran, the American press was encouraging; they were oblivious to the hype – at least until much later. The backlash in England was expectedly brutal. None of the write-ups had anything positive to say about the Brinsleys' performance. At best most of the press coverage said very little about the band and focused almost entirely on the trials and tribulations of the trip itself. Dave Robinson concluded that, despite the bad press, the Fillmore trip had achieved what he most wanted. The band's name was now known and they had a profile. The album sold surprisingly well and, while I'd never adhere to the adage that there's no such thing as bad press, there was an awful lot of it. You couldn't escape the name Brinsley Schwarz and quite possibly people checked them out, if only out of curiosity. They could do nothing but bide their time. The way they reacted once the dust settled was to consciously turn it around by adopting an anti-hype stance that was far more in keeping with what they were about. They had the great presence of mind to be seen to put it behind them.

The cost of flying out nearly 140 people, providing a convoy of Cadillacs, several floors of hotel rooms, seats in the Fillmore, food and other sundries – not to mention the budget covering a film crew making a documentary that never materialised – came to an estimated figure somewhere between £35,000–£50,000. Our advance of £22,000 was paid to Famepushers. Most of it was swallowed up to cover the debts. I didn't see Molton and Warwick again. The *Sunday Times* published an exposé of their various nefarious enterprises six months later.

Dave Robinson severed any links with them and carried on managing Brinsley Schwarz. They went back to basics musically and in their lifestyle. They all moved into a house at 10 Carew Road, Northwood, Middlesex, sold the big Marshall amps Famepushers had bought for them for something smaller. It paid some bills and also fashioned an intimacy in their performances. The trip could have defined them, but they weren't about to let that happen. Our deal was for a second album after which they signed to United Artists direct. The follow-up album came in late November. Calling it *Despite It All* was a way of owning up to what had happened without actually apologising for any of it.

Despite It All was a much better album; Nick's songwriting improved, the songs were more melodic and direct, and they moved away from the heavier sound Famepushers had encouraged. They gradually found their feet, leaning heavily towards the Band and Van Morrison for inspiration. I think a lot of people in the press and the business now understood that they'd been hapless victims of the hype and been given a raw deal. That helped them turn things round.

Chapter 11

Nobody in Britain is Playing This Kind of Music

Brinsley Schwarz's album was released two weeks after the Fillmore frolics and serviced throughout the sceptical media. There was nothing more we could do except leave it in the hands of fate. I had plenty of other albums already stacking up throughout the summer, the first of which was the third Groundhogs album which I knew was the one to take them to the next level. Then, at the end of April, I had a phone call from Terry Ellis. He was one half of Chrysalis Records with Chris Wright and, following a successful licensing deal with Island Records, they were now setting up a new independent label. I met with Terry, who basically offered me a job on the spot as their head of A&R. I'd been feeling uncomfortable about my working relationship with Noel Walker, which was the only thing that didn't feel right for me at United Artists.

The Chrysalis offer was totally unexpected. I'd be coming in at the start of something new but with a tried and tested team. So I said I'd like to do it. Money was never an issue because I thought I was being paid well enough but Terry asked what I was earning and said, 'I'll double that.' I was either being underpaid or they were being generous. We shook hands on it, I went to see Martin and gave in my notice. He said he understood but was very sorry to see me go. My brain was whirring all weekend because I knew I wouldn't be able to follow through on so much I was emotionally involved with.

It had been three years since I started out at Liberty, the transition to United Artists had been remarkably smooth and I had great relationships with Martin and with Alan Warner. I was torn. The Groundhogs had been my first ever signing, I liked the guys in Brinsley Schwarz and felt for them. I'd also be letting Doug and Wayne down over Cochise and Hawkwind. So I spent the weekend worrying that I'd made the wrong move. Luckily, the decision was made for me. Martin called me into his office on Monday morning and said, 'Noel's left the company, so we need a head of A&R and we'd like it to be you.' I didn't take long to accept.

He asked what Chrysalis were going to pay me and I said, 'Double what I'm getting now.' Martin didn't even pause before saying, 'We'll double that.' I'd quadrupled my salary in the space of three days. I went to see Terry and he was very good about the turnaround. It was a huge relief, which left me wondering if that had been my intention all along, to force the issue over Noel. He'd left the building and clearly he'd been pushed. Martin's only instruction was, 'Carry on what you're doing but we do need more product.'* 1970 was the year I really came into

---

* It wasn't long after that Pete Swales arranged to see me, and he used a band called Gypsy as a bit of a carrot. I'd already intended to catch up with Gypsy – the vibe on them was Moby Grape meets Buffalo Springfield. Pete was working for the Rolling Stones management, which may have helped fund him. He had the finished self-titled album by Gypsy, and another by a group called BB Blunder (*Worker's Playtime*), who formed from the ashes of Blossomtoes. The third album was by Reg King, formerly the singer in the Action. Both had a history that interested me. Pete wanted to do a deal with his Sahara Productions covering management, publishing and recording. It was a straightforward arrangement and all three albums came out during 1971. We did a second album with Gypsy, but we never really captured what they had going for them live.

my own as an A&R man. Four of the bands I'm most closely associated with at United Artists were all signed that year, and the Groundhogs' breakthrough album *Thank Christ for the Bomb* was released in late May.

The Groundhogs needed their third album to shake off their dependence on the blues once and for all. They also needed to carve out an identity to separate them from the other bands leaving the 1960s behind. *Thank Christ for the Bomb* did just that. It was recorded in February 1970 at De Lane Lea Studios; it was Tony McPhee's choice, having been blown away by what Peter Green had achieved there on Fleetwood Mac's grand single 'Oh Well'. The album was produced by Tony, but we brought in engineer Martin Birch, who'd recently done a great job with Deep Purple, and between them, they got the sound just right. As soon as I heard the tapes I knew we were on to a whole different thing, which was less about dispensing with the blues than creating a multi-layered, textured sound that had real depth. It provided a heavier backdrop to Tony's outstanding playing.

Tony had also come up with a surprising set of lyrics that explored class issues and alienation in an anti-war context, all of which was brought to life by commercial artist Alan Tanner's striking artwork. It had been Roy Fisher's idea to position the group in a First World War battlefield that matched Tony's lyrical themes. Everything came together to create a successful concept that managed to avoid the usual pitfalls of 'the concept album'. It was never something we flagged up, but the underlying themes were definitely there and Tony's lyrics rammed home the pointlessness and bloody-mindedness of war without losing the spontaneity and power of the band.

Thank Christ for the Bomb wasn't recorded on the usual small budget in a couple of days. I'd made sure they could spend more time and more money on getting the crucial third album right. I was going out on a limb, though fully backed by Martin. I was shocked when it charted immediately and quickly became the bestselling British album I'd released. I'd had greater success with Creedence Clearwater Revival and Canned Heat, but this was my first Top 10 album by a British band. The Groundhogs had never been within sniffing distance of the Top 75 before.

It was loud too. Soon after I'd been made head of A&R the test pressings came in and after the rest of the building had cleared, I sat in the office and played it at ear-splitting volume. The Ground-hogs wanted to carry that power through on stage too. They were one of the first groups who didn't rely solely on often poor club and college PA systems. We'd given them a further advance and put money into getting a decent PA system. They invested in big cabinets which had been modified by Tony so they could be in total control of their own sound in the clubs. Pre-Motorhead, the Groundhogs were as loud as anything I'd ever heard.

I was really proud to see the Groundhogs grow into some-thing that nobody would have predicted after the first two albums. It had taken only two years to get a Top 10 album by a group which many in the press regarded as, at best, a 'solid' blues group and, at worst, mediocre. They continued to have detractors in the press, but *Thank Christ for the Bomb* won them plenty of new allies and an increasingly younger club and college crowd began flocking to gigs. John Peel didn't like the first two albums at all. He and John Walters came to see them after *Blues Obituary* and said they were boring, but he loved *Thank Christ for the Bomb* and particularly 'Soldier', which he played repeatedly.

I'd signed Hawkwind and Cochise a week before going to America with Doug, and sent round an internal memo to all departments about them when I got back. Cochise were easy to explain but Hawkwind less so. When Hawkwind played the Marquee, John Gee, who co-ran the club, described them as 'the

147

biggest load of pretentious rubbish I've seen in my life'. I thought if I used that line in the memo it would intrigue everyone in the company enough to wonder just how bad they were. Most of them actually got it straight away. Seeing Hawkwind was always an experience. Dave Brock was effectively the band's leader. He'd originally been a blues guitarist and had been a member of piano-led acoustic blues outfit Dharma Blues but, for the last couple of years, he'd been earning a living busking in and around Ladbroke Grove and cinema queues in the West End.[*]

Dave, bass player John Harrison, drummer Terry Ollis and guitarist Mick Slattery made up the original four-piece that rehearsed in Dave's flat. Dave and Mick Slattery had met Nik Turner in the Netherlands in 1967 where Nik was part of a loose free jazz-rock outfit called Mobile Freakout. He was part of the fringe rock and jazz scene in Berlin for a while, before ending up living in Notting Hill. He had his own van and was hired originally as a road manager for Hawkwind. Before long he graduated to playing blasts of free jazz on stage with the band, adding another dimension to their sound. Nik brought in a friend of his from growing up in Margate as replacement roadie. Dik Mik (Richard Michael Davis) then found himself inducted into the band when he began using an audio generator – used for testing radio valves – to create primitive, eerie electronic sounds over the barrage of feedback and sax that was becoming the band's signature sound.

Hawkwind continued to evolve in this random way, their ever-fluid line-up changing immediately I signed them. Original guitarist Mick Slattery went off on the Moroccan hippy trail and

---

[*] After busker Don Partridge had two Top 5 hits with 'Rosie' and 'Blue Eyes', there was a Buskers' Concert at the Royal Albert Hall in January 1969, which Dave Brock took part in, later joining a tour that travelled around the country in a red double-decker bus.

was replaced by Hugh Lloyd Langton. Dave and, increasingly, Nik Turner were the driving forces behind the band. Dave was more clued in to the practicalities of a rock 'n' roll band, whereas Nik was a completely open spirit. They complemented each other, even though they'd occasionally rub each other up the wrong way – and would always do so.

We made the first album very quickly. They went into Trident studios in March and April. We recorded a single first, comprising two of Dave's busking numbers, 'Hurry on Sundown' and 'Mirror of Illusion' from the original demos. The two more conventional songs weren't typical of the rest of the album which they bookended. The first album is all Dave Brock credits – but arranged by Hawkwind – and I remember being surprised how cohesive it was compared to their shambolic live gigs. Aside from the two sides of the single, the rest is a continuous rumbling, pulsing barrage of sound recorded live. They did various takes of their live set, saving the best, which were then edited into songs. We did a few overdubs afterwards, and an uncomplicated mix. We wanted it raw and alive because that's what they were about.

The sessions over three or four days were produced by Dick Taylor, who was simultaneously producing the Cochise album at Trident. Dick had years of studio experience as guitarist and founder member of the Pretty Things. He'd left at the end of 1969 after *SF Sorrow*. Dick just wanted to do something else. It made total sense to me; like Hawkwind, the Pretty Things were rough and ready when they started out and I was such a huge fan. Apart from Dave, nobody else had been in a studio before, and Dick steered them through it and did a great job isolating the best performances without undue interference.

'Hurry on Sundown' was released on 31 July and Hawkwind's self-titled debut followed two weeks later. The single aside, *Hawkwind* revelled in a new brand of heavy psychedelia. Hawkwind were never sophisticated and, much like High Tide's debut, the album was aimed at an underground scene that wanted barely controlled experimentation and spontaneous jamming and in that, Hawkwind's debut album delivered.

We gave it a psychedelic gatefold sleeve – all purple, orange and green colours. The band's photo took up the whole of the inner gatefold with them playing in front of an array of tall speakers stacked and arranged in the shape of a stone circle. The artist we used was Arthur Rhodes – as far as I know it's the only album cover art he did; he's now well known as Arturo Rhodes and is a highly collectable British surrealist painter living and working in Deia in Mallorca. I'd wanted a sixties West Coast vibe about the sleeve and it's the perfect statement. The band added their own mission agenda: 'Now we are trying to freak people, now we are trying to levitate their minds, in a nice way, without acid, ultimately a complete audio visual thing, using a complex of electronics and environmental experiences.' It's a pretty good summation of Hawkwind, although they never did anything 'without acid'. The package set out their philosophy at that moment in time without any reference to the 'space rock' that was just around the corner.

Hawkwind didn't really need any encouragement; they played any gigs they could and welcomed the exposure, but gigs were invariably aimed towards helping people or supporting causes. They were playing enough paid gigs to make that possible, whether locally or playing off the back of a lorry at the Aldermaston CND marches or in front of Wormwood Scrubs. It was very community led. They believed in what they were doing. They weren't doing it to get publicity, even if that was a corollary.

Between recording the album and its release three months later they played around fifty gigs and immediately after its release they hijacked the Isle of Wight Festival during the last week of August 1970. Hawkwind (with their friends the Pink Fairies) played a series of alternating and seemingly non-stop shows over the five days of the festival outside the perimeter fence. Their free alternative festival was a widely publicised anti-establishment stance which generated more attention than most of the bands playing inside could hope to muster. I was all for that; that's who they were. The timing couldn't have been better with the album just out; it went down expectedly well in the underground press and more subjectively in the music press.

Hawkwind ended the year with a prestigious BBC broadcast, recorded at the Paris Theatre, and introduced by John Peel, who'd been supporting them all year on radio and in *International Times*. Sales of the album were healthier than I could have hoped for. They just needed that something to propel them even further outwards. Something was always happening – or about to happen – around Hawkwind, not through any preconceived intentions but as a result of the volatility and creative impulsiveness among the band's extended family.

High Tide had played their part. Without them and my friendship with Wayne, I might not have connected with Clearwater and, without High Tide, Hawkwind might not have done so either. We recorded and released a second album with High Tide more or less at the same time as *Hawkwind*. Just called *High Tide*, it wasn't as impactful as *Sea Shanties*. As a band, they didn't easily fit in anywhere. There weren't many other heavy metal improv bands with loud guitar and distorted violin. They moved to a place called Puddletown in Dorset, living just up the lane from Arthur Brown. They were working on a third album, but the drummer had a breakdown and they broke up soon after.

After having the initial conversation with Gerhard in the New Year about Can – or the Can as they were then – Siggy was on the verge of signing them. He said he'd send over a copy of

their debut album. A couple of weeks later Martin Davis asked if
I could come to his office and he introduced me to Abi Ofarim. I
must have done a double take. Abi Ofarim was the Israeli singer
and producer who with his wife Esther had an unlikely No. 1
novelty hit two years earlier with 'Cinderella Rockefella'. When
I met Abi he was clutching a copy of Can's debut album *Monster
Movie*. It was one of the original limited edition of 500 copies
on Music Factory. I assumed he'd just been asked by Siggy to
bring it over as he was coming to England but, as I much later
discovered, he had a management and publishing deal with
Can. It was called PROM, which does appear on the original
pressings of *Monster Movie* where the credit reads 'Inner space
for PROM production'. Beyond a few polite niceties all Abi did
was to pass over a package which also included the even rarer
Canaxis 5 album, an electronics project by Can's bass player
Holger Czukay and Rolf Dammers.

I had no other dealings with Abi and I was never made aware
that there was an ongoing dispute between him and the band.
In one interview I've seen since with Can keyboard player Irmin
Schmidt, he's asked about Abi and he jokingly replied: 'Forget
him; don't mention the war. It was a war and don't mention it.'
Apparently, Abi's name was on the original contract by default;
he signed on behalf of the band's unofficial manager Kalle
Freynik. Abi used that as a kind of leverage in an ongoing legal
dispute that was only finally settled after Can left us and signed
to Virgin.

It wasn't till early in the New Year that Gerhard told me
Can really wanted to get a UK deal and a positive commitment
from us to clinch the deal with Liberty in Germany. That was
never an issue with me. Can were ambitious and thought a
UK deal would provide a springboard to getting a release in
America. My copy of *Monster Movie* was 115. I played it as soon
as I could that afternoon and it completely blew my socks off. At

the end of the day I was playing it again, this time at blistering volume, when underground club DJ Andy Dunkley wandered in. He said, 'That's the best thing I've heard in years', and was almost demanding I make him a copy. He wanted to play it that weekend at a festival, but I didn't want to risk anybody else hearing it. I knew straight away I wanted to release it. I can't think of too many other records that excited me that much on first hearing.

The more I learned about Can, the clearer it was that they weren't by any means a conventional rock band. All bar guitarist Michael Karoli were in their thirties and they were all well-educated musicians and had backgrounds in modern classical, electronic experimental and free jazz circles. Michael was ten years younger and the most rock 'n' roll. The others had only come to rock 'n' roll more recently. Black American art student Malcolm Mooney had joined just before they were ready to record *Monster Movie* and his attitude and vocals tipped the scales even further towards pre-punk. He'd never sung before, so his vocals and lyrical input were just as improvised as the music. At times he's literally screaming and moaning.

The only thing to equate *Monster Movie* to was the Velvet Underground, but it was a superficial comparison. Can's music had broader perimeters. Critics always picked up on the fact that Irmin Schmidt, credited just as playing organ on *Monster Movie*, studied under Stockhausen. It was a link to the Velvets; John Cale having worked with John Cage and La Monte Young. The most amazing track on *Monster Movie* though is 'You Doo Right'. In hindsight it pointed the most to Can's future sound. It had two of Can's trademarks – Holger Czukay's metronomic bass lines and Jaki Liebezeit's machinelike drumming.

Can's music became a lot more challenging but what people heard first was *Monster Movie* and that was as close to a re-cognisable rock album as they'd ever get. Four months later

153

we released Can's *Soundtracks*. It was always meant to be an interim album, a selection of title songs and other music for soundtracks they'd composed. It wasn't their second album proper, although it has classics such as 'Soul Desert' and 'Mother Sky'. *Soundtracks* also documented the changeover from Malcolm Mooney, who departed after a mental breakdown, to new vocalist Damo Suzuki. They'd discovered the Japanese Damo busking outside a café and plunged him immediately into a live performance that night. Like Mooney, he'd never sung before and he also used his voice as an instrument in a sometimes incomprehensible linguistic babble of English, French, German and Japanese. Can were different people from different backgrounds. Finding Damo wasn't a like-for-like replacement. He added something different, but the others were intuitive enough musicians to be able to adapt to anything. They were playing for each other – not themselves.

With both Can and Amon Düül II we always tried to release their albums as closely as possible to the original German release date. Sometimes we lagged behind a few months, and Amon Düül II's second came out in England a year after *Phallus Dei* in November 1970. *Yeti* was the album that announced them as a force to be reckoned with; it offered up more identifiable songs by individual writers rather than extended jams. *Yeti* really got them noticed here, then in France and back in Germany, where they went from playing underground clubs, academies and universities to become a major band. Leading German magazine *Music Express* voted *Yeti* Album of the Year, and Renate Knaup Best Female Vocalist of the Year.

Yeti featured the band's definitive line-up – future recordings would always reflect some changes – guitarists Chris Kerrer and John Weinzierl, vocalist Renate, new bass player and computer programmer Lothar Meid, Dave Anderson played bass on *Yeti* before leaving. Artistic and lighting director and occasional

154

synthesiser and keyboard player Falk-Ulrich Rogner was crucial
to the band. *Yeti* was singularised as much by Rogner's stunning
artwork as the music. It was the first of many gatefold sleeves
he designed using a blend of collage and photography, highlighted on *Yeti* by the woodcut figure of the grim reaper wielding
a massive scythe across a misty blue and yellow landscape. The
reaper represented the band's former soundman, who'd recently
died. Rogner designed eye-catching artwork for all Liberty/
United Artist albums, aside from *Live in London*, which I origin-
ated. Amon Düül II albums never got much airplay outside of
John Peel's shows, and their greatest visibility probably came
from Rogner's striking artwork in record racks.

Significantly, *Yeti* gave Renate a prominent role. She'd been
living in London and working as an au pair and was little
more than a backing singer on *Phallus Dei*. *Yeti* features their
best-known song 'Archangels Thunderbird', which I released
as a single. The combined impact of *Monster Movie* and *Yeti* in
1970 reinforced the idea that German rock music was no longer
something to snigger about. Both albums were insightfully
reviewed by Richard Williams in *Melody Maker*, followed by a
piece he wrote in June 1970 about the rise of Euro-Rock focusing
on Amon Düül II, Can and Danish band Burning Red Ivanhoe.
Williams' Can review ended by saying, 'Nobody in Britain is
playing this kind of music.' In 1970 I wasn't aware of any other
label in Britain releasing it either.

Guided by Gerhard, I was checking out other albums coming
out of Germany and usually on import here. I was drawn to Ohr,
a Berlin-based rock, electronic and experimental label, which
was part of the multinational company Metronome. That was
where I finally heard the original Amon Düül. I was staggered at
how much the early albums by the non-musical branch of Amon
Düül collective reminded me of the communal freak-out on
Hapshash and the Coloured Coat. It was nothing but excessive

chanting and percussion. Ohr also released *Electronic Medita-tion*, the first Tangerine Dream album in 1970. None of their first four albums were released here till they signed to Virgin in 1973. The first Kraftwerk album appeared on Philips in Germany in 1970 as well; it was eventually released on Philips' UK prog outlet Vertigo two years later.

I get the kudos and the credit as the man who signed Amon Düül II and Can in the UK. I was in the right place at the right time. That's not me putting myself down; I know plenty of A&R men and label managers would have passed on both albums. I had a sympathetic ear when *Phallus Dei* came along when nobody was telling me you can't release that. I did pass on releasing Popul Vuh's first album *Affenstunde*, which Gerhard released on Liberty in Germany in 1970. Today you'd say Florian Fricke's pioneering use of the Moog synthesiser was an ambient album, but I couldn't see who would understand *Affenstunde* here, let alone buy it. I did spend a very convivial evening at Florian's flat with Gerhardt smoking and drinking wine and I remember his parting shot. He said: 'Remember, Andrew, that Germans play in concert halls; Americans play in bars.' That was pretty good context for what he was doing. It may have been a Moog masterpiece but wouldn't have been recognised as such at the time. There was never any pressure to put it out and I didn't want to push my luck any further with a third different German release.

With Maureen moving over from the States, I'd gone to look at a bigger flat in Kensington, and a guy called Barrie Marshall was living there. We got round to what you do for a living. I told him what I did, and he said, 'I'm in the music business too.' He added, 'And I'm managing this group you may have heard of called Man', which sent shudders through me. I wanted to be enthusiastic about the flat but, as far as Man was concerned, I'd never thought too much about them. My negativity towards them was because they were signed to the Dawn label, which was Pye's progressive label and the worst of the various major label progressive spin-offs. I knew they were Welsh and used to be a harmony group called the Bystanders that had a run of singles on Pye's Piccadilly label. They'd changed their name to Man a couple of years later and become more of a blues-based underground band. The Bystanders were the first Welsh band to break away from just playing the Welsh circuit. It was a bold move when they gave that up – and an income of a grand a week from touring – to reinvent themselves. Man was a completely different-sounding band whose name meant nothing. Both their date sheet and income plummeted overnight.

Barrie said they were in Germany, where they were a popular live band, having had a hit there, and in France with a track from the first album, *Revelation*. It was a very Doors-like bluesy instrumental called 'Erotica' which started with a girl saying 'please love me', after which she acts out a four-minute orgasm. It was clearly inspired by Jane Birkin and Serge Gainsbourg's 'Je t'aime'. The girl on it was a record plugger who was engaged to a friend of mine.

Barrie told me the band had changed the line-up since the two Pye/Dawn albums. Terry Williams had come in on drums, and I soon found out how good he was and what a difference he made – as did recently recruited bass player Martin Ace. So Man had the two newcomers plus Deke Leonard and Micky Jones on guitars and Clive John on keyboards. Micky and Clive were the only survivors from the original Bystanders.

They were keeping a low profile in England and working exclusively in Germany because Barrie wanted Pye to lose interest and drop them. I got on really well with Barrie straight away and his enthusiasm was hard to ignore, so I went back and listened to the Pye albums. I could hear what they were trying to do but the production was lumpen. In the meantime, Barrie sent me tapes of the current group where the songs now came to life. I didn't take the flat, but I did sign the band.

It seems odd, thinking about it now, but I didn't see them play before making that decision because there were no UK dates. I didn't see them play until the following year. So it was a leap of faith that really paid off, because playing live was what Man was really about. I'd not met them either till I signed them at the end of the summer. Man simply didn't have a following in the UK outside of Wales. They regularly toured Germany, Belgium, Switzerland, and France where, especially in Germany, they were playing sizeable venues usually to around 2000 people and even more at European festivals. In Germany they were also expected to play for three to four hours, so they began jamming and extending their existing songs. They definitely wanted to make it in England where, from playing to thousands in Germany, they'd return to play the Greyhound or Cooks Ferry Inn. They'd probably have got no bookings here at all if Barrie wasn't working for Arthur Howes Agency. He went out of his way to push Man. His belief in them never wavered and that always rubbed off on me.

Once I met the band, we hit it off immediately – they were a great bunch. Very funny and totally down to earth. We talked about music, of course, that was our common language and we loved the same bands. They were greatly influenced by various Californian bands, particularly Quicksilver Messenger Service, but also the Airplane, the Dead and the Steve Miller Band, all masters of stretching out their songs. When I finally got to see them play I thought they were outstanding and I liked that they just stood there and played freely. There was no posing during guitar solos – no posturing whatsoever.

Chapter 12

As Long as You Keep the Smoke Extractors

Creedence Clearwater Revival's extraordinary run of success couldn't be matched by any other band at the beginning of the decade. By September 1970, when *Cosmos Factory* topped the UK album charts, they'd become the bestselling band in the world since the Beatles. Creedence Clearwater Revival was focusing so much on making the records, getting them out and touring all over the world that nobody was keeping an eye on the business too closely. If anything, John Fogerty was the group's de facto manager.

By the time they eventually toured Europe in April 1970 it was straight into headlining major venues and capital cities every-where, and here it was the Royal Albert Hall. I'd end up lurking around at these high-profile gigs with limited access to the group. I learned more about them through a colleague in America who had closer contact. John Fogerty was a loner and something of a disciplinarian when it came to how the group functioned. They were always well organised before going into the studio and on the road. Creedence had a 'no alcohol' rule when they were on tour. Despite coming from San Francisco, they had no time for the city's drug culture. They were the antithesis of rock stars, their image typified by John Fogerty in jeans and work shirts.

The deal with Creedence Clearwater Revival was Andrew's
first major coup

I found it extraordinary that there was no manager and no
entourage to speak of on the road. With Creedence it was John
Fogerty and family; rhythm guitarist Tom, of course, brother
Bob who was a photographer, and another brother who tour
managed. There'd be a couple more roadies, but that was it even
at the height of their fame. The band was like a small family
business that went global so quickly that there was no infra-
structure in place to deal with the consequences of such rapid
success. It stood mostly on John Fogerty's shoulders and, by all
accounts, he wouldn't have had it any other way.

They had so many hit singles and albums in such a short
space of time that it was so obviously not going to last beyond
three or four years because nobody was there to put the brakes
on. On the surface it was going swimmingly, and that continued
through 1970. I knew they'd been saddled with a contract that

was never properly renegotiated. They were delivering record after record almost without taking breath. It's what happened time and time again in the 1960s: successful acts believed that if they ever went out of the charts, their careers would be over and they'd be forgotten. And as with so many 1960s groups the problems came to a head later.

Never was this more apparent than when I went to the grand opening of the new Fantasy offices on 6 February 1971. Their sixth album, *Pendulum*, had just been released and still made No. 5 in the US but only 23 here. I was never going to write Creedence off but there were signs that they'd peaked. It was only a year since I'd visited the humble Fantasy offices on my trip with Doug. Now the new Fantasy offices amounted to a multimedia complex that took up the whole block on 10th and Parker Street in the western industrial area of Berkeley. Everyone who went to the opening had the same thought and it became known as 'The House That Creedence Built'.

Zaentz had built Fantasy Studios to accommodate its expanding roster, which remained primarily jazz artists but included some investment in rock, soul and other genres. Studio C, one of three, was at least purpose-built for Creedence, with their own private entrance. Except that they weren't around for much longer to make use of it. Zaentz was also laying the groundwork for his move into the film business.

Fantasy did sign another rock group I was particularly taken with – and that was Clover. They'd formed in San Francisco in 1967 when Johnny Ciambotti joined up with John McFee, Alex Call and Mitch Howie, who were members of a group called the Tiny Hearing Aid Company. I'd seen Clover's name on posters, usually third on the bill, long before they had a record out. I loved their self-titled debut album and released it in 1970. It was very low key, recorded in the old Fantasy studio, but it had a great feeling to it. It reminded me of Brinsley Schwarz, and I

161

knew they'd really like it. I gave them all copies of the Clover album and said, 'These guys are on the same wavelength as you.' Like the Brinsleys' albums, it didn't sell particularly well.

I'd been invited over because I'd done the Creedence deal in Europe, and they put all the invitees up in the Mark Hopkins Hotel in San Francisco on Nob Hill. I had a list of who was playing live in the warehouse and the first band on was Clover. They were the band I most wanted to see and I told the Brinsleys, who asked me to take along copies of their albums to pass on. They sent a bus to pick everyone up from the hotel and I was sat next to Calvin Carter. I was deep in conversation with him. He'd produced that unreleased Groundhogs single and lots of blues artists for Vee-Jay and was now working for Fantasy's bluesy, R&B label Galaxy. Suddenly he noticed we'd taken a wrong turn. The driver had got lost and we arrived late, so I dashed into the warehouse just as Clover's set was finishing. I ran to the side of the stage and grabbed John McFee, the guitar player, babbled away and thrust a box of Brinsley Schwarz records at him. It was a brief, but as it transpired, a surprisingly prophetic encounter.

Lee Mendell, who'd left United Artists and now worked at Fantasy as head of international, said you must come over to the office the next day because they were announcing some very exciting news. The exciting news was that Tom Fogerty had left Creedence, and I remember saying, 'This is good news?', and he said, 'Yes, now we've got two great artists instead of one.' I wasn't convinced. Lee handed me a copy of Tom's debut single 'Goodbye Media Man', which did nothing for me. Fantasy remained loyal to him for the next ten years, but his self-titled debut reached only a respectable No. 78, which was as good as it got.

Only four months before I went to the Fantasy complex opening, *Cosmos Factory* had been a No. 1 album in the UK, but after a final Top 20 hit with 'As Long as I Can See the Light' at the end of 1970, all subsequent singles in the UK barely scraped

162

into the Top 40. Performing as a trio, they did what turned out to be a final European tour in September 1971 which included another Royal Albert Hall show. Live, they could still carry it off, but their first and last album without Tom was a disaster. *Mardi Gras* was released in March 1972 and lived up to reports that there were growing tensions in the band. *Mardi Gras* was John's demonstration of democracy where he, Doug Clifford and Stu Cook all wrote and fronted three songs apiece. Even John's three songs were hardly vintage Creedence. Depending on which story you believed, John was either agreeing to give the other two greater involvement or was proving a point by giving in to their pressure, knowing the results would be below par.

Mardi Gras was the first Creedence album since their 1968 eponymous debut to fall short of the US Top 10. It received an almost universal kicking in the press. Famously, writing in *Rolling Stone*, Jon Landau declared it 'the worst album I have ever heard from a major rock band'. I'm sure they could have made great records again – even as a three-piece – if relations between them hadn't soured so irreversibly. It was very acrimonious and was never resolved satisfactorily. The band split up in October 1972.

Zaentz was the making and the breaking of Creedence Clearwater Revival, but without strong management his association with the band and John Fogerty was a disaster waiting to happen. I don't know any more than I've read and little beyond the fact that Fogerty and Zaentz spent decades tying each other in legal knots culminating in Fogerty being unsuccessfully sued by Zaentz for plagiarising his former self.

The deal I'd brought about in 1968 which brought Creedence Clearwater Revival to Liberty in the UK and Europe came to an abrupt end following the release of *Mardi Gras*. Fantasy went to EMI, who paid a serious amount of money for the catalogue. We thought we'd already had the best of it during our highly productive five-year tenure and now there was no longer a band anyway.

Canned Heat's re-working of Wilbert Harrison's 'Let's Stick Together', featuring Bob Hite as vocalist, came out of nowhere to reach No. 2 in the charts in January 1970. A month later the compilation *Canned Heat Cookbook* reached No. 8 and hung around for three months. I always thought it was quite remarkable that a motley-looking American blues band with an overweight frontman made such an impact in the UK, and not just among blues fanatics. Measured by the charts and a succession of regular sell-out tours, Canned Heat were far more successful than more feted bands such as Jefferson Airplane or the Doors.

Then tragedy struck ahead of their next album, *Future Blues*, which was released to coincide with their third European tour that year, beginning in mid-September. I wasn't alone in being amazed that the tour went ahead, because Al Wilson died on 3 September. The group only got wind something was wrong when Al missed the flight to Europe. They figured he'd catch a later plane. They were holed up in Germany when they heard that Al had been found dead due to an overdose of barbiturates on a hillside behind Bob Hite's Topanga Canyon home; he was twenty-seven years old. It's still open as to whether he committed suicide. From what I heard, I wouldn't have been surprised if he had taken his own life. Bob Hite certainly believed so, because he'd attempted suicide before and recently been admitted to a psychiatric hospital.

Al had been depressed in the months before as a result of personal problems, and being such an avid conservationist further added to his despondency. He was a very troubled and concerned soul who carried the feeling he was going to die young. His particular passion was in preserving the natural world, particularly the giant redwood trees. His body had been found in an area surrounded by the trees he was so fretful about.

Al was the group's primary songwriter and *Future Blues* featured more songs written and sung by him than before, including the prophetic 'My Time Ain't Long'. It was their last great studio album. Without Al, the subtleties he brought to the band's recordings were gone. I don't think they ever recovered from his death and, thereafter, rarely maintained the same line-up from one album to the next. On record it was mostly Al who differentiated Canned Heat from other blues bands, particularly where his voice was featured. Visually he was a shy presence on stage, the perfect counterpoint to the prowling Bear-like Hite.

Hooker 'N Heat – released in April 1971 – was completed not long before Al's death and his photo appears on the wall behind the band on the front cover. It was the last Canned Heat album that sold at all over here and it gave John Lee Hooker his first ever *Billboard* chart entry – at No. 78. The music is split between solo Hooker, full band workouts and duets with Wilson. John Lee spoke generously about Al Wilson as the best harmonica player he ever worked with, which is quite some compliment. Canned Heat meant a lot to me as the first American group I got to know personally, and they helped establish me as an A&R man in my first couple of years at Liberty. I'm not sure I'd have got away with releasing so many blues albums but for Canned Heat's success. It was good to be around them for those few years when their music reached so many people. It's always surprised me that they were – and still are – so widely unsung and particularly in the press. Al Wilson's death came just two weeks before the death of Jimi Hendrix, four weeks before the death of Janis Joplin, and ten months before the death of Jim Morrison; all four died at the age of twenty-seven. Yet when people theorise about the so-called '27 Club' – and it wasn't long before Brian Jones made the list – it's very rare that anybody remembers Al Wilson.

After the Bonzo Dog Band split up in March 1970, Neil Innes

didn't waste any time putting together a new group called The
World. It was a surprisingly conventional band; they split up at
the end of the year just as they released an album called *Lucky
Planet*. Viv threw himself into a series of short-lived, daftly
named projects, only the first of which was for us. The Sean Head
Showband's curiously titled 'Labio Dental Fricative' featured his
mate Eric Clapton on guitar. He recorded a couple of singles for
other labels before he had a serious breakdown and was in a
mental hospital for several months at the end of the year. I saw
Viv on and off during the summer of 1971 when he was taping
Radio Flashes at the BBC, filling in for John Peel for a month.
The BBC was close by Mortimer Street. Viv's visits were always
unannounced and always great fun. One day Viv turned up and
produced a terrapin from a satchel he had under his arm. He kept
bringing them out till there were a dozen crawling about all over
the table, everywhere, in fact. 'Don't worry, old boy,' he assured
me, 'take no notice, they won't harm you.'*

Over the years the story behind the Bonzos' reunion album
has become muddied. They owed us a certain number of tracks,
but it made most sense to make an album. I don't remember that
we had to twist anybody's arm. The onus was almost entirely on
Neil and Viv. There was no manager and I left it to them to speak
to the rest of the old band. I heard through Legs Larry Smith,
who lived in Oxfordshire, that Richard Branson was opening up
a residential studio nearby called the Manor. The studio wasn't
fully up and running yet and the Bonzo Dog Band were the first
to record there. Richard Branson called me and said they were
still equipping the studio and asked if I could pay a chunk of the
recording costs up front towards paying for the recording desk

---

* Viv was part of GRIMMS with Neil that year, a kind of musical comedy
supergroup with key members of the Bonzo Dog Band and the Scaffold. Viv was
the S in the acronym of founding members, although he never recorded with them.

and console. He gave us a good rate for the studio and accommodation, and I thought it was ideal to have the group under one
roof and just see what they came up with.

There has been some griping since because the album was
so dominated by Viv and Neil. Larry and Roger were hardly
featured. Rodney was absent and listed as there 'in spirit'. Viv
and Neil brought in various other musicians they'd been working
with, which included bass player Dennis Cowan. They wanted
to record it quickly and there was one story floating around that
they went in and recorded an entire album in forty-five drunken
minutes the night they arrived. They woke up the next day and
quickly realised it was too awful to release. In the end they were
there for at least six weeks. It was coming up to Christmas.

Both Neil and Viv said they were happy with the record at
the time. It includes the first appearance on record of 'Rawlinson
End', featuring Sir Henry, Viv's best-loved character. His narrative was set to some delightful music by Neil. *Let's Make Up and
Be Friendly* was released in March 1972. They did no promotion
for it and all went their separate ways. People are often swayed
against it because it was a contract filler. It is mostly made up of
songs by Viv or Neil, but that was true of all the earlier albums
too. They always wrote separately, and Viv and Neil's tracks are
very identifiable.

It was within days of arriving at the Manor that Viv made
his unplanned contribution to Mike Oldfield's *Tubular Bells*.
The studio was being constructed in an old manor house in
Shipton-on-Cherwell. Richard Branson brought in a couple of
engineers, one of whom, Tom Newman, produced the Bonzos'
album. Mike Oldfield was already there. He was working on
demos and helping them get the studio together. That's how
Viv came to be asked to be the MC for what was then called
'Opus One'. Mike was a Bonzos fan and wanted something
along the lines of 'The Intro and the Outro', and he wrote out

the list of featured instruments in order, indicating where Viv should introduce them. It took more than a few takes. Viv by all accounts was pissed and swaying about as he took his cues from Mike Oldfield, and it was the exaggerated tone Viv used when he said 'plus . . . tubular bells' to introduce the final instrument that gave Oldfield the album's eventual title.

I worked closely with Viv on a two-LP compilation called *The History of the Bonzos* that we released in 1974, but he didn't record for United Artists again. I did two low-budget albums with Roger Ruskin Spear in 1972 and '73 – *Electric Shocks* and *Unusual*. His mad professor was a very English comic stereotype and he developed his own stage show as his Giant Kinectic Wardrobe. Neil in the meantime quietly became integral to the Monty Python team, touring with them and providing music for their films. His partnership with Eric Idle on *Rutland Weekend Television* led to what is arguably the finest pop parody of all time, *The Rutles*.

I never wanted to cut Neil loose; he made a few singles for UA and one final album, *How Sweet to Be an Idiot* in 1973. It brought out the more poignant and introspective side of his writing. The songs were subtle and often very sad. He wanted it to be an album where he didn't have to be funny. Then, typically, for the cover, he was photographed sat on the floor in dungarees, with a blank expression on his face and a customised yellow plastic duck he'd bought in Woolworth's on his head.*

United Artists was more a mini-major label but the way I operated was closer to an independent. Martin allowed me complete freedom to do whatever I wanted and trusted me not to go mad. What made it possible was that, outside of my particular

---

* Neil had something of a windfall when it was noticed that Oasis borrowed portions of 'How Sweet to Be an Idiot' on Noel Gallagher's song 'Whatever', released as a single in 1994. EMI resolved the matter and Neil received a writing credit and a 20 per cent share of royalties.

domain, there was a whole other side to United Artists' roster, which always had a steady stream of hits. The day we moved offices they were enjoying a No. 1 pop hit with Peter Sarstedt's faux-French sophisticated pop song 'Where Do You Go to My Lovely' that I soon grew very tired of hearing.

United Artists usually had at least one chart record active at any time, whether it was Bobby Goldsboro's maudlin 'Honey', or hits by country stars such as Crystal Gayle and later Kenny Rogers, or Don McLean, who was phenomenally successful in Britain for several years after 'American Pie' in 1972. Even Slim Whitman and Bing Crosby recorded new albums and found themselves back in the charts, while Alan Warner issued 'The Trail of the Lonesome Pine' by Laurel & Hardy, a big hit around Christmas 1975. Shirley Bassey had the occasional hit single too, but her albums sold consistently well, including a run of twelve Top 20 albums, some of which Martin produced.

I was holding my own. It wasn't as if my signings were being subsidised by Shirley Bassey and Don McLean. The company was doing well, and it was a credit to Martin Davis that United Artists was so laissez-faire and eclectic in its outlook. I was able to get on with the things I wanted to do in a very harmonious and very social environment.

If Ike & Tina Turner, Don McLean or Bobby Womack was in town, it was usually Alan, Ronnie Bell or the press office that tended to look after them. Ronnie was in his element at United Artists and remained there till he retired in 1980. He would often go on tour with Canned Heat and Ike & Tina. Ike used to give him a briefcase to carry through customs. He thought, 'They'll never stop Ronnie' because he was such a straight-looking older gentleman. I don't think Ronnie had a clue what he was carrying. Ike and Tina had reinvented themselves in the 1970s with hits such as 'Proud Mary' and 'Nutbush City Limits' and they toured here, year in, year out, with their fabulous soul revue.

I had more to do with them through Gerhard Augustin, who managed and even produced Ike & Tina Turner in the mid-seventies. Ike was a workaholic. When he wasn't on tour he was making records every day in their live-in studio complex Bolic Sound in an old furniture store in Inglewood, California. He had a reputation for recording for two or three days non-stop until he'd finally collapse on the studio floor. He'd wake up the next day and go right on recording. I spent an evening hanging out with them. There was a lot of cocaine about. Ike put out lines that stretched the whole of the recording desk. You had to run at them to get to the other end. Gerhard had warned me not to use the studio bathroom because Ike had installed a camera in there with a screen by the console. He said best use one of the private bathrooms – so I went through one of the bedrooms where Tina was putting the Ikettes through a new routine. I regret not hanging round. A few years later Bolic Sound burnt to the ground under, shall we say, mysterious circumstances.

Martin would ask me to work out a budget based on what I thought I'd be doing each year and it was as simple as looking at all the bands and what each album would cost with them. It was invariably two weeks recording and a week mixing, and for overdubs. None of our groups were spending months in the studio but God knows if what we spent bore any resemblance to the budget. Martin was never tapping me on the shoulder and saying, 'You've gone over on this.'

I never got into any bidding wars for groups. I just told Martin what I was doing, and business affairs would deal with the contract and any adjustments. There was a rule of thumb that each album sold well enough to warrant doing another one. In business terms it was a form of low-level, long-term investment. I can't think of any titles which didn't break even eventually. And we were always getting released in America and throughout Europe. Very little didn't get picked up.

I did put a lot of records out in a short space of time, especially during the first few years of the seventies. I do wonder if I
put out too many spin-off albums, which I did with Man, Hawkwind, the Bonzos and even with Cochise. *Swallow Tales* is the
best of Cochise's three albums but none of the so-called English
country rock groups were able to rise above the thinking behind
them. It wasn't enough to have the intent or to have a pedal
steel guitarist, even one as good as B.J. Cole. I don't regret doing
a solo album by guitarist Mick Grabham or with B.J. His album,
The New Hovering Dog, featured string arrangements by Robert
Kirby. It sounds as much a complete one-off today as it did in
1973. I always felt a sense of loyalty towards those I signed; I
was giving them the chance to do something they wanted to do
and B.J.'s timeless, idiosyncratic album deserved to be made.
I was creating my own catalogue, so it was Alan Warner who
took charge of releases coming through from Liberty and United
Artists in America. I did get more involved with some of the
country rock releases which I liked personally and which were
compatible with Cochise, Brinsley Schwarz and Help Yourself.*

When Martin appointed me head of A&R, he said that
whatever I wanted to do with my office was fine by him as long
as I kept the smoke extractor fans. I moved into Noel Walker's
larger office and set about creating an homage to the Charlatans
and the Red Dog Saloon in Nevada. I adorned the walls with bull
horns, several Charlatans posters and framed the 1969 *Rolling*

---

* That included the Nitty Gritty Dirt Band, seminal bluegrass band the
Dillards, Country Gazette, another bluegrass band briefly absorbed into the
Flying Burrito Brothers, and two albums by Chris Darrow, who'd been in
the Dirt Band and the eclectic Los Angeles based Kaleidoscope. United Artists
also distributed the Grateful Dead's label between 1972 and 1975, which
included band albums and spin-offs. Unfortunately, the Dead didn't play
outside the US during those years so I couldn't make a case for greater
involvement.

Stone cover and even had western-style swing doors installed. The swing doors weren't very practical for me blasting out Hawkwind and the Groundhogs at deafening volume when people outside were on the phone. They only lasted a few months, during which time Richard Olsen brought Dan Hicks over to the office when he was here doing promotion. Dan was a bit freaked out walking into a shrine dedicated to his early career.

Martin was very good at turning a blind eye to the various comings and goings. Pretty much everyone was smoking dope at that point – Hawkwind, Man, Brinsleys, and recent signings Help Yourself weren't the only culprits, but if they were in the office there'd be a fog of marijuana by the time they left. There'd always be somebody rolling a joint at the end of a big table that everyone sat around; I bought a big Victorian lamp from the Lacquer Chest in Kensington as a centrepiece; it's still in our living room at home now.

Not everything went to plan. Bringing the Flamin' Groovies over from America was certainly a bit of a misfire. I was a fan of all three of their Epic and Kama Sutra albums. *Teenage Head* was their best. I thought they'd be able to build on that album, but they were dropped by Kama Sutra the same year it was released. I was convinced that if the Flamin' Groovies came to Britain they'd really shake things up. I spoke to Martin and sold him on the idea that they'd come over and blow everyone away with their high-energy rock 'n' roll.

They were a band with a history unlike any other band that had come out of San Francisco. They'd always played short and snappy three-minute songs; even live they didn't stretch out. They were able to get a deal with Epic even though their style of rock 'n' roll conflicted with the prevailing psychedelic scene of the day.

They sent me tapes and demos which I liked. I was in touch with Mike Wilhelm, former guitarist with the Charlatans, who'd formed a group called Loose Gravel which included a young singer

172

called Chris Wilson. He was now in the Flamin' Groovies. Only guitarist Cyril Jordan and bass player Dave Alexander had been there from the start. Cyril was the leader, so I brought him over first. He stayed at my flat with Maureen – we'd moved to Queensgate at that point next to Baden Powell House, owned by the Boy Scouts.

Cyril was so excited about coming to London and he loved the idea of working with Dave Edmunds and recording in Rockfield. It was difficult putting Cyril up because he'd be out all night or arrive back at two in the morning and then start playing very loud music, usually the Rolling Stones' recently released 'Tumbling Dice' on repeat. We felt like parents with a troublesome teenager in the house. That should have been a warning sign, but I decided to bring the rest of the band over in April anyway.

I asked Roy Fisher to take them on; it was soon after he'd been dumped by the Groundhogs. He found them a farmhouse in Chingford, Essex; they were fish out of water in the country and drove Roy nuts. He put a crew together and began getting them decent dates, including a tour in France. They probably did around sixty or so dates in the seven months they were here, including one date on the Spiders from Mars tour at Friar's Aylesbury, the Bickershaw Festival and dates with Man. They did the Roundhouse a few times as well. Cyril later claimed they'd been worked to death and played some 250 gigs – which mathematically was a complete impossibility.

The recordings with Dave went well but in two stints at Rockfield and further London studio time, they managed only seven tracks. They loved Rockfield and the nearby pubs and even wanted to call their album *Bucket of Brains*, named after Welsh local brew, Brains' beer. I was chuffed with the recordings though, and decided to release 'Slow Death' from the first batch at Rockfield. It was a song about mainlining that Cyril had written with former singer Roy Loney. I thought, 'fuck it'; it was such a great record, driven by a riff even the Stones would have killed for. I knew it was never going to get airplay, but I really thought it would blow all the right people away.

The Flamin' Groovies were hard work, taking up a lot of my time. They could be an absolute nightmare. There'd always be problems they really could have taken care of themselves. We put a second single out in December, a great version of Frankie Lee Sims' 'Married Woman', but I couldn't justify keeping them here for another year. They were too high maintenance. Cyril wanted 'Shake Some Action' out but I wanted to hold that back. In the end it served the band well and became the title track of their Sire debut in 1976 – again produced by Dave Edmunds.

I don't regret bringing them over even though overall costs probably came in around the £40,000 mark. We didn't have enough for an album, and I felt we'd be pouring good money after bad to take it any further. They hadn't made the impact I'd expected and I couldn't see a bigger picture where that was likely. We paid for them to return home at Christmas and called it quits after that. The tracks were never released in my time at UA, aside from the two singles. They were always a step out of time and whenever it didn't happen for them, they'd put the blame on somebody else; the record company was usually first in the firing line.

I gave them a master copy of the tracks they'd done for us to shop around back home but there were no takers. Writer Greg Shaw came to the rescue. He was now putting out singles on his Bomp label and asked if he could release one of the United Artists tracks. I let him have 'You Tore Me Down', which sounded like an unreleased Lennon and McCartney song. Through Greg they signed with Seymour Stein's Sire Records at the end of 1975. I was really pleased for them. *Shake Some Action* looked like it might be the charm that did the trick until the Ramones and Talking Heads came along. Almost overnight the Flamin' Groovies found themselves pushed to the back burner and unable to compete against the onslaught of punk.

Chapter 13

Who Will Save the World . . . and Hartlepool FC?

The Groundhogs were back in De Lane Lea studios with Martin Birch again within a year of recording *Thank Christ for the Bomb* and this time Tony came up with *Split*. It was only half a concept album; side two offering up 'Cherry Red', the fans' favourite ever Groundhogs song, 'Junkman', influenced by Tony's vegetarian beliefs and ending with Tony's wild electric solo 'Groundhog'. The four-part conceptual side definitely broke new ground; it described a traumatic schizophrenic experience Tony had been through himself where he'd say, 'One moment I felt all right, the next I didn't know who I was.' It was a bold statement about a subject nobody spoke openly about and was delivered amidst a stream of jagged riffs and frenzied solos that collapsed into feedback and distortion. The ferocious and uncompromising *Split Parts One to Four* definitely buried the blues once and for all. The Groundhogs sounded like no other British band from the late sixties fallout and, challenging as it was, *Split* did even better than its predecessor on release in April 1972. It made the Top 10 again, spent six months in the chart and was one of the ten bestselling albums of the year. It was the Groundhogs' only gold album.

They got a serious break when they were invited to tour with the Rolling Stones ahead of its release. It was the Stones'

so-called farewell tour before they went off to be tax exiles
in France. After the tour the Stones gifted Tony a tape of the
Groundhogs' own *Live at Leeds* which had been recorded on
their mobile. Within days of the tour ending, the Groundhogs
headlined the Lyceum in London, easily their biggest solo show.
It was a real test of how far they'd come but the Lyceum was
absolutely rammed. They sounded great, very loud, and they
commanded the stage with an authority I'd not seen before and
without a hint of self-indulgence.

They were fast becoming the thinking man's power trio and
it seemed as if the whole world found this out after seeing the
Groundhogs do the *Top of the Pops'* new 'Album Spot'. They
blasted out a pile-driving version of 'Cherry Red' that people still
talk about. The television cameramen inadvertently helped with
jagged camera angles and severe close-ups of the hairy trio; it
was a relentless barrage of noise that looked both violent and
exciting. The Groundhogs made so many new fans that day; far
more than those who gawped and complained. I was never more
convinced that the Groundhogs were going to be a truly mega
band than in those five minutes.

That didn't stop the Groundhogs and Tony being dismissed by
a lot of music journalists as a 'poor man's Hendrix', which was a
ridiculous comparison. They were totally different in just about
every way beyond a blues background and both fronting trios.
The third Groundhogs album of the seventies was *Who Will
Save the World? The Mighty Groundhogs* which appeared a year
later. Some saw it as the last in a loose trilogy, if only because
of yet more inspired artwork. It was Roy Fisher who thought
of depicting the band as superheroes with a sleeve designed by
Marvel Comics illustrator Neal Adams. Musically, it was a shift;
Tony wanted it to be more melodic and used a mellotron which
defused some of their usual power riffing. It did less well here,
but still almost cracking the Top 10. It sold better in America,

where interest had been building up steadily and where the cover art was an even greater talking point. They were finally about to tour there for the first time too.

It had been bang, bang, bang with the three seventies albums until a guy called Wilf Pine called me just as *Who Will Save the World?* was released and bluntly proclaimed, 'We're now managing the Groundhogs.' I couldn't believe it and asked, 'What's happened to Roy?' Wilf said, 'We've been talking to Tony and he agrees it's time for a change. So from now on you'll be dealing with me.' I was dumbstruck, and in the silence he added: 'Don't bother phoning Tony, he won't want to hear from you.' Of course I tried to phone Tony straight away, but he never picked up. I kept trying, but clearly he was under instruction to lay low.

Wilf Pine taking over management from Roy was the first time I thought, 'Hang on, things aren't going to plan here.' I hadn't seen it coming. Wilf Pine's Worldwide Artists (WWA) was a management organisation and he'd basically set out to steal the group. He did everything to make that happen by shamelessly pulling out all the stops to win over Tony personally. It's usually the singer or chief writer or the focal guitarist/musician that gets singled out, and Tony was all of these. Their pitch to him was 'Why don't you have your own home studio, a bigger house, a new car? We'll sort all that out for you.' Tony already wanted to explore synthesisers and the clincher was that they promised to help him set up a home studio. It was the classic ploy of creating a division within a group by effectively saying you're carrying the rest of them and you should be reaping the benefits. WWA had come late to the party, seen something happening and exploited the situation to their advantage.

It was devastating for Roy, who'd put in all the hard work to get them to where they were. I'd never seen any chinks in Tony's relationship with him at all. Wilf Pine had never even heard of them till a few months earlier. It was only much later I found

177

out that Wilf was the adopted son of Joey Pagano, head of one of the major New York crime families. Wilf had started out running a team of bouncers at drinking clubs on the Isle of Wight, before working for Don Arden. He'd worked with both the Move and Black Sabbath early on. One of his associates within WWA was none other than Pat Meehan, the man who'd scared the pants off me in Don Arden's office five years earlier.

Now, with Roy gone and Tony very much under Wilf Pine's spell, I was being frozen out. One of the things that had dogged the Groundhogs was that various US tours kept eluding them until they finally made it there in June 1972. After being a support act to Edgar Winter, Humble Pie and Black Sabbath, they were meant to play their own dates till I received a call telling me the tour was cancelled. Some bright spark in regional promotion at United Artists suggested the band go horse-riding in the Catskills during a day off. It's not the story that was released, but Tony actually fell off a horse and broke his wrist. We had a good tour lined up and were using their *Live at Leeds* as a US-only limited edition promo. For the first time, there was even a good deal of anticipation from United Artists in America. Neither the Groundhogs – nor Tony in any capacity – ever toured the States again. The Groundhogs had the potential to really break America – not just to do endless tours but to become a major band. It wasn't to be, and it soon began unravelling in the UK as well.

Once Wilf Pine focused on Tony and got in his ear, the result was to isolate him and demotivate the people who'd been behind the Groundhogs from the start. That's certainly how I felt. You can only do so much if you're being shut out. Ken Pustelnik left the band after the cancelled US dates. Ken wanted out but he may well have been pushed. They brought in a technically better drummer in Clive Brooks, from more progressive band Egg. Ken was more of a basher. There were no thrills in his playing; he 'walloped the life out of the kit', as Tony would say.

Back from the States, and once Tony's cast was off, they recorded a new album at Advision studios that autumn. Tony was still maintaining a low profile around me and the record company. *Hogwash* was released in November 1972, where they reverted to the formula of being heavy and bluesier again but with a sound tempered by synthesiser effects. It was unpleasant dealing with Wilf Pine, but that wasn't why I thought *Hogwash* wasn't their best. The synths couldn't disguise that *Hogwash* was more one-dimensional and lacked lyrical depth. I may be judging *Hogwash* unfairly, but the fans did too. It sold poorly compared to the previous three albums.

Contractually, *Hogwash* was the band's last album with United Artists and I wasn't about to re-sign them. WWA was setting up its own label, whose first release was *The Two Sides of TS McPhee*. It was recorded at the studio Tony built in the first half of 1973 at his home in Haverhill, Suffolk. If the Groundhogs always tended to divide critical opinion then Tony's solo album saw the lines drawn even more firmly. One side returned to the acoustic blues format, the other was a synthesiser suite called 'The Hunt', laudably in support of animal rights and anti-foxhunting but considered by many as unlistenable. Others saw it as a brave, forward-looking classic. I wasn't one of them. A second album on WWA, this time by the Groundhogs, *Solid*, didn't turn things around when it finally appeared in summer 1974. Before the year was out, Tony and Wilf mutually agreed to call it a day. The Groundhogs had lost all momentum and soldiered on till Tony split up the band the following year.

I did re-sign the Groundhogs after Tony put together a completely different line-up six months later. It was a four-piece with a more multi-instrumental approach. I should have thought twice. I saw the Groundhogs as unfinished business, but the two albums recorded and released in 1976 – *Crosscut Saw* and

Black Diamond – didn't claw back many of their old fans. I had Dr Feelgood turning it on by then and they signalled the change that was coming, and the 'new' Groundhogs were clobbered by punk. Rather ignominiously, and putting much of the blame on United Artists, Tony split the group up again. Now, of course, they are feted by exactly the same people who were rendering them redundant.

Kurt Cobain may not have been the first to speak out, but once he said somewhere that *Thank Christ for the Bomb* was an important album for him. The Groundhogs became forebears of grunge, just as they had punk beforehand. Others like Steven Malkmus, Jim O'Rourke and Queens of the Stone Age cited the Groundhogs, and over here Julian Cope, Karl Hyde of Underworld, Captain Sensible, and Mark E. Smith of the Fall all spoke up for them. The Fall even covered both 'Junkman' and 'Strange Town'.

The only occasion the Groundhogs and Man played together was when they took part in a fundraising weekend to save Hartlepool United Football Club. Mum used to send me the Saturday *Hartlepool Mail* every week, which early in 1972 reported that the club was not just having its usual financial difficulties but might actually struggle to stay in business. Having sworn allegiance to the 'Pools back in 1957, I thought there must be something I can do, and the obvious thing was to organise a benefit concert. At the time it was only the Groundhogs that could sell tickets in any great numbers and, though none of them were paticularly football fans, they were happy to do me a favour for expenses and hotel accommodation. I knew that Man and more recent signings Help Yourself were free and they completed the line-up. There wasn't a hall in Hartlepool that was big enough, but we managed to get Middlesbrough Town Hall on Saturday, 3 March. The gig sold out even though the Groundhogs had played there only a month before.

I wasn't the only Hartlepudlian at United Artists at the time; Richard Ogden had recently joined the press office and he followed the 'Pools as well. Richard's dad was the bank manager for my dad's timber business and Richard turned up at his door asking if he'd put him in touch with me. Richard had produced an impressive music magazine at Leicester University called *Fast 'N Bulbous*, which gave him a taste of the music business. He joined the press office, where the Hartlepool FC benefit was one of the first things he organised.

There was no stopping him and from a benefit gig headlined by the Groundhogs it grew to become a 'Save Hartlepool Football Club' fundraising weekend. Richard suggested a folk night on the Friday at Longscar Hall in Seaton Carew, where he was born. I never released too many folk albums, but we'd recently put out the first of three albums by Allan Taylor (backed by Dave Swarbrick, Dave Pegg and Dave Mattacks from Fairport Convention) and another by Colin Scot (which featured the likes of Peter Gabriel, Robert Fripp and Jon Anderson). So we asked them to play.[*]

United Artists was about to release the Frank Zappa film *200 Motels* and we also had the soundtrack. Richard came up with a Northern Premier at the Gaumont in Hartlepool at midnight on the Sunday, which was almost laughable and definitely a first. He also thought we should have a charity football match that afternoon with ex-Hartlepool players against a music biz eleven and that naturally led to us thinking, 'Why not come up with a specially recorded single?'

---

[*] I used Trident Studios a lot. An American guy called Jack Nelson ran the studios and he'd started a production company which the Colin Scot album came through. They were also behind the first Queen album, which I really didn't like. It just wasn't my kind of thing, although I thought they'd probably be successful. Trident Productions wanted to do a full production deal, which I wasn't comfortable doing anyway. Queen played down the bill with Hawkwind a couple of times and nothing they said was about to change my mind.

Our publisher's in-house writer/arranger/producer Ed Welch came up with an A-side called 'Who Put Sugar in My Tea', but it was the B-side 'Never Say Die' – for which Richard wrote more direct, stirring lyrics – that went on to become a club anthem. The phrase 'Never Say Die' is still featured on the corner flags and team shirts. We put the record out in a picture sleeve of the team in the studio, which included a young Neil Warnock, whose playing career has long since been eclipsed by his managerial exploits and who has just announced his retirement after forty-two years. We shipped five or six thousand copies of the single to the club to sell in local shops and at the ground. They took all the money from those sales, and we'd press more singles when they needed them.

'Never Say Die' is still the 'Pools rallying cry

We had one meeting with club secretary, Nattie Armstrong, who couldn't understand why we wanted to do it, and there was an underlying feeling of 'What's in it for you?' It was only the Groundhogs gig where the proceeds made any substantial profit after expenses, the other events were all pretty calamitous. The match on the Sunday certainly didn't get much of a turnout, which wasn't helped because it clashed with a then rare live match on television – Chelsea versus Stoke. The 'Pools team included 1950s heroes Kenny Johnson, the club's record goal scorer, Bobby Lumley and Tommy McGuigan as well as several players from the current squad. The celebrity side included members of various pop groups – the Fortunes, Vanity Fair, the Ivy League and Plastic Penny plus J. Vincent Edwards from Hair. Several journalists from *Melody Maker*, Ed Welch, and Sean Tyla then with Help Yourself, completed the team. There was a suggestion that certain musicians had something more than a few orange segments at half time, but the 'Pools team trounced them anyway.

The *200 Motels* screening wasn't well attended either. Frank Zappa wasn't exactly a household name in Hartlepool. It was a drunken and rowdy affair that degenerated into a food fight at one point and few managed to sit through Zappa's surreal tale of life on the road. I was staying at Mum and Dad's that night and was thankful I decided to give it a miss. Richard did get carried away and he was grilled by BBC TV's *Look North*, accusing us of staging the whole thing to get publicity for *200 Motels*. Frank Zappa would have chuckled at that. Then, for all his efforts, Richard also got a hard time from Martin for spending too much money. Hartlepool United started winning after our weekender event and, having been firmly at the foot of the table, we finished sixth from bottom that year. For once we didn't have to apply for re-election. I'd like to think we helped motivate the team and our efforts were vindicated.

Chapter 14
Space Rock and Sonic Attack

Hawkwind didn't record again till May 1971, by which time the line-up that had recorded their debut album a year earlier and had played around a hundred or so gigs had shed two members. Being in Hawkwind was an intense experience and everybody was doing drugs, which took its toll. Huw Lloyd Langton and founder member John Harrison had left. Hawkwind would never go back to a two-guitar line-up, but Dave Anderson was brought in as Hawkwind's third bassist; he'd been in Amon Düül II. Between making the new record and it coming out, there were a number of others who were sucked into the Hawkwind vortex; they all proved to be crucial members of the band or major collaborators. Nothing about Hawkwind was ever formulaic in the way all the pieces fell into place. Dik Mik left temporarily after being involved in an accident in the equipment van and they brought in Del Dettmar. He was another non-musician but proved more proficient than Dik Mik and was soon playing one of the early VCS 3 synthesisers. They both played on the second album and when Dik Mik returned Del stayed on, giving Hawkwind a greater electronic assault.

Most days Hawkwind used to hang out at the *Friendz* office on Portobello Road and it was there they met Robert Calvert and Barney Bubbles. Both worked for the magazine. Calvert was another of Nik Turner's old acquaintances from Margate and *Friendz* regularly published his poetry and short stories. He began performing on stage with the band from time to time before becoming an official member in October as their 'space poet'. His key role, however, was in hatching conceptual ideas with the group and with Barney Bubbles for the artwork, notably the Hawkwind Log, the 24-page booklet that came with the group's second album *In Search of Space*.

Barney would be instrumental in creating an amazing visual identity for Hawkwind over the next four years. He designed and crafted the sleeve artwork and elaborate fold-outs for their albums during the group's classic years with United Artists, as well as designing posters and helping visualise Hawkwind's immersive stage appearance, painting and fashioning the stage and the backline equipment. Barney and Nik shared a house for a while, and with Bob Calvert they were the chief architects of Hawkwind's space rock odyssey that framed all the new songs Dave and Nik were coming up with.

Barney's designs were central to translating Hawkwind's narrative. His artwork was so immaculately and intricately worked out and, however complex, Barney had already figured out how it needed to be printed. He had a background as a commercial artist as well as being a genius illustrator, graphic artist and designer, able to contextualise Hawkwind's counter-cultural spirituality and cosmology. There were never going to be any arguments from me, nor were there any from the art department, however much of a challenge the artwork might present, or the potential cost of manufacture. Doug would make sure all the information was correct and it was good to go. No other band was coming up with anything like Barney's designs, which said 'This is Hawkwind' as much as the music.

By the time *In Search of Space* was released on 8 October, the final parts of the classic line-up were in place and, most significantly, Dave Anderson had made way for Lemmy, who was

suggested to the group by Dik Mik. Lemmy was another character around Ladbroke Grove who'd been in Sam Gopal's Dream,
then a group called Opal Butterfly and before that he'd roadied
for The Nice and Hendrix. He'd never played bass before his first
gig with Hawkwind in September, but he developed a distinctive chord-based style influenced by playing rhythm guitar in
Blackpool beat group the Rockin' Vicars. It wasn't long before
his rock-biker image and physical on-stage presence made him
a natural frontman. Although Bob Calvert was in the line-up by
then, both he and Dave Brock tended to blend in more with the
dark shadows created by Hawkwind's portentous light show.

The touring entourage had also expanded to include spontaneous dancer Stacia Blake, who was very popular with both male and
female fans. DJ Andy Dunkley went from warming up the crowd
to take on a greater role as master of ceremonies during *Space
Ritual*. Hawkwind had a very loyal road crew too, most of whom
had been there from the early days, including lighting and effects
specialists Liquid Len and his team. From a makeshift start, they
got more sophisticated and adventurous. *In Search of Space* was
only the beginning. Hawkwind had arrived at the classic line-up
that would remain intact for three years. The only change came
early in 1972 when drummer Simon King – who'd been in Opal
Butterfly with Lemmy – replaced the flagging Terry Ollis.

There were no star turns in Hawkwind, nor were any of them
outstanding musicians. The reviews of *In Search of Space* were
very good, sometimes begrudgingly so, but I remember Richard
Williams picking up on how they were the first British band to
display a recognisable influence of German rock and specifically
their label mates Can and Amon Düül II. The fifteen-minute 'You
Shouldn't Do That' was a blueprint for their cumulative power
of repetition. Hawkwind were never acknowledged as innovators,
but who else was attempting what they were achieving? They
pre-dated Roxy Music too. Hawkwind were becoming a phenom-

enon and were growing fast even before 'Silver Machine' tipped the scales.

Doug Smith was totally committed to them, which brought problems within Clearwater Productions and he left that year to set up his own management company Western Productions. I always thought the band had a point to prove that they were not just the spaced-out hippies as they were often cast. *In Search of Space* was a Top 20 album which remained in the charts till well into the New Year. Its success and sell-out shows took the music press and people in the industry – including some within United Artists – by surprise. From doubting and dismissing Hawkwind, there was no denying they were now a major band in the making.

In Search of Space's amazing sleeve was now there for all to see and pore over in awe – marvelling how that middle section on the front of the jacket slotted perfectly into the die-cut serrated edges, opening out to reveal portraits of the band. Then inside was the Hawkwind Log with Bob Calvert's chronicles interspersed with pictures, comic strips and illustrations drawing from astrology, cosmology, Eastern religious philosophies and iconic hippie images of Stonehenge and Glastonbury Tor. Lyrically they drew from the same well, though with a sense of foreboding rather than optimism and idealism.

By the time we did the *Greasy Truckers Party* on 13 February 1972, Hawkwind could easily have sold out the Roundhouse without any extra acts. The Greasy Truckers benefit was Doug's idea to support a Ladbroke Grove community organisation led by *Friendz* editor John Trux. I likened them to the Diggers in San Francisco. The gig was a major turning point for Hawkwind because it featured a relatively new song called 'Silver Machine' that they'd been playing for a couple of months. I'd agreed to put out a double album with a side given over to each act on the bill; two of the others happened to be United Artists acts Brinsley Schwarz and Man. Hawkwind dropped acid in the dressing room in the afternoon ahead of the Roundhouse performance and then had to delay going on stage because of a power cut. The Roundhouse date was during the three-day week. So the entire audience had to leave and return once the power was restored. At least three hundred additional people came back in amidst the chaos.

Hawkwind really stood out. There was something about them that appealed to a more grounded audience that had no time for ELP or Yes or Genesis. However much they were out in space, Hawkwind were down to earth and they'd come a long way from playing free gigs under the Westway in Notting Hill. The *Greasy Truckers Party* double LP was released on 28 April. We'd already decided that we'd press an initial 10,000 records and then delete it from the catalogue. We also sold it as cheaply as possible, which created a real demand for it. The ploy worked perfectly, and we actually pressed up 20,000 in the end.

Hawkwind's rock-biker frontman Lemmy at the BBC in 1972

It had never occurred to me that 'Silver Machine' was a hit single. Doug had a hunch it would work and said, 'If I can have a couple of hours in the studio, let me have a go.' He and Dave took the tapes from the *Greasy Truckers Party* – and 'Silver Machine' wasn't on the album – asked Lemmy to re-do Bob Calvert's vocal, did some edits, added some guitar, and that was that. Even Tony Blackburn was playing it from day one. It was quite something to hear Hawkwind blasting out from every-where rather than expecting just a few plays from John Peel. It was released on 9 June, charted three weeks later and reached No. 3 at the end of August, three years to the day since Group X made their debut at All Saints Hall. Having a Top 3 hit was such a buzz and made a lot of people eat their words.

They did *Top of the Pops* too and we made a film recorded at Friar's Aylesbury. We all thought the idea of Hawkwind actually playing in the BBC's studio wasn't right. If they had done it, I'd've loved to have been there but it went against their outsider image. Quite possibly the producers were wary of having a wild bunch like Hawkwind being let loose among the kids herded into the studio. People from both sides of the fence were talking about the film the next day; their appearance shocked some viewers, but the fans loved it. The band hadn't sold out – so it worked on every level. It was broadcast four times during its chart run and even re-broadcast on the Christmas special.

Hawkwind were still at the heart of the Ladbroke Grove community, but their success created even more demands upon them. They found it hard to say no and it put them under even greater pressure. To give them some breathing space we decided to record the next album at Rockfield, the residential studio in Monmouthshire, which became my studio of choice over the next four years. *Doremi Farso Latido* was Lemmy's first album with the band and it captured them in full flow. It was the same sonic assault, had the same driving rhythms, but new drummer Simon

King was more powerful than Terry Ollis and with Lemmy's bass and Dave's choppy guitar propelling the band to an even higher level of raw energy. The electronics were more upfront too – less about creating atmosphere – particularly Del's EMS synthesisers. Nik Turner had already added a few new tricks, taking a leaf out of Miles Davis's book by using wah-wah and echo effects. Yet there was nothing flashy about Hawkwind's drug-fuelled space rock, no showing off and nothing predictable in the way Pink Floyd had become.

The new album coincided with the *Space Ritual* tour kicking off in November. The group were now playing to 2000 people a night. Bob and Barney had created a magnificently painted stage with the musicians all standing in positions relative to their astrological signs. Barney was also working closely with Jonathan Smeeton (aka Liquid Len), so the visual feast was all-encompassing. They upped their entourage, now stretching to three dancers and a mime artist, more lighting and stage personnel. Everybody was pulling together and pulling everything together. The money they were making was ploughed back into their own new PA, an expanded light show and a couple of Mercedes vans that wouldn't break down. I thought the *Space Ritual* was amazing and very loud, particularly the pulse of Lemmy's bass just a register below Dave's crunching guitar riffs, and all totally in sync with the lighting effects. The set drew largely from *In Search of Space* and *Doremi Farso Latido*, which had peaked at No. 4; it goes without saying that it came in another opulent sleeve.

People used to mock the Grateful Dead in the same way as they did Hawkwind, but all these so-called freaks were acting together to make this thing work. As with the Dead, none of it would have been possible if they lived up to the cliché that they were spaced out all the time. They'd become street-smart hippies. And like the Dead, Hawkwind had a reputation for the amount of drugs they took, a reputation that was completely warranted. After 'Silver Machine' was a hit they were getting raided backstage almost every gig and crossing international borders, being stopped and searched became arduous and time-consuming. They had to find ingenious ways to hide their stash. If it was a theatre or venue with a rigging system, they'd tape it to the fly bar high up at roof level. That was safe from sniffer dogs and the police were never going to climb up there. Sometimes they buried the stash outside.

Space Ritual Alive became the best seller of the lot. It was recorded on the Pye Mobile before Christmas 1972 in Liverpool and London and released 11 May 1973. Surprisingly, it's the first album to feature Bob Calvert. It was a double album with an exotic front cover of a space goddess that folded into six panels; it may have been Barney's most extravagant creation yet. The spoken-word pieces by Bob Calvert included Michael Moorcock's 'The Black Corridor'. Bob's own public service announcement 'Sonic Attack' was always a scary highlight; we used it as a promo 7-inch contained in a cloth bag. This was Hawkwind's peak, not only their highest chart entry but when the *Space Ritual* tour picked up again in February that was capped by them playing the Empire Pool at Wembley to an incredible 10,000 people. Hawkwind shows had become an unmissable event.

We decided that this was our best opportunity to bring out another single that might realistically do as well as 'Silver Machine'. 'Urban Guerrilla' was the only contender, but it only got to No. 39. It wasn't going to shoot up the next week. I have to own up here and say that because it coincided with a series of bombings as part of the IRA's campaign in mainland England, we used that as the excuse for pulling the single. I could see that 'Urban Guerrilla' was going to peter out, so we withdrew it. I feel a little ashamed about issuing the statement that 'the record was selling very well but we didn't want to gain sales by association with recent events'.

191

Although both bands are associated with 'space rock', I always thought the parallels between Pink Floyd and Hawkwind were more coincidental than anything else. Pink Floyd's experimental sound and mixed media approach had evolved playing shows at All Saints Hall where Hawkwind had made their bow as Group X. For Pink Floyd, though, once Syd Barrett left, their lengthy space rock songs such as 'A Saucerful of Secrets' initially served to give them breathing space, having lost their chief songwriter. For Hawkwind, space rock had been integral to developing their countercultural slogans and science fiction and fantasy stories, but they didn't want to become wholly reliant on it.

They made their first US tour in November, after which the *Space Ritual* was phased out. It was like Bowie killing off Ziggy. Their next UK tour on their return – beginning 10 December – was ironically called *The Ridiculous Roadshow*. Tired of being on the road, Dik Mik left at the end of the year and Bob Calvert also moved on, perhaps seeing his role in the band soon diminishing. America was becoming a priority, with two US tours in quick succession by spring 1974. Hawkwind were making inroads in America, even if that wasn't reflected in record sales, and by the third tour in the space of twelve months they were playing to 6000 people in some major cities. It helped that Greg Lewerke loved the band and he was now Head of International A&R at United Artists in the States. Promoters wanted them too. There wasn't another band in the States anything like Hawkwind.

Del Dettmar also announced that he wanted to leave the band after the third US tour. Simon House had been playing in the Third Ear Band since High Tide and joined the tour to ease his way towards replacing Del. He joined Hawkwind officially in April. The loss of their two electronics wizards, and then replacing them with a violinist/keyboard player, did change the balance of the sound. Simon was also by far the most accomplished musician ever to join the ranks. Once Simon

became crucial to Hawkwind's range of sounds they operated
at a much lower energy level.

Bob Calvert's *Captain Lockheed and the Starfighters* was
released 10 May 1974. Paul Rudolph from the Fairies was musical director and it was produced by Roy Thomas Baker. I knew
him from Trident Studios and he'd been working with Queen
from the start and was soon to help overhaul Queen's sound on
their breakthrough album *Sheer Heart Attack*. We recorded three
albums with Roy producing during 1974. Bob's album was about
death-trap Lockheed planes in the German air force. It featured
most of Hawkwind and at times sounds like it; particularly
'Ejection', released as a single ahead of the album. The album
is part Monty Python in its craziness with skits featuring Viv
Stanshall and Traffic's Jim Capaldi.

Bob was friendly with Viv, who does a brilliant turn as an
over-the-top German commandant. They were quite similar characters; Bob was also well educated, well read, but prone to mood
swings and mental instability. He was very into role-playing
and one time turned up in the office the same afternoon as Viv.
Bob arrived totally in character in a German air force uniform
and wearing ludicrous goggles. He and Viv began speaking in
cod German accents and goose-stepping round the room. Brian
Eno is one of the other musicians on the album and he produced
Bob's second album *Lucky Leif and the Longships*, released the
following year. It imagined what would have happened if the
original Norse settlers had colonised the continent. It was Eno's
first outside production job, much praised at the time although I
didn't care for it.

Captain Lockheed was holding a place for Hawkwind fans
with no new studio album because of their relentless touring
schedule. The album they recorded in June – *Hall of the Mountain Grill* – was another produced by Roy Thomas Baker. It was
the last album Del contributed to and Simon House's first. His

presence brought greater melody and harmony and the lyrics
were less cosmic. The greater prominence of keyboards and even
mellotron signified prog to me; *Hall of the Mountain Grill* was
leaning more in that direction. Released on 6 September 1974,
it reached No. 16 in the UK charts. They toured the UK again,
now featuring two drummers but even that failed to halt the
transition towards a more considered approach.

Hawkwind returned to Rockfield to record the next album
before yet another scheduled American tour in April. This time
Michael Moorcock was integral to the underlying concept and
appeared on a Hawkwind album for the first time. He effectively
replaced Bob Calvert as a source of ideas although he didn't
tour with the band. Moorcock's 'Kings of Speed' was released
as a single on 7 March to flag up the new album but Lemmy's
'Motorhead' on the B-side would soon have far greater significance. Hawkwind were now out of contract with United Artists,
but Doug agreed to an interim licensing deal for us to press and
distribute *Warrior at the Edge of Time* – which was released on
9 May. Its chart position at No. 13 didn't suggest things were
slipping but Hawkwind were a band in transition and I wasn't
sure where they were heading.*

Doug was renegotiating with Martin Davis but as it turned
out *Warrior at the Edge of Time* was the band's final album for
United Artists. If things were already in a state of flux, then
two days after the album release the walls came tumbling down.
Lemmy was arrested on the Canadian border and found to be
in possession of white powders that turned out to be speed not

---

* I put out a Michael Moorcock album with a group named after his fictional
band Deep Fix. There was some Hawkwind involvement in *The New World's
Fair*. Although we gave it a glorious Barney Bubbles sleeve it was a flop
sales-wise and indifferently received critically, causing Moorcock to damn
United Artists for being useless compared to his book publishers.

coke. That didn't stop him being carted off to jail before the charges were dropped but it led to him being sacked.

The circumstances surrounding his dismissal heralded the beginning of the end for my involvement with Hawkwind. When Lemmy was arrested, the band phoned Doug in London and asked him to get Paul Rudolph on the next flight. It made sense to bring him over as cover but, despite Lemmy making the next scheduled gig in Toronto, he was still sacked that night. Paul Rudolph took his place for the rest of the US tour and remained in the band for a couple more years. Apparently Nik Turner declared that he'd leave if Lemmy was allowed back in the band and he wasn't alone in that. There'd been no outcry in the press or among fans when Dik Mik or Del or even Bob Calvert left, but Lemmy was both a fan favourite and a media favourite. Once Lemmy had gone, Hawkwind were less of a rock 'n' roll band. I know some of my enthusiasm left with Lemmy.

The dates kept coming and I was already feeling that the money-making touring had long since taken precedence over recordings. After headlining Reading on 22 August, Stacia left to get married. Bob Calvert had guested with the band at the festival and ended up staying on. Lemmy's departure was the beginning of a series of hirings and firings. By the end of 1975 Doug Smith had left too. He thought sacking Lemmy was a serious mistake and there were now too many internal squabbles within the band. There was also a dispute with United Artists over unpaid royalties due to an accounting error – and a failure to agree on a new offer was the final straw for Doug.

When Doug departed only Dave and Nik remained from the early days and I was well aware of the power struggle between them. I could see that for the band to survive one of them had to go. It wasn't my problem any more. The new management decided to take Hawkwind to Charisma. Their first for the new label was *Astounding Sound, Amazing Music* in September 1976.

195

I was a little sad when Nik left a few months later. That left only Dave Brock from the original group. I released *Roadhawks* that year; it was a 'best of' with elaborate packaging that Dave Brock was involved in. He compiled and segued all the tracks, which gave it a definite Hawkwind spin. We'd had the best and most exciting period with Hawkwind and it was going to be more expensive to keep them. I felt like a football manager who builds up a team and then all the players start leaving so it's not your team any more.

I remember Michael Moorcock saying it's not science fiction, it's science fantasy – and that's what Hawkwind were for their fans – something escapist. For a few years they were a true phenomenon and it was something they achieved against the odds. The music press was always sniffy about them. When they started out, you'd see headlines about them being a joke band; then they became the joke band that made it. It was an 'us against the world' situation, battling against the mainstream. I can't think of any other band that captured people's imaginations the way Hawkwind did at that time. I used to feel quite righteous being part of it.

They'd inherited that Ladbroke Grove scene from the mid-sixties but what Hawkwind achieved was to take that spirit of the London underground out to the provinces. It travelled well to Glasgow, Liverpool, Manchester and the Midlands in what was a pretty miserable few years for the country politically and a miserable time for music. Hawkwind were definitely the antithesis of glam and prog – there was no 'look at how great I am'. In that I think they did open up a gateway for punk; Hawkwind was about attitude and intent and never about instrumental virtuosity. John Lydon wasn't alone in being a fan. The Sex Pistols even had a crack at 'Silver Machine' after they reunited in 2002.

I'd got to know Lemmy pretty well because he used to come in

196

and hang out in the office. He had this dream of being in the loudest, dirtiest, nastiest rock 'n' roll band in the world. It was a great calling card, but he hadn't thought it through. It was too soon for what he had in mind but I was excited about starting something new with him just as I was losing Hawkwind.

The first trio came together quickly with Pink Fairies' guitarist Larry Wallis and drummer Lucas Fox. Doug Smith was going to manage them too, and I wanted him around because Lemmy could be a handful. He was still under contract to us. We all agreed on Dave Edmunds producing the band and, having been talked out of calling his trio Bastard, Lemmy decided upon Motorhead. It was the title of the last song he'd recorded with Hawkwind as well as slang for heavy amphetamine use. I'd already put Lemmy in touch with American artist Joe Petagno who'd done artwork for Dr Feelgood's *Malpractice* and he came up with the first version of the now familiar skull logo, so it was beginning to fall into place.

They started recording at Rockfield in late September and I went down after the first week. They'd got four tracks done with Dave Edmunds that sounded great. Dave didn't look at all well, though. He'd turned green and said: 'This is going to kill me. I haven't slept for five days and can't keep this up.' Lemmy said later that it wasn't down to Motorhead's excessive behaviour or the long hours but because Dave was really stressed out. He'd just done a solo deal with Swan Song – Led Zeppelin's label – and Peter Grant was pressuring him to get his own stuff together.

We had the studio time booked so I brought in Fritz Fryer. He'd been in the Four Pennies – just about the antithesis of Motorhead – and was now an engineer/producer at Rockfield. It was a tough ask for him to try and match what Dave had done as closely as possible. Fritz at least finished the tracks, which would have been enough for an album, but while Dave's tracks still sounded great the rest were more like demos.

We mixed the tracks in January and by then Lemmy was coming in to see me every day wanting this or that because Doug had pulled out. He did return to manage Motorhead again but for the time being the band had no manager. As a result, Lemmy was taking up more and more of my time and we had nothing to show for it. Lemmy hated the album. We couldn't salvage it in any workable way and he even made me promise I'd never release it. I said, 'As long as I'm here it won't come out.' Next thing he'd brought in a new bass player and drummer in what would become the classic Motorhead line-up with Eddie Clarke on bass and Phil Taylor on drums. At that point I knew the album we had was definitely a dead duck because two thirds of the recordings weren't good enough and it was a different band anyway, so even Dave Edmunds' tracks were now redundant.

I've not regretted much. The exception was Motorhead. That was the one that got away. I'd always thought we'd recorded too early and didn't trust my instincts that the band was under-cooked. I should have given it more time, but the Feelgoods were really happening in 1976 and I felt like I was becoming Lemmy's stand-in manager' so I cut them loose.[*]

---

[*] You can't lose sleep over things that later became successful. Andy Dunkley recommended King Crimson to me in 1969. They hadn't played any gigs but I went to see them at a rehearsal room and what I heard was pretty impressive – more or less the first album. A deal was already being discussed so I never followed through. I missed out on Roxy Music a few years later as well. I met Brian Ferry when I sat next to him at a Sun Ra concert at the Royal Festival Hall. We had a few conversations about things that we liked. He was a couple of years older than me and also born in County Durham, in Washington in rural Sunderland. Martin Davis knew their management well and said, 'Leave it with me', but it was destined to go where it was going. Both bands were with EG Management and both went to Island. I knew that neither band was right for United Artists, nor was it the right label for them.

A few years later I was in Los Angeles and I went to the Rainbow Rooms and there at the bar was Lemmy. This was in 1980; Motorhead's crucial second album for Bronze – *Bomber* – was out and they'd had a Top 10 EP. United Artists couldn't resist releasing the 'original' first album under the intended title *On Parole*. Lemmy saw me and shouted across the bar: 'Oi, you bastard – you promised you wouldn't put that out.' I shouted back: 'I'm not there any more.'

Motorhead had actually started playing dates in July 1975, usually to pretty indifferent reactions. The only thing they had going for them was that they were loud. I used to wake up the next day after Groundhogs' gigs with a ringing in my ears but it would fade away during the day. When Motorhead opened for Blue Öyster Cult at Hammersmith Odeon in October I was standing by the sound desk. It was situated on the ground floor in the centre where the first rows of seats ended. Motorhead started quietly to a point where people in the crowd were shouting to turn up the volume. Lemmy wasn't living up to his claims and he was getting some stick. So he kept gesturing to the soundman to make it louder and louder until at one point I felt a stab of pain in my head and yelped. The damage was done and I've had tinnitus ever since.

Chapter 15
Do You Like It Here Now?

I'd expected there'd be a certain amount of resistance to Man. I knew I had to get people to reappraise the band as I'd done but it was a slow process building something out of nothing. The first album we did – simply called *Man* – was patchy but it was important to get something out quickly. I needed to make people aware they were now signed to United Artists because as a label we were establishing a good reputation through the Groundhogs and Hawkwind. I knew Man slotted in perfectly and were part of my masterplan even if I didn't have one. True to form, *Man* got poor reviews and we rushed the second album out only six months later. *Do You Like It Here Now, Are You Settling In* was recorded at Rockfield Studios in Monmouthshire on their home patch and that was a marked improvement.

I got the Rockfield bug because of Man. I knew Dave Edmunds had recorded a worldwide hit there in 1970. 'I Hear You Knocking' had been recorded in the potato loft. Rockfield was a working farm owned by the Ward brothers, Charles and Kingsley. I got on really well with them both and with Kingsley's wife Anne. Kingsley was amazed that I actually had a copy of the Charles Kingsley Creation's Columbia single 'Summer Without Sun', the only release by the brothers' band in 1965, which was produced by Joe Meek. It was Kingsley who mostly ran the studio. Since using it for local groups in the mid-1960s they'd built it up from an eight-track to a sixteen-track studio now fitted with a custom-designed mixing console. Between 1971 and '76 Rockfield was almost a second home. I recorded just about everybody there for a while, including Hawkwind, Brinsley Schwarz, Help Yourself, Motorhead, the Flamin' Groovies, Dr Feelgood, even Del Shannon and much later the Stone Roses. Kingsley would give us great deals.

We'd usually book in to record for one or two weeks and mix back in London. Groups loved it because they could work at their own pace, spend the day in one of the pubs down the road if they wanted and then work through the night. If they wanted to relax, the rural surroundings and fresh farm food added an experience that could be as restful as it was productive. Kingsley was a great character too. His forte was doing Elvis Presley impersonations standing on the table in whichever of the local pubs he wasn't banned from at that particular time. The home-from-home recording in Rockfield definitely contributed to *Do You Like It Here Now* getting closer to capturing what Man was about – writing a song in the morning, recording in the after-noon, completing and mixing at night. They were still derided by the press or at best completely ignored. The problem was that so few journalists had ever seen them play. I was frustrated that everybody I spoke to about them reacted exactly as I'd done when Barrie Marshall first mentioned them to me. It took the *Greasy Truckers Party* to make the breakthrough, by which time Clive John had left and they were down to a classic twin-guitar four-piece line-up of Micky Jones, Deke Leonard, Martin Ace and Terry Williams.

When Doug Smith first mentioned *Greasy Truckers Party* the line-up was Hawkwind, Brinsley Schwarz and Byzantium. I'd agreed to release an album from the Roundhouse show and told Doug I really wanted to add Man to the bill, which he was fine about. Man went on in the middle of the afternoon because they had another gig later that night, which turned out to be a real stroke of luck. The event took place during the three-day week and we expected there'd be at least one power cut during the day. As it was, Byzantium missed out. It was the best I'd ever seen Man play. I don't think they went into it thinking this is going to change everything, but they were fantastic and the rest of the day people were coming up to me saying, 'Wow – I'd no idea Man were that good.' At last, I thought. The Notting Hill underground contingent who were there for Hawkwind totally got what Man was about, this tight, free-flowing jamming band with that classic West Coast dual guitar sound. It came over brilliantly on record – a side-long twenty-two-minute version of 'Spunk Rock'. *Greasy Truckers Party* finally steered Man to the right audience and almost overnight they took a huge step towards burying their chequered past. It was my favourite Man line-up – just the four-piece and the same set-up as Quicksilver Messenger Service – with Micky and Deke a parallel version of John Cipollina and Gary Duncan.

I wanted to get something more out of that line-up and moved quickly to get a full live album out there. We wanted to record in Wales and *Live at the Padget Rooms, Penarth* was organised within two months and released in September. The band suggested the venue, familiar stomping ground for them at the southern end of Cardiff Bay and a typical municipal hall that had seen better days but with great sound. We used the same marketing trick as for *Greasy Truckers Party* but pressed up only 8000 copies this time which sold out in a week. It topped the mid-price chart, which I'd never even considered but, significantly, Man also made the *Melody Maker* Top 30. We were finally making inroads with the music press. To their credit, the Man band didn't actively court the press. They were so resigned to being dissed or ignored that it no longer bothered them.

Deke Leonard was the only one in the band who'd hang

around in London. I got to know him better than the rest and I
knew that at some point he'd go off on his own. What I wasn't
expecting was that Deke would be asked to leave. Barrie knew
I'd be disappointed, so he waited till they had a new line-up
confirmed before he told me. Martin Ace had also left the group.
I was gutted and was convinced it would set the band back.
They brought keyboards in again with Phil Ryan. He was in
Neath-based band the Eyes of Blue, who were very popular on
the Welsh scene. Another fellow Welshman, Will Youatt, replaced
Martin on bass and Clive John returned but mostly playing
guitar this time around. So in what soon became a typical Man
game of musical chairs only Terry and Micky remained from the
band that had made the breakthrough. The only album in this
particular line-up was *Be Good to Yourself, At Least Once A Day*
produced with Dave Edmunds at Rockfield in August 1972. It
yielded two more classic improv vehicles, 'C'Mon' and 'Bananas'.
Man now had a rolling set list of frivolous titles such as 'Many
Are Called But Few Get Up' and 'Daughter of the Fireplace' that
maintained a movable feast over the years.

Despite the changes, *Be Good to Yourself* kept up the momentum and I started to push the Welsh thing as we needed a
talking point. The artwork came in a gatefold sleeve that opened
out to a giant cartoon map of Wales that was both funny and
a comprehensive history of the Man band, and Welsh rock. It
was conceived by Deke Leonard who, of course, wasn't even on
the album. It didn't seem to matter who was in the band; they
were playing bigger venues, three times the size from a year
ago and record sales were on the rise. To keep things moving
we recorded Man's end-of-year party, *Christmas at the Patti
Pavilion* on 19 December 1972 and released it in April 1973 as a
double-gatefold 10-inch. That was a first in itself as a format and
built on the notion of Man's extended family with performances
by various Man alumni in the Flying Aces – Martin Ace and his

wife George, Deke Leonard, Dave Edmunds, and as a sign of
the camaraderie between label mates it included tracks by Help
Yourself and B.J. Cole from Cochise. The album also marked the
first recorded appearance by Ducks Deluxe, all somehow part of
my United Artists family tree.

With Man everything focused around albums and touring.
If they weren't on the road, they were probably in the studio.
There'd be some rehearsal time but even that was minimal. So
I wanted to rush another album out to keep things ticking over.
True to form, Clive John left again, and Alan 'Tweke' Lewis
replaced him on *Back Into the Future*. Typically, it was written
and recorded at Rockfield within a month, then straight out on
the road again. I recorded Man's show at the Roundhouse on
24 June 1973 so we could make the next release a half live/half
studio double album and sell it for the price of a single album.
The bonus of what was effectively a free live album helped Man
finally reach No. 23 in the official chart in October 1973. It was
the fourth album they'd released in thirteen months but the fans
were still coming back for more.

It was during a full British tour in September and October
that I had an inkling, yet again, things weren't right. Man got
their only ever music press front cover in *Melody Maker* with
a photo of Micky Jones on the front. Phil Ryan was so furious
he set fire to the paper in the dressing room in front of Micky.
The power struggle came close to the unthinkable when Micky
declared, 'It's him or me.' Phil did the decent thing and left,
taking Will Youatt with him. Watching from the wings on that
tour had been Deke Leonard, whose band Iceberg was supporting. I'd made two albums – *Iceberg* and *Kamikaze* – with Deke
during the twenty months he'd been out of the band. I kept on
making records with other past members – one with Clive John
and two with Phil and Will's group the Neutrons.

*

I've always thought that if Help Yourself had been an American group they'd have a huge cult following by now. As it is, they have a modest cult following. Given their instability, and particularly keyboardist, guitarist and chief songwriter Malcolm Morley's fragile state of mind, it's a wonder they were able to record four albums for United Artists between 1971 and 1973. Unlike so many groups coming together at the end of the sixties, Help Yourself didn't have any damaging back story. The Bystanders and Kippington Lodge typically suffered from that hangover. Help Yourself carried very little of that sixties baggage of failure and underachievement but they had plenty of their own personal hang-ups.

Dave Robinson produced both the first Help Yourself album and an album by Ernie Graham, who'd been in the Irish group Eire Apparent. I knew about Help Yourself because drummer Dave Charles was involved in the Brinsley Schwarz New York launch. He was there to record the group at the Fillmore. John Eichler was an old friend of Famepushers' Stephen Warwick and he'd been supervising the film crew around the ill-fated event. Once he and Dave Robinson put that episode behind them, they formed a no-nonsense management company called Down Home Productions and John was responsible for Help Yourself.

The quartet of Malcolm Morley and Dave Charles, who'd been friends since schooldays, was completed by bass player Ken Whaley and an extraordinarily talented guitarist called Richard Treece. He was so gifted and versatile but had no idea how good he was. They hadn't played any proper live shows before recording their debut album with Dave at Olympic at the end of 1970. I particularly liked *Help Yourself*, which was a very melodic combination of elements of both English folk and American country rock. *Rolling Stone* later described it as sounding more like Neil Young than Neil Young. We released it in April 1971 but almost immediately, Ken Whaley felt left out in the cold and left once Ernie Graham was drafted in with his friend, guitarist JoJo Glemser. Richard switched to bass, which was a ridiculous move, but it was always such a loose set-up. They all lived together, along with John Eichler and his wife Sue at Headley Grange in Hampshire, where Led Zeppelin had recorded much of their runic fourth album. It was a grand-sounding place but very run-down and rudimentary. They had the gear permanently set up so they rehearsed and played all day – or sometimes not at all – which frustrated Dave Robinson.

We made Help Yourself's second album at Rockfield; by the end, Ernie and JoJo had drifted away, so Richard rightfully switched back to guitar. Paul Burton, who was part of the road crew, took on playing bass. *Strange Affair* followed a year after their debut and saw a shift from country rock to a more spacey rock sound. It included their first full-on psychedelic epic 'The All Electric Fur Trapper', which was inspired by an essay by Sean Tyla. Sean was a live wire character who used to hang out in my office but I could never steer him towards the right project. He met John Eichler there and a few weeks later invited himself down to Headley Grange and ended up sticking around. The more trippy direction Help Yourself took was a measure of Sean's presence.

We'd arranged a short tour of Switzerland under the umbrella title of *All Good Clean Fun* – a song from *Do You Like It Here*. The dates were headlined by Man and with Help Yourself and another of my recent signings, Gypsy, on the same bill. Man and the Helps really hit it off and Deke, in particular, became very protective towards Help Yourself and Malcolm in particular. Malcolm was an enigmatic character who'd have dark mental interludes which occasionally prevented him going on stage. Both Sean and Deke covered for him at different times. He was prone to lapses in confidence and began struggling to write enough songs. The others might chip in with ideas but couldn't originate songs. Sean contributed one particularly memorable co-write, 'American Mother', on their next album, *Beware the Shadow*. It's a genuine classic West Coast psychedelic track – as good as anything in that vein. The 'shadow' is credited. It was the band's way of acknowledging the shadow of depression hanging over Malcolm. They'd produced it down in Rockfield again, where Sean was present when it was completed in four all-night sessions. Unfortunately, the band was rarely in good enough shape to promote it in any concentrated way and it slipped through the cracks again.

After Deke Leonard left Man, he began hanging out with Help Yourself and sharing their new house in North Finchley. Sean Tyla had moved on to form Ducks Deluxe, which left Malcolm once again shouldering most of the creative responsibilities in the band. Deke picked up some of that slack after Sean left. He was another motivational force around the band. Deke was very fond of Malcolm and definitely a shoulder for him to lean on. Dave Robinson used to have a go at John Eichler for giving the band too much rope, but John knew they could never be pushed. Help Yourself were more a social unit than a working band. They had the talent but not the determination or the focus to become a consistently roadworthy outfit.

I never thought twice about making a fourth Help Yourself album, but we needed 'something' to raise the level of awareness. They were too flaky to do that for themselves. Their original bass player Ken Whaley returned early in the New Year but calling the album *The Return of Ken Whaley* was a little too knowing. I decided to add a bonus album as a marketing ploy. To that end we recorded *Happy Days* which brought in Martin Ace's duo, the Flying Aces, with his wife George, who joined the band at Rockfield. Martin also came up with most of the songs, which took pressure off Malcolm. *Happy Days* was packaged in the same envelope as *The Return of Ken Whaley* and released in July 1973. The idea backfired. Hardcore Help Yourself fans were foxed by the diversity of the extra album.

Help Yourself were always hard to pigeonhole but the *Happy Days* tour was completely mystifying. It was presented as a kind of psychedelic pantomime with a host of guests, mixing sketches and music in the spirit of how I imagined Ken Kesey's Merry Pranksters operated. The entourage also included Roger Ruskin Spear and his Kinetic Wardrobe with all his dolls, mechanical creations and explosions. It was the most consecutive gigs they ever played. Even Malcolm was enjoying himself, and they were despondent that I had to call a halt after two months. There was no way to make it financially viable. Even though they started another album, the recordings just fizzled out and the group split up by the end of the summer. It wasn't something we could complete and release without a group. It was a shame; we even had a title – *Wrench Boy* – and the cover was a striking painting by Rick Griffin. They'd split up after Malcolm quit; you couldn't have the Helps without him. He joined Ken Whaley in the final line-up of Deke Leonard's Iceberg. When Deke was invited back into Man he took Malcolm and Ken along with him for what was Man's sixth line-up change in six years.

The cliché about Man was that whenever they started getting anywhere they'd reshuffle the line-up and end up at square one again. That wasn't strictly true. I'd always go 'Oh no, not again', but in a strange way the personnel changes re-energised the band. Their repertoire always included Man staples such as 'C'Mon', 'Angel Easy', and 'Romain', and each line-up brought something different to those songs. Over the years Deke or Clive or Martin came and went and came back again, and guys from other Welsh bands came in. Man as a group were the very definition of the phrase 'greater than the sum of its parts'.

The Man band were never great at doing interviews, so the regular shake-ups in personnel were as much their calling card as any. There'd been a succession of press stories that said third time lucky, fourth time, fifth time and now sixth time around. I was thrilled at the prospect of this particular line-up. They recorded one album together, then a second without Malcolm. The first of these was *Rhinos, Winos and Lunatics* which was as near to a commercial-sounding album as Man ever made. It was exactly what I'd hoped for since there were now two songwriters in the band in Malcolm and Deke. Deke had definitely honed his writing skills for his two solo albums.

I brought in Roy Thomas Baker as a producer because I thought the combination of Malcolm and Deke would benefit from some assistance with arrangements and a different approach to recording. The band was taken aback; they'd never worked with outsiders. Once it was underway, they could see the sense of it. Micky and Deke both thought *Rhinos, Winos and Lunatics* was one of their better studio albums although, as usual, it was written, recorded and mixed in just three weeks. It maintained their modest chart record, reaching No. 24 on release in May 1974.

Before its release, the Man band finally made it to America, which had long been an ambition. The tour – from 3 March to 14 April – was with Hawkwind, now playing sizeable venues. It was the perfect way to introduce Man to American audiences and I wasn't about to miss out on attending some of the shows. Never one to pass on an opportunity to go to San Francisco again, I went along to a *Tribute to Dr Tim Leary* at Berkeley University. Leary was an American psychologist who became famous as an advocate of LSD in the 1960s. I was quite chuffed that the five-hour programme actually featured two British bands who were no strangers to the drugs Leary had championed. During Man's set the plan was to hook up with Leary, who was currently in prison. There was a window during which he'd be able to speak to his wife on stage. Unfortunately, when his wife got up to talk to him the phone connection was so bad that she was left standing repeating his name with no response from her husband. The crowd picked up on this and began chanting Leary's name while the band stood around waiting to continue playing.

We'd hired a mobile in Chicago to record both the Man and Hawkwind shows on 21 March at the Auditorium Theatre in Chicago. I'd just stepped off the plane and turned up at the hall where we had the mobile truck parked outside before getting a message that somebody from the local police would like a chat. It was United Artists paying for the mobile studio and the police came on strong saying, 'We're here to make sure there aren't any problems with the mobile truck.' It was nothing less than a shakedown, although they insisted they were just making assurances. I forked out a couple of hundred dollars, which I had to borrow from Doug. We did the sound checks and then a couple of hours later I was called out to the truck again. Another police officer started coming out with the same routine. We want to make sure everything goes fine blah blah blah. I said thanks very much, but we sorted this with your guys earlier. 'Sure,' he said, 'but we're the night shift and we're here till midnight.' So that was another couple of hundred dollars. The tapes then sat on a shelf; none of the recordings were ever used in my time at United Artists.

On their return from the States in April, Help Yourself were asked to reform for one day only to play a benefit for *Zigzag* magazine at the Roundhouse headlined by Michael Nesmith. I'd written a few articles for *Zigzag* about the beginnings of the San Francisco scene, the Charlatans and Mad River under the name Alan Lord. The concert was to mark its Fifth Anniversary. Help Yourself got an amazing reception as good as anybody on the bill. In the cold light of day Malcolm came away disturbed by their triumphant return. It brought him down wondering, 'Where were all these people when we needed them?' He thought it was only because he was now in Man, which triggered a wave of negativity. He left Man once they'd completed their scheduled UK dates that summer. They recorded *Slow Motion* at Rockfield as a four-piece but this time it failed to keep the momentum going. Malcolm's departure did at least ensure that no two studio albums featured the same line-up of Man during the years they were signed to United Artists.

The tour with Hawkwind had definitely opened up American audiences. Let down by the reaction here to *Slow Motion*, they needed little encouragement to return to America. They began another extended tour, initially supporting the Strawbs. It was during that leg of the tour that Ken Whaley quit. The call went out to Martin Ace, who arrived on the next plane. Man was back to my favourite four-piece line-up again. They played a dozen shows in California, including some huge support shows, most notably at the Winterland Ballroom, with the likes of Peter Frampton, Montrose and REO Speedwagon. Rather than return home they remained in San Francisco to do their own shows. It was ironic because they were more or less taking coals to Newcastle. There were no local bands summoning up the spirit of San Francisco in its heyday in the way Man was doing. Bill Graham loved the band and put on several local shows with them. They also came to the attention of Deke and Micky's all-time guitar hero John Cipollina. After hanging out and jamming with him, they invited him to tour the UK as a special guest. The climax of these dates was a trio of concerts at the Round-house between 24 May and 26 May 1975. It was billed as a West Coast Weekend. I was always going to record the shows and the results were released as *Maximum Darkness* in the autumn.

The tour with John Cipollina was the culmination of my working with Man. We all went out on a high. I often wondered what more I could have done, and it was fitting that the last thing was the tour with John Cipollina. Quicksilver was so special to us all and particularly to Micky and Deke, who'd spent years trying to emulate what they called 'the growl', the snarling guitar he played on 'The Fool' from Quicksilver's first Capitol album. *Maximum Darkness* was the final album Man released on United Artists. Appropriately, Rick Griffin, who had designed the sleeve for *Slow Motion*, came up with the lettering for the title and created a new Man logo. Their contract was up and MCA made an offer we couldn't better. If I'd said, 'OK' we'll match it', they'd probably have stayed but I knew it was time to let go. Perhaps instinctively, I could see the band was nearing an end too. After one studio album for MCA in 1976 and a farewell live album, Man called it a day.

Man went out on a high playing with their guitar-hero
John Cipollina

There was never any considered strategy with Man. Their style was simple and direct. There was never any degree of pretence, reflecting the unassuming personalities of all the

different musicians who passed through the band. They seemed
to be most happy on the road, playing to anyone who'd listen,
with no thought of becoming stars. They always looked more like
roadies than a rock band. Yet Terry was a fantastic drummer
and had great stamina, which set up hypnotic back beats and
build-ups that freed the rest of the band. Deke Leonard was
instantly recognisable usually wearing a black leather jacket
and playing a zebra-striped Telecaster. He and Micky, slight
and quiet by comparison, were perfect foils. Micky never played
the same twice and when he'd drift into a spacey jam you'd
never know where it would take him. He was such an inventive
guitarist and always different from Deke, who was a lot better
than the 'random thrasher', as he'd describe himself.

The band never worried about not having an image. It was
only the music and the playing that mattered. The rest was
bullshit. You had to admire them for that, even if some people in
the business found it frustrating. Man never had a leader. You
could argue it should be Micky because he was the only constant
in all the line-ups till they split up in 1977. Terry was also there
for the whole of the United Artists period, but Micky had been
on the Pye albums, and in the Bystanders before that.

There's not many of them left now. They took a lot of drugs
and did some serious drinking – and they were pretty wild in a
boisterous 'all good clean fun' kind of way. Martin Ace and Terry
Williams are still with us; but Micky's gone, Deke's gone, Phil's
gone, Will Youatt, Clive John . . . they all embraced the lifestyle
and always managed to be a lot of fun. That's why I liked
hanging out with them. I remember Micky announcing from the
stage that 'we may not be the best band in the world but we
smoke the most dope.' That's a pretty fitting epitaph, although
sometimes I genuinely thought they *were* the best band in the
world. They could be so good, it was scary.

Chapter 16
Germany Calling

I can't remember exactly when I first heard the term krautrock but I shuddered. I would never have used it as a way of describing Can, Amon Düül II and the growing swell of German bands during the seventies. I always thought it was insulting and far too derogatory. I soon found out that there was never a scene as such either. What you had was bands of like-minded musicians mostly born during or soon after the war operating in different parts of Germany. They often included musicians from a more classical or jazz background, but the key factor was that the bands felt the need to create music utterly anew. Their aim was to fashion something German in origin, often rejecting Germany's own past but, crucially, no longer imitating British and American bands.

To begin with the groups we now know as frontrunners were unaware of each other's existence. Can were from Cologne; Kraftwerk, Neu! and Cluster were from Düsseldorf; Tangerine Dream came out of Berlin, and Munich, where Liberty/United Artists was based, was home to Amon Düül and Amon Düül II. 1974 and '75 marked the commercial and international breakthrough by many of these groups, notably Tangerine Dream with *Phaedra* and then Kraftwerk worldwide with their album *Autobahn*. There's a view that we did all the hard yards at United Artists and there's some truth in that. It was Siggy

Loch and Gerhard Augustin who were the prime movers. When we started putting out Amon Düül II and Can in 1969 and 1970 they were part of what was a very broad underground scene in the UK where there was never much breathing space between albums. Somehow you were supposed to progress every time. Both those bands definitely progressed in very different ways. A year on from *Yeti*, Amon Düül II produced a second double album, *Dance of the Lemmings*, which abandoned the spacey, Floydian influences of *Yeti*. Its sequel presented an album of sprawling improvisations coupled with a second album of near straightforward songs. Then came *Carnival in Babylon* which was an often surprisingly commercial-sounding Teutonic take on folk rock. It was the group's least favourite of the albums we released. These albums were all graced with fantastic Falk Rogner sleeves. Falk's artwork was now becoming as identifiable as Roger Dean's covers were for Yes or Hipgnosis and Pink Floyd.

We finally managed to bring Amon Düül II- over to tour between *Carnival in Babylon* and 1973's *Wolf City* when they undertook a series of extensive European tours. We'd tried several times but they always had visa problems. Amon Düül II's dates began with support slots to Roxy Music, at the end of which I recorded *Live in London* on the trusty Pye Mobile with Vic Maile at the Croydon Greyhound on 16 December. I did it as a budget price release in time for their next scheduled tour, which included a show at the Rainbow on 1 June with the Pink Fairies. The bands seemed to be trying to outdo each other for loudness. I was trying my best to really promote Amon Düül II and decided to simultaneously release *Phallus Dei* on our budget label Sunset – priced at only 99p. The ploy backfired this time. I may well have saturated the market by releasing their debut album and *Live in London* – effectively a retrospective live journey through their past – at the expense of *Wolf City*.

215

Amon Düül II isn't given the credit for pushing open the door in 1969 to the initial recognition and gradual acceptance of German rock. By 1973 Amon Düül II were becoming sidelined as a rock band because they were less experimental than most of their contemporaries. *Vive la Trance* early in 1974 was their last for United Artists and they shifted to Atlantic Records where that run of classic albums came to a close.

The new climate in the music press towards more intelligent and more expansive features was reflected in 'Deutsch Rock', *Melody Maker*'s comprehensive look at all the German bands. It ran just before Can's first British tour in April 1972, their first dates outside Germany. Rival paper *NME* ran a series of articles by Ian MacDonald at the end of that year – this time headlined 'Germany Calling' and coinciding with Amon Düül II's first UK dates.

Can's more rarefied recordings were attracting the greatest attention in the press. Their second album proper, *Tago Mago* in 1971, completely shook off the Velvet Underground comparisons. It sounded nothing like *Monster Movie* either and seemed to be purposely challenging the framework of what constituted rock music. I thought it was astonishing once I could get my head round it. Can's albums were always demanding. I was inclined to leave it to music critics to try and describe them and with each album they seemed to be running out of superlatives.

I obviously didn't have any input over the music, but I did change the cover art for *Tago Mago*. It was a double LP and gatefolds were expensive, so we came up with a single envelope format with a flap at the top.* I also changed the original

---

* I used the same envelope format later that year for a triple LP Liberty/ United Artists sampler called *All Good Clean Fun*. I went back to the Lacquer Chest for the cover idea, adapting it from a vintage 1895 *Boy's Own* annual. The boy on the cover was originally reading the *Boy's Own Paper* but we substituted the schoolkids' edition of *Oz*.

abstract image to a photograph of the band playing live but shot from the back of the stage. I added notes by Duncan Fallowell, an Oxford graduate who'd written about Can in the *Spectator* and went over to meet them in Cologne. I thought the notes would help introduce the band to newcomers.

A year after *Tago Mago* came *Ege Bamyasi*, which was a much more approachable album. It was more subdued – some might say bleak – but with more identifiable songs. It included 'Spoon', which was the theme music for a hit television detective series in Germany where it even made the Top 10; it sold 250,000 and became their bestselling album there. I missed Can's first UK tour, so the first time I saw them was at Imperial College on 15 March 1973, part of a month of dates here. The tour fell between *Ege Bamyasi* in November '72 and the more spacious and atmospheric *Future Days* the following year when they toured yet again.

Irmin Schmidt and his wife Hildegarde, who managed Can, used to come over to meet with me and Martin to discuss advertising, dates and tour support. The thinking was always that Can fans were either music obsessives or more intelligent, discerning listeners, so it was Social Secs booking college and university gigs that we targeted. The assumption was that college audiences would find them less taxing, which was some-what judgemental. Can became a very hip name to drop but never an easy band for the uninitiated when they played live. They never had set lists and never promoted 'the new album' other than by being there. Their sets were improvisational; even familiar pieces, if you were able to recognise them, were simply springboards for further improvisation. As musicians they were like a married couple who knew each other so well they'd finish each other's sentences. Audiences were either transfixed or bewildered and often probably both.

Over the course of their albums for United Artists – and *Soon Over Babaluma* was our last in November 1974 – Can's music was never anything but in a field of its own. Apart from *Monster Movie*, which had an immediate and recognisable wow factor, their albums always took a while for me to get my head around. *Future Days* and *Soon Over Babaluma* appeared to be more accessible but perhaps I was simply more accustomed to the shifting complexities of the music by then.

I can't pretend I really got to know the entire band that well. It didn't help that I spoke no German; Irmin and Holger had a really good command of English which made a difference, but I always found them all very friendly and amenable. They defin-itely weren't as intense as they appeared to be on stage. United Artists' deal with Can ran out in 1974; *Limited Edition* was the last thing we put out. I'd heard there were disagreements within the band and Damo left after *Future Days*. When they signed to Virgin, I found the albums less focused. They were more straightforward, certainly by their standards if not by anybody else's.

I can't claim to have had any significant involvement with

218

Can beyond releasing the records. So I do find it a little mislead-
ing that being 'the man who signed Can' is almost my calling
card. It's definitely stood me in great stead with so many groups
I've met or signed in the years since. It certainly got me the
Buzzcocks. I'd put in an offer and it was all agreed. I was on my
way to Manchester on the train with the contract in my hand
when, very belatedly, CBS came on strong offering more money.
The band stuck with me basically because of my involvement
with Can.

Eno's oft-quoted comment that 'The first Velvet Underground album only sold 10,000 copies, but everyone who bought
it formed a band', probably applies even more to Can. Their
influence or more likely inspiration was first acknowledged
by the punk and post-punk generation of musicians such as
John Lydon, Mark E. Smith, Julian Cope, Pete Shelley, and the
Jesus & Mary Chain. By the late seventies all the above were
bringing what they'd first heard five years earlier into their own
post-punk and early experimental electronic outfits. Can had put
down a marker for anybody trying to be innovative.

I instantly liked the first Neu! album when I heard it; it
was released on Brain – a label that started up in 1971. Neu!'s
repetitive rhythmic drive totally got to me, right from the opening track 'Hallogallo'. It was driven by a single beat with trancey
fuzz guitars and it ran for a hypnotic ten minutes. I thought
Neu! would have a broad appeal because, even though it was
pure electronic music, it was so relentlessly catchy. I loved that
it was simple and strange. Licensing *Neu!* wasn't going to be
expensive; Brain was happy to get a release in the UK and I was
happy to put it out. We reversed the sleeve from the German
original, making its very direct image even brighter and gaudier.
I also asked Dave Brock to write some notes because I thought it
would appeal to Hawkwind fans.

Neu! was Michael Rother and Klaus Dinger, who'd played

guitar and drums in a short-lived line-up of Kraftwerk.
Effectively, there was a third member of the group in producer
Conny Plank whose participation was almost certainly as
crucial. I didn't think twice about releasing 1973's *Neu! 2* either.
It featured only twenty minutes of new material coupled with
sped-up and slowed-down alternate versions of both sides of a
single – 'Super', coupled with 'Neuschnee' – which I'd released
earlier that year. It was an ingenious way to finish an album
after they'd run out of money to pay for further studio time.

Neu! didn't tour here but they came over once for a meeting. Michael was early and was really friendly and easy-going.
Then Klaus arrived. He was wired to the mains, very animated,
standing on the desk waving his arms about while Michael just
sat there. They had a chemistry that worked because they were
such opposites. That was even more obvious when they got back
together at the end of December 1974 and released *Neu! '75*,
which gave Michael and Klaus a side each. Michael's ambient
meditations weren't too far from the music that Brian Eno was
experimenting with. Klaus Dinger's side featured two extra
drummers (his brother Thomas and Hans Lempe) and was more
abrasive and aggressive with distorted vocals and guitars that
are now regularly identified as a precursor for early punk. The
same trio became La Düsseldorf after Neu! split up again.

I find it hard to get a take on Neu! because when we put
the records out there wasn't a particularly positive reaction to
their propulsive, stripped-down sound. Now there's considerable
retrospective appreciation. I never thought much about it at the
time. The Neu! albums were something I was in a position to put
out – so I just did. Sometimes it's that simple. It emerged much
later that Brian Eno and David Bowie were both fans of Neu! –
and particularly *Neu! '75*. When I first met Midge Ure in 1979
– the Radar Records offices were next door to the Blitz Club and
he used to drop by – he told me how much he loved Neu! The

exclamation mark after Ultravox! was an homage to the German duo even though it was dropped after their second album.

When the music press first began writing about the German bands they'd often mention Nektar. They were actually a group of British musicians who'd been permanently living together in Southern Germany since the late sixties. I probably first heard about them through the Man band. Nektar often did dates with Man in Germany – their drummer had to deputise for Terry Williams on one occasion. They knew each other very well, but signing them came through a different connection.

Marty Scott ran Jem records in association with Seymour Stein, a record import company based in New Jersey. Jem imported a lot of German albums into the US. Marty would come into my office because he was always interested in importing stuff that wasn't getting a US release. He'd been importing Amon Düül II, Tangerine Dream and Kraftwerk long before *Autobahn* opened up the floodgates over there. Marty then set up a separate record label called Passport and began releasing Nektar's albums directly. So following his lead, I did a deal with Bellaphon, the band's label in Germany, and licensed four albums between 1971 and '74, beginning with *A Tab in the Ocean*.

They were interesting because they recorded epic, often side-long suites of songs which had all the trappings of progressive music but they were never as studiously complex musically. Nektar were much more reliant on the basics of 1960s rock, with more riffing than you get in the usual prog stuff. There were none of the pseudo-classical pretensions either that came with the Nice and ELP. They appealed to Man and Hawkwind fans in a way that most prog bands didn't. They were very much like early spacey Pink Floyd to begin with, but I always thought their lengthy jams were also reminiscent of the San Francisco ballroom bands.

Nektar were really self-contained. The bass player Derek Moore acted as manager and Mick Brockett ran the lightshow in the same way Liquid Len did with Hawkwind. They really took off in America after gambling on taking their full light show and entourage with them on their first tour, by the end of which they were playing to huge crowds, not hundreds but thousands. They even had chart albums there with *Remember the Future* and *Down to Earth*.

Here they were much more under the radar; the deals with Bellaphon were simple to do and we easily recouped, especially once they began touring here. Like Amon Düül II, they had really distinctive artwork; Helmut Wenske has since acquired a cult following of his own as an illustrator and writer. Nektar benefited from all the trappings of being a prog band without actually being a prog band. I remember somebody once said that Nektar was the band that gave prog rock a good name. Now that name often comes up in a much more unlikely context. It's assumed that Joy Division's Ian Curtis must have been a fan based on the evidence of a photograph where he's wearing a Nektar T-shirt. You can even buy replica T-shirts on eBay now where the tag line is 'as worn by Ian Curtis'.

Chapter 17
They Sound Like Johnny Kidd and the Pirates

American country rock band Eggs Over Easy made their debut at the Tally Ho pub in Kentish Town in May 1971. After Dave Robinson saw them play there he suggested that Nick Lowe and Billy Rankin should go along to check them out. Eggs Over Easy closely mirrored Brinsley Schwarz's new anti-hype musical approach, but what struck Nick and Billy was that it looked like as much fun for the group as the audience. Brinsley Schwarz were moving towards a more diverse take on American roots music: the Band, of course, but also Dr John and other New Orleans stuff, the Grateful Dead's *Workingman's Dead*, and they still liked Clover a lot. They began to play pubs and began their own residency at the Tally Ho in January 1972, a month before their third album *Silver Pistol* was released. They'd added Ian Gomm by then, offering another voice, another guitar and another song-writer to ease the load on Nick. It was by far their best album so far, recorded in their communal house on mobile equipment, even recording outside in the garden. It's a really timeless album, far more assured and the closest on record to seeing them live.

Throughout 1972 more and more pubs added regular rock nights where bands such as Chilli Willi and the Red Hot Pep-pers, Ace, Clancy, Ducks Deluxe and Kilburn & The Highroads were among the first wave. The number of venues stretched to include the Lord Nelson, the Kensington, the Hope and Anchor, the Greyhound, the Red Lion, the Nashville and plenty more. Pub rock was injecting 'good time' values back into the music scene. It was the antidote to mega tours and a rock mainstream that was weighted down by pretension and self-importance, but it was more a diversion than solving the problem. As much as bands, fans, journalists and A&R men loved the idea of pub rock, none of the bands on the circuit were going anywhere or selling significant amounts of their records.*

In April 1972 Brinsley Schwarz began recording their fourth album *Nervous on the Road* at Rockfield where they met Dave Edmunds for the first time. Nick was immediately in awe of Dave in the studio and was itching for him to produce Brinsley Schwarz. *Nervous on the Road*, though, stuck to their usual formula and great songs like 'Surrender to the Rhythm' and the aptly titled 'Happy Doing What We're Doing' didn't have the oomph they deserved.

In early 1973 the band moved to a new community base at Wilton Park Farm in Beaconsfield. We all thought things were looking up when Paul and Linda McCartney asked them to support them on the first Paul McCartney and Wings tour. It ran from 11 May for two weeks and ended with a series of shows at Hammersmith Odeon. Touring with Wings merely offered a brief taste of what might be but never was. They parted with Dave

---

* I wanted to get our bands into smaller venues outside London. Rather than buying onto tours by bigger bands – which was never money well spent – I wanted to give our bands a chance for a fraction of the cost, so I hired Martyn Smith. He was a very funny Welshman who'd been working at Charisma and loved Brinsley Schwarz. He ran our Iron Horse agency out of my office. There were plenty of venues, especially pubs, in and around London, but he was able to organise little tours and find out-of-the-way gigs for bands such as Gypsy, Cochise, Help Yourself and Country Gazette.

Robinson perfectly amicably soon after and Dai Davies took over. I first met Dai in the early seventies when he was doing PR for David Bowie. Dai was moving into management and was soon running some of the leading pub venues, notably the Nashville Rooms. In the absence of any kind of 'Plan B', I pushed to release yet another album and October's *Please Don't Ever Change* was cobbled together from new and existing tracks. Dave Edmunds' busy schedule meant that he couldn't record the band until the following spring. To bridge the gap, I decided to release a 99p retrospective overview called *Original Golden Greats* in the hope it might broaden sales.

I was feeling generally disillusioned at the time. Most of the groups I'd signed had already left United Artists or were within a year of being out of contract. There were very few albums coming out here and even in America that excited me. I was very fortunate that United Artists in America had an account with Tower Records in Los Angeles and Lee Mendell said I could order anything I wanted. I didn't need much encouragement and placed an order every two weeks, which carried on right up until I left at the end of 1977. I was apparently the biggest individual customer at Tower Records. It sounds ungrateful but diminishing returns set in – far too many dreary confessional singer-songwriters and a lot of mellow country funk that today is described as yacht rock. The best stuff coming through was by the so-called outlaw country singers and writers such as Willie Nelson, Waylon Jennings, Guy Clark and Townes Van Zandt and what later came to be known as Americana.

I've always enjoyed putting compilations together and with nothing else to excite me I'd been putting a Mersey Beat collection together in my own time, so it took a couple of years. Martin Davis sorted all the contracts as we went along. I'd go round to Bill Harry's flat and he'd regale me with stories about the heyday of the Liverpool beat scene before it all exploded. *Mersey Beat*

225

'62–'64 covered an era that was distant enough to revisit – ten years ago – and I didn't include too many of the obvious groups or familiar hits. I was dipping into the two *This Is Merseybeat* albums on Oriole, which I used to play to death at Wellingborough. *Mersey Beat '62–'64* was a double LP that was tapping into the thinking behind Elektra's great *Nuggets* album – *Original Artyfacts from the First Psychedelic Era: 1965–1968*. That was definitely a game changer; it revolutionised how catalogue could be done. Catalogue was mostly a budget line, all very cheaply done. *Nuggets* was the first time it was treated seriously and imaginatively as something of historical interest and importance. It definitely inspired me and Alan Warner to follow suit.[*]

The Mersey Beat album sold well enough that I decided to put together a companion volume called *The Beat Merchants 1963/4*. It focused on the rest of the country and all the regional scenes where odd groups had sprung up and had mostly been forgotten. Once again I was looking back to what excited me when I was at school. Both those albums were labours of love, and that was

---

[*]   Marty Cerf, who was Head of Creative Services for United Artists in the US, instigated a great double-LP series called *Legendary Masters*, releasing albums by Fats Domino, Eddie Cochran, Ricky Nelson, the Ventures and Jan & Dean, all of which we released. Seymour Stein was doing the same thing with Greg Shaw at Sire – the Vintage Series (including comprehensive Troggs and Pretty Things collections) and a *History of British Rock 'n' roll* series. Marty also edited a magazine called *Phonograph* run out of his office.

I used to correspond with a lot of American writers such as Bud Scoppa, Ed Ward, Greg Shaw, and Lenny Kaye. Many of them were certified Anglophiles, so I started a regular mail-out for writers, DJs and producers for college radio and underground stations. It was originally promos, photos, biogs, but I started adding stuff I bought from the Lacquer Chest in Kensington – copies of late 1800s magazines and Victorian postcards – just to be different. Those packages helped get to get Cochise, Brinsley Schwarz or Help Yourself reviewed or played on a cool station. I tried to make each package more interesting than the last, so it eventually became too expensive and time-consuming. I had to bring things to a halt when it reached about sixty people.

certainly reflected in artist Tony Wright's wonderfully evocative
cover art for *The Beat Merchants*. Another double LP, it wasn't
actually released till 1976 but Nick Lowe dropped by the office
one day in late May 1974 and asked what I was listening to. Martin had just cleared the rights from EMI for a rare Pirates single
they'd made when Johnny Kidd had a bad throat and couldn't
record. The Pirates used the studio time to record live favourites 'My Babe' and 'Casting My Spell' with bass player Johnny
Spence singing. And Nick said, 'That's weird because I've just
seen this band that sounds exactly like Johnny Kidd and the Pirates. You'll love them.' They were called Dr Feelgood. I saw them
at the Kensington a week later and I was totally blown away.

I had to pinch myself because Dr Feelgood captured everything that got me into music in the first place, but this wasn't
a throwback. After two years playing locally in and around
Southend and Canvey Island, they'd come in from the outside
fully formed. They already had a great look as well, especially
singer Lee Brilleaux in his grubby suit and demented guitarist
Wilko Johnson. John Sparks (Sparko), the bass player, and
drummer John Martin (the Big Figure) were right on it too
– as tight as you like. By the end of the evening I sought out the
manager and we started talking about a deal the next day. I
knew before the second number that I wanted to sign the band,
and that had never happened before. I didn't need to see them
again or get demos done. They were exactly what I needed to
shake off the drabness of everything else I was hearing.

It was just as we signed Dr Feelgood that Dennis Knowles,
our sales manager, hired Judith Riley. Richard Ogden had left
and I wanted a music fan in the PR department. Judith had
a column called 'Jude's Jottings' in a St Albans paper. She
was thrown in at the deep end and was very soon running the
department. We had major albums due from Hawkwind, Man
and Brinsley Schwarz. Judith wasn't just working on my stuff;

she also had to take on Ike & Tina Turner, Bobby Womack and we soon had ELO through a deal with Jet Records, so she was also taking on Don Arden's charges. This was during ELO's most successful period with global selling albums such as *A New World Record* and *Out of the Blue*.

I was on a high from discovering Dr Feelgood, and even feeling optimistic about the new Brinsley Schwarz album. At the back of my mind, though, I was hopeful rather than confident that *The New Favourites Of . . .* was the album that would finally do the trick. Dave definitely gave it a kick; it was the Brinsleys' sound with just the right amount of polish and it sounded like something you'd hear on the radio. The album exploded into life immediately with the power chords that announced '(What's So Funny 'Bout) Peace, Love and Understanding', one of Nick's finest ever songs. It was the obvious single but, once again, we didn't get the airplay we needed. The line from radio producers was 'If it had been a new band it would have been different.' And the press had run out of things to say about them too. I even started to think we were the wrong label. It was my sixth album with Brinsley Schwarz but in my heart of hearts I knew that even a hit would only prolong the band's life by another year. Nick already wanted to do something else, but he didn't have the heart to call time – nor did I.

Dave Edmunds enjoyed working with them so much that he decided to tour for the first time in five years. It was the perfect set-up. Brinsley Schwarz would play a set and then back Dave for his set. The timing was spot on too, with dates in June ahead of the release of *The New Favourites Of . . .* Dr Feelgood joined them for a couple of dates including Cardiff Top Rank on 19 June 1974. I brought in the Pye Mobile to record everybody but mainly to get something down early with the Feelgoods. As good as Dave Edmunds and Brinsley Schwarz were, the Feelgoods simply blew them both off stage. It was awkward. I could see what was happening before my eyes; Dr Feelgood was the future. This wasn't lost on the Brinsleys, and Nick in particular. I was thrilled at the prospect of getting the Feelgoods in the studio as soon as possible. It was the start of something new but the beginning of the end for Brinsley Schwarz, even though we went ahead to make album number seven.

They returned to Rockfield, this time with an American producer, Steve Verroca who'd recently made albums with Link Wray and Juicy Lucy. The band thought he'd make a difference but album number seven was never completed. We released several more singles and tried a couple of things under different names which hadn't worked before and smacked of desperation. They did a tour supporting Al Stewart before playing their final show on 18 March 1975 at the Marquee. It was largely at Nick's instigation, but the others – or some at least – felt let down at not being able to carry on. Once they'd split up, I thought there was no point in putting those final recordings out. Calling it a day was something of a relief. Retrospectively of course Brinlsey Schwarz has become a very pivotal band because of what they went on to do – and Nick Lowe in particular.

I'd taken the draft contract for Dr Feelgood down to Cardiff only a few weeks after I'd seen them at the Kensington. It was signed on 8 July. Even that went smoothly because the band had a really good, plain-speaking manager in Chris Fenwick; he wasn't on the make, he just wanted the right deal. He was also from Canvey Island and had been at school with Lee. Meeting the band had involved the usual chat about records and favourite groups; Lee was a real blues fan, and although it was obvious Wilko's simultaneous rhythm and lead guitar style was a trademark of Mick Green in the Pirates, I saved that conversation for a while. Their name came from Piano Red's 'Dr Feelgood' but it was Johnny Kidd and the Pirates' version they heard first, the B-side of their last record to chart, 'Always and Ever'.

I did consider asking Dave Edmunds to produce them, but the Feelgoods music was so stripped down and basic that I didn't want anybody to tart it up in any way. Wilko was suspicious of record companies, and rightly so, but we both wanted to approach recording the same way. He didn't want to be seen as revivalist or play on nostalgia. It was only about the edge, the excitement and the energy they conveyed on stage. We went straight into making the album in the last week of August down at Rockfield. The majority of the songs were their own, and that was important too. Nine out of thirteen were written by Wilko; three R&B classics and the great 'Cheque Book' by Southend legend Mickey Jupp completed the album.

I'd used the Pye Mobile a lot over the years and Vic Maile was the engineer who came with it. He'd recorded Hawkwind, Man, Greasy Truckers and Amon Düül II for me and, famously, *The Who Live at Leeds*. I'd never used him in the studio but had a feeling he'd be right because he wasn't in any way dictatorial. The band wanted to work with someone who'd get the record exactly how they wanted it. Even Wilko, always wary of anybody outside the band, got on with Vic. We kept it simple. *Down by the Jetty* was released in February 1975. The sleeve was in black and white, and it was in mono, as they wanted. That did become a bit of an issue with Wilko, because he didn't want to make a point of it being in mono. He thought it would be taken as a gimmick, but he had to accept that we had to specify mono or stereo because of the Trade Descriptions Act.

The album didn't chart but they were fast becoming a major live proposition. I genuinely thought that nothing could stop Dr Feelgood and they'd fire up live rock 'n' roll in the UK again. Everybody I took to see them play saw it immediately. What came over on stage was an attitude that wasn't so much menacing as saying 'we mean business'. Nothing was contrived. They didn't smile or engage with the audience between numbers, they just played.

They recorded *Malpractice* with Vic again, although the credits read 'Produced by Dr Feelgood'. First time round they knew exactly what they wanted; now they knew how to get what they wanted. If somebody says 'play me a Dr Feelgood album', then *Malpractice* is the one for me. It came eight months after their debut, and it was a measure of their popularity as a hard-gigging live act that the album reached No. 17.

Wilko was the most serious. He had a university background and was well read and into poetry and he was married with a young son. He was also teetotal, which did come between him and the rest of the band to a greater degree as time went on. They were all very intense on stage but the dynamic focused equally on Wilko and Lee. Off stage Wilko was more exacting; the others couldn't have cared less about some of the things that bothered him.

Dr Feelgood was the nearest thing I ever came across to compare with the beat boom. That's why, from day one, I just wanted to make a record with them. I never sat around worrying if anyone was going to buy it. I didn't care if they did or not. I always thought there'd be somebody who'd love it in the same way as I did. I soon found out I wasn't alone.

I first met Andrew Jakeman in 1972. He came into Mortimer Street with Barney Bubbles. He'd been working for Revelation Enterprises, a West London co-operative that released the *Glastonbury Fayre – The Electric Score* triple LP that was part soundtrack to the second Glastonbury festival but featuring other bands that donated tracks including Bowie, Pete Townshend, and the Grateful Dead. We gave them tracks by Hawkwind and Brinsley Schwarz. Barney's artwork was as extraordinary as anything he came up with for Hawkwind, not least a 'build your own pyramid' insert as a part of a six-panel fold-out jacket. Revelation's only other release was the debut album by Chilli Willi and the Red Hot Peppers, a blues duo which featured ex-Mighty

Baby guitarist Martin Stone. Nick Lowe, Bob Andrews and Billy Rankin played on the album. The band was soon managed by Jake, as everybody called him. He'd been hanging out and trying to make himself useful to Brinsley Schwarz since the end of 1974. Nick and Jake really hit it off and Nick had taken to crashing at Jake's Queens Gate Terrace flat in South Kensington rather than return to the group's Beaconsfield farm. It was the first indication that Nick was pulling away from the others.

Still managing Chilli Willi, Jake launched the *Naughty Rhythms Tour* in January 1975, which put them on a joint equal bill with Kokomo and Dr Feelgood. Just as they had in Cardiff, the Feelgoods left their fellow bands standing in awe. The headline act was supposed to change each night, but nobody wanted to follow the Feelgoods, who became de facto headliners. With the pub rock scene on its last legs, Chilli Willi split up soon after.

After Brinsley Schwarz called it a day Jake soon began looking after Nick's career. We held Nick to his United Artists contract, happy with Jake managing him. Nick already had other ideas beyond just writing and recording songs; inspired by Dave Edmunds, he wanted to try his hand at producing. I was loath to let Nick go because I knew it was only a matter of time before his many talents would align and he'd make it. He was always going to be important somehow. Plus I really liked him – as I did Jake. You could never doubt Jake's passion, self-belief and his belief in Nick. He wasn't strictly conventional in his methods and at times he deliberately set out to rub people up the wrong way, but I could live with that.

Nick and Jake were usually out on the town every night and their shared flat in Queens Gate Terrace was rapidly becoming something of a fun palace. The main thrust of their scheming was to find ways to get Nick out of his deal with United Artists. With that in mind, Nick recorded a Bay City Rollers tribute single as the Tartan Horde – called 'Bay City Rollers, We Love

You'. Probably the last thing they wanted was for me to put it out – which I did – and to compound matters it was almost a hit in Japan. Japan was such a huge market that Nick actually made a few bob out of that. The Japanese company had wanted an album, but Nick recorded just one further single, 'Rollers Show', before moving on. He recorded another track at Rockfield with Dave Edmunds, this time as the Disco Brothers, called 'Let's Go to the Disco'. Nick was still treading water, although his post-Brinsley Schwarz career was on the brink of taking off.

Nick had been hanging out with the Feelgoods, now being tour-managed by Jake. He'd just done a new publishing deal with Pink Floyd's publishing outfit and was flush enough to pay for his flight to join the advance touring party for Dr Feelgood to play at the CBS Convention in San Diego. Nick's hotel bill was covered as part of the entourage under the name Dale Liberator, Equipment Handler. We'd held *Down by the Jetty* back from United Artists in America and placed *Malpractice* with Columbia, where I thought they'd have a better shot. Their US debut was going to be at the Convention in January 1976. It was a typical corporate jolly held twice a year for all the regional sales teams, press and promo guys, and all the execs from every department. It was easy for me to justify being there too.

The first thing we all noticed on checking in was large notices in all the rooms at the Rivermont Hotel expressing the availability of TOTAL UNLIMITED CREDIT. The gift shops were looted for shades, fashion accessories, clothing and whatever else they sold but, most importantly, it meant room service round the clock and a bottomless tab in the bars. I remember seeing Sparko and I don't think I've ever seen anybody as pissed as he was. The band wasn't at all impressed by the other bands being showcased, which ranged from Texan country singer Michael Murphy to the Charlie Daniels Band. Chick Corea was playing on the first night; the band walked out during his set, explaining to their company chaperone that 'we're not into that jazzy stuff' before hitting the bar. The next day they had to play themselves. The sales guys really didn't know what hit them. They were too hungover and too laid back for the full Dr Feelgood onslaught.

On his return, it was Nick's old manager Dave Robinson who came up with a proposition that went a long way to re-setting his career. Dave asked him to produce the debut album by Graham Parker and the Rumour. Dave had been running a studio above the Hope & Anchor where his former managerial partner John Eichler had been installed as the landlord. Dave recorded demos with Parker that led to a deal with Phonogram. He recorded the first demos by Declan MacManus there too, another part of the puzzle that was shaping up. Graham Parker's album reunited Nick with his old bandmates Brinsley Schwarz and Bob Andrews, now members of the Rumour. *Howling Wind* was the first step on the way to vindicating Brinsley Schwarz. Parker himself wasn't a product of the pub rock era – Dylan and Springsteen were his touchstones – but the album received such universal acclaim that it signalled something that was a breath of fresh air in much the same way as the Feelgoods had been.

You could feel that something was in the air by early summer 1976 and that something was punk. I had signed the Feelgoods and they were definitely part of that rebooting process, but as an A&R man you couldn't sit on the fence about punk. There were stories about the Sex Pistols' exploits every week and how they couldn't really play and there was a lot of violence at punk gigs – *NME* writer Nick Kent getting hurt, for example – and DJ Bob Harris being roughed up. So my initial feeling was that this wasn't something I wanted to be involved with, but there were people I trusted saying, 'No, you have to look beyond that because it is going to be a whole new thing.' Dai Davies was one such and he was already in my ear about a group called the Stranglers that he was managing. I'd seen the Stranglers supporting Patti Smith

234

in the spring and then the Flamin' Groovies at the Roundhouse in July, and on both occasions they'd had terrible sound problems and didn't make any impression either way.

It was in those heady months that Jake began hatching a plan that really played to both his and Nick's strengths. He played me 'Heart of the City' and 'So It Goes', which Nick had recorded at the tiny Pathway Studios in Stoke Newington. He said they were starting a label together and wanted 'Heart of the City' to be its first single. That was the point when I knew it was time to let Nick go. Both sides of the single presented a very 'now' kind of smart pop that had no place on United Artists. I didn't want to hold him back and I said I'd help with the new label, which they were calling Stiff Records.

Stiff was to some extent inspired by Beserkley Records, founded by Matthew Kaufman in Berkeley, California in 1974 and which I'd briefly licensed. The label had two things I wanted at the time. One was Earthquake, a San Francisco group who'd been known as the Purple Earthquake before that – and the other was the fantastic Jonathan Richman and the Modern Lovers single 'Road Runner'. Matthew came over and I did a modest deal for a few singles, the *Earthquake Live* album and the *Beserkley Chartbusters* album, which had four tracks by Jonathan Richman, Earthquake and Beserkley's other main acts, the Rubinoos and Greg Kihn. For a while Beserkley's singles were the hippest thing to own in pre-punk days. The label's declared aim was 'To have fun and make interesting records', summed up by the cheeky slogan 'Home of the Hits'. At one point Jake was talking to Matthew about Beserkley being an outlet for Nick until deciding they were a bit too West Coast laid back. Jake wanted to go his own way; he took Beserkley's exuberance and moulded it in his own image – witty, irreverent and audacious and with a lot of mischievous British traits.

When Stiff started, I agreed to press up the initial singles.

We couldn't distribute them through United Artists. That was never Jake's plan anyway. The singles were sold directly to independent shops or through mail order. There was no contract with me; the arrangement was 'You make the records, we'll press them and you sell them.' Once they'd recouped the money on the Nick Lowe single, they'd pay us back, then move on to the next one. Whether they ever did pay for the pressings I can't say because I never looked into it. Nobody in accounts questioned it, so I figured best not to ask.

Stiff records also brought Barney Bubbles in as their in-house designer and Dave Robinson came on board as Jake's partner. Nick took charge of most of the production. Dave had given up the Hope & Anchor studio and was now managing Graham Parker and the Rumour out of offices in Alexander Street in West London. Stiff Records moved into the same premises. The next four singles were very much born out of the embers of the pub rock scene; Nick's single had been BUY 1 – released on 14 August 1976 – and the next four were by the Pink Fairies, Roogalator, the Tyla Gang and Lew Lewis, and we pressed them up as agreed.

When it came to BUY 6, which was the Damned's 'New Rose', there was too much interest since the race was on to release the first official British punk single. We pressed 'New Rose' as before, but we did a dealer mailing as we would for one of our own releases. We put it out as if it was a United Artists single – but it was on Stiff and there was no mention of United Artists on the sleeve. BUY 6 was released on 22 October and was the last Stiff record I was involved with. After that Jake fell into a deal with Island Records, which was fine by me. Stiff Records thrived with its ingenious packaging and marketing, risqué humour and brilliant slogan-mongering. Jake not only reinvented himself as Jake Riviera but also needed a company name and with typical aplomb came up with Riviera Global. Before the year was out, they'd signed Declan MacManus and renamed him Elvis Costello.

Another of those seemingly unrelated circumstances soon came into play, dating back to my releasing the Clover album in 1970 which Brinsley Schwarz had fallen in love with. Clover never toured the UK when they were signed to Fantasy but eventually came over in 1976 to record at Rockfield. Clover by then included Huey Lewis and was a different-sounding group. They sent me a tape which didn't appeal to me as much as their earlier recordings and I gave a copy to Jake who, by coincidence, got the chance to see them play in their hometown of Mill Valley, outside San Francisco, where he, Nick and the Feelgoods went after the CBS Convention. Next thing I knew, Jake was managing Clover, and they'd been signed by Nigel Grainge at Vertigo. While they were here, guitarist John McFee, bassist John Ciambotti and keyboardist Sean Hopper were called in to rehearse and record some songs with Elvis Costello – which Nick Lowe was producing. The original idea had been to use those recordings to persuade Dave Edmunds to produce Elvis. That never happened, which is how Clover came to be featured – uncredited – on Elvis Costello's debut album *My Aim Is True*, released in summer 1977.

Everybody was saying why don't you make a live album with Dr Feelgood? On the face of it, that was the obvious thing to do. I wanted to wait a while. *Malpractice* had done well but now they were selling out bigger and bigger venues here and in Europe. It was the right time to record the live album. This wasn't the usual stopgap between studio albums, nor was it going to be a double LP, which had become the norm. The Feelgoods were lean and mean, so a single album would make greater impact. I never considered doing it as a budget album either. We thought it would do well but I never thought we'd have a No. 1 record.

There were a few days of me and Wilko locking horns over the mix. We all agreed it would be warts and all. There'd be no replacing a dodgy vocal here or a bum note there. We were having

none of that. Wilko had heard some earlier live recordings where
we'd used ambient audience microphones and he wanted to keep
the crowd noise in throughout. The usual option was to push up
the crowd noise level at the end of each song. Wilko was insistent
that we keep the buzz of the crowd for the entire mix. I thought
that muddied the sound and he'd say this is what it's like if you're
in the middle of the crowd. I'd argue that you don't want to be in
the middle, you want to be at the front. I was never going to win.
I was hoping for some support from the others, but they weren't
fussed. Wilko, on the other hand, relished disagreeing with the
record company and getting his way. It became a bigger issue in
his mind than mine and we put *Stupidity* out the way he wanted.
Then, after it went to No. 1, he said, 'There you go, I told you so.'
To which I said, 'But my way it would have stayed there longer.'

I thought he'd be against including a limited shrink-wrapped
7-inch single on the first 10,000 copies, but he was fine with
that. It's what made the difference in it going to No. 1. Fans had
to rush out and buy it week one. The sales team made sure it
was in the chart shops and it worked. The only issue for me was
finding a way to shrink-wrap the 7-inch. It added to the process,
plus we had to add a sticker, all of which bumped up the costs.
Shrink-wrapping was common in America but not here. It was
worth the extra expense and effort and became very much a
marketing tool in the punk era. *Stupidity* was my first and only
No. 1 with a UK act that I'd signed.

It hit the No. 1 spot the same week the Damned's 'New Rose'
was released by Stiff. There was always an opinion that Dr
Feelgood hastened the advent of punk rock, but I think it was
more that the Feelgoods primed fans and even the media for punk
with their edgy, spiky songs, their attitude and their look. Wilko
hated that so few of the punk bands could play. He never wanted
to be lumped in with punk rock any more than he did pub rock.

Chapter 18

Dark, Mysterious and Not a Strangled Victim in Sight

Dr Feelgood wanted to pay more attention to America, where they'd made very little headway, and Columbia stressed that radio play was crucial. They suggested bringing in producer Bert de Coteaux, who'd had considerable success producing various blues, soul and even Tamla recordings. There weren't any dissenting voices in the band, but we did hedge our bets in going back to Rockfield.

I started to get wind that there was something wrong when I heard they were arguing in the studio over a Lew Lewis song called 'Lucky Seven', which Lee wanted to record and which they began recording without Wilko. As it was, Wilko had been keeping more to himself at Rockfield and complained that the others were always going to the pub at lunchtime, leaving him sitting round waiting. They'd return late and end up working long past midnight. The fact that Wilko didn't drink had never been so divisive before. I didn't want to take sides but the issue over the Lew Lewis song was blown up out of all proportion and became the trigger for Wilko to announce he was leaving the band. There was nothing I could do once Wilko had made up his mind. I think his leaving was on the cards anyway and he left immediately after they'd finished recording the album in March.

As the record company, we chose to continue working with the band. We had a finished album, after all, and it had the impetus of being the last one Wilko would play on. It was a clean break; he wanted no involvement in promoting the record.

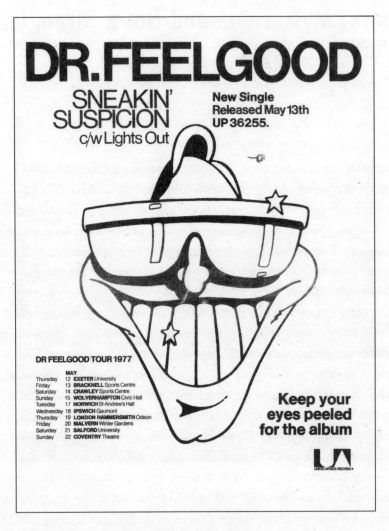

After Wilko's sudden departure, the tour featured new guitarist 'Gypie' Mayo

Janet Street-Porter was doing a feature for London Weekend Television about punk and they wanted to film me and brought a crew up to the office. We'd only recently released *Sneakin' Suspicion* and I was sitting in the office waiting to speak to Janet when there was a phone call from Wllko, who I'd not spoken to since the split. The message relayed by the girl on reception was that 'Wilko's coming round, and he's got a knife'. I was told this in front of Janet, who was licking her lips. I thought, 'Great – she's going to get the first ritualistic murder of an A&R man on film.'

Wilko was impossible to deal with, which he's since freely admitted. There was nothing I could do. He'd made his decision and we'd made ours. I was impressed just how quickly they found another guitarist and gutsed it out. Some groups would have crumbled. *Sneakin' Suspicion* was released in June and made the Top 10. Dr Feelgood's name still meant something but the next one was going to be the real test. They brought in John 'Gypie' Mayo, who was a great guitar player. He wasn't as individualistic as Wilko, which nobody was, nor did he try to copy him. Gypie came up with his own licks and hooks and brought with him a greater variety of sounds. Lee was always a great frontman and hardcore fans went with the transition because, for them, Lee and Wilko were equally important. They were prepared to see how it panned out with Gypie.

The band now followed Lee's lead towards a more broadly commercial style which they could never have done with Wilko. They needed to be seen to move on and didn't hang about. The Nick Lowe-produced *Be Seeing You* appeared only four months later in October. Nick had maintained a strong connection with the Feelgoods, so he was the obvious choice and he gave them a first Top 40 single with 'She's a Windup'.

The Feelgoods continued to make it work by constantly touring, although they were never the same draw as the original line-up. The albums came thick and fast too. Sire Records co-founder and New York new wave producer Richard Gottehrer produced *Private Practice*, for which Nick Lowe and Gypie had co-written 'Milk and Alcohol'. It gave Dr Feelgood their only Top 10 single in February 1979. It never got any better after that. The touring took its toll and Gypie left in January 1981; the following year Figure and Sparko were gone, too. Lee Brilleaux continued with the band almost until his death from lymphoma, aged forty-one, on 7 April 1994.

Dai Davies wasn't about to give up on me over the Stranglers. He gave me a tape of four or five tracks and I knew I wasn't the first to hear them. I still wasn't sure what to make of the band. Were they part of the punk movement or just using that as a way to get noticed, or was it an accident of timing? They'd been called the Stranglers for a while (and before that the Guildford Stranglers) so they hadn't suddenly adopted a punk-ish sounding name. The other anomaly was that having formed as far back as 1974, they were more professional and polished than your average punk band. I just couldn't put my finger on what they were about.

I'd already signed two bands in 1976 that were floundering because of the impact punk was making. One was the George Hatcher Band, which came about through my thinking 'What can we do that nobody else is doing in the UK?' For some reason I came up with the idea of a British-based 'Southern Rock band'. At least frontman George Hatcher was from Florida and had been in the Marines. They were convincing enough but I knew my heart wasn't in it. I'd also signed The O Band, who'd already made an album as the Parlour Band and two for Epic as A Band Called O. They were a really intelligent bunch, all very good musicians and all originally from Jersey. That definitely made them unique, but it was difficult to give them any recognisable style or image beyond them being 'a really

242

good rock band'. They were managed by Barrie Marshall and I spent a lot of time with them in the studio. I liked them a lot as people. Both acts were building up nicely in 1976 but became an anathema a year later.

Dai Davies kept telling me the Stranglers were 'an Andrew Lauder band – you will get it'. We knew each other well enough that I never doubted he believed that. Finally, he said, 'What if I hire a rehearsal room, get in some decent equipment and the Stranglers can play just for you? If you don't get it, then I promise I won't bother you again.' So I agreed to that and went along. There was a chair in the middle of the room with the equipment set up in front. I never sit down at gigs, so I stood at the back, hardly inconspicuous, watched and listened. They started playing and in no time at all I began thinking, 'Right, now I'm getting it.' As the set went on it was obvious that they actually had tons of really catchy tunes. The sound was retro, but that appealed to me because it was a 1960s garage band retro that definitely chimed with punk. By the time they'd finished their set, all my concerns had melted away.

They were a distinctive-looking bunch too, with a sinister disposition that suited the times. Keyboard player Dave Greenfield looked like he'd come out of a progressive rock group – which he had; bassist Jean-Jacques Burnel was dangerous looking but not without mean and moody pop star looks – a kind of punk Jet Harris. He was an economics graduate from Bradford University whose parents owned a French restaurant in Godalming. Guitarist and singer Hugh Cornwell looked like he'd just stepped out from a police line-up, and former jazz drummer Jet Black was knocking on forty but carried it well. He was running a pub and had previously been an ice-cream salesman. They used to drive to gigs in his ice-cream van. Hugh had been in a band at school with former Fairport Convention guitarist Richard Thompson and was only two years younger than me. Between them they

had a very strange collective band CV. Once we started talking –
about music, as usual – we hit it off.

Signing the Stranglers coincided with Martin Rushent becoming my assistant at United Artists. He was an experienced
engineer, usually working out of Advision Studios, and Martin
Davis knew him from working with Shirley Bassey. Strange
credentials to be producing a band like the Stranglers on paper,
but he was a fantastic engineer. The Stranglers were his first
assignment for me. I kept quiet about Shirley Bassey. The band
had already been rebuffed by various other labels and were
champing at the bit to finally make a record.

They were due to play at the Nashville, which Dai and Derek
Savage at Albion ran, so this was another job for Vic Maile and
the Pye Mobile. I wanted to get a live recording under our belts
so that Martin Rushent could assess the material. It wasn't a
difficult deal to sort out; nobody else was interested. We decided
to record in the claustrophobic TW Studios in Fulham. It was
more a demo studio, but they had a very good engineer there
called Alan Winstanley and he and Martin became a team for a
while. It was very basic, with flaking tiles coming away from the
walls. The next day you'd be scratching like mad from the dust,
but despite that it was also kind of funky. It was the perfect
studio to record the Stranglers' debut album.

My personal situation had changed because Maureen and I
were splitting up around the time we signed the Stranglers. We'd
bought a house in Muswell Hill, which was a long way to get
home to from most venues and places we used to go to. Maureen
left United Artists soon after we moved there. She was already
growing tired of going to so many gigs anyway and probably
of driving me around. I guess we'd been drifting apart without
realising. I tended to stay at the office when I was visiting studios
after hours or going to gigs, so we were seeing less of each other.
At the same time Judith would be going to the same gigs so we

started getting cabs together and grabbing something to eat. It wasn't long before we got together, and Maureen and I separated. We sold the house in Muswell Hill and rented a flat in the Barbican where we stored all our stuff, including all the records, but I never stayed overnight there once. I'd moved in with Judith.

A week either side of Christmas, Judith and I would go down to the studio in Fulham most days. Martin played me the roughs from the first day's session, but it wasn't the sound I'd heard in the rehearsal room. The broad stereo felt distant to me. It wasn't suffocating enough. I was trying to explain what was wrong and Martin said, 'Oh, you mean like this—' and flicked one switch at the desk and I said, 'That's it!' They could really play but I wanted it to sound like you were locked in a room with them. It was a different, more oppressive sound than the Feelgoods but just as tight. JJ was a fabulous bass player, Jet the perfect drummer for the band and Dave was a really accomplished player, so he was reining himself in to make it all sound more urgent. Hugh's attitude to playing was almost dismissive but he made every note count.

We chose '(Get a) Grip (On Yourself)' as the first single because, intentionally or not, we were definitely going to get sucked into the punk scene. Even within United Artists I was hearing cries of 'Why have you signed one of these dreadful punk rock groups?' As word came out in January 1977 that we'd signed the Stranglers, the first Buzzcocks EP had been released while the Jam had signed to Polydor and the Clash confounded a lot of speculation by signing to CBS. The Stranglers' single was released at the end of January and came in at No. 44. We were more than happy with a Top 50 slot but due to a cock-up by chart compilers BMRB, the Stranglers' entry never appeared in print. I knew I'd signed the Stranglers at just the right moment. If I'd delayed, we'd have been caught up in a bidding war as every label now wanted a piece of the action. Instead, I knew we had a great album almost ready to go. I'd accepted the inevitable – the Stranglers were going to be perceived as a punk band and we were on course for them to be one of the first to unleash a debut album.

In the meantime, having signed them outside Buckingham Palace on 10 March, A&M became the second label to scrap a Sex Pistols' contract. I'd met and spoken to Malcolm McClaren a couple of times and he came by the office a few days later. He asked if I'd be interested in signing the Sex Pistols. My first thought was, 'Maybe I'm the person that can handle them.' I'd already signed the Stranglers, and that was going well, and dealing with Lemmy and Hawkwind had primed me for dealing with an outsider band. It was about half seven, and after Malcolm and I had the conversation, I said I wanted to sleep on it. Nick Mobbs at EMI had told me about the grief he'd had with them. So I was wary, but kept thinking, 'Well, maybe?' Malcolm made no attempt to reassure me that it was going to be any different this time. For a brief while I made up my mind to sign the Sex Pistols, but by the time I got home I'd talked myself out of it. The clincher was that I knew how much the Stranglers would resent it. Both bands hated each other so it would have been really unfair. The Stranglers I could talk to and, more to the point, they'd listen. I also doubted the Sex Pistols were going to last. I spoke to Malcolm the next morning and within a couple of days they'd gone to Virgin.

We'd been right to make a record with the Stranglers so quickly and have an album in the shops by April. The Stranglers were going to be tarred by punk anyway, so I wanted to make the most of that. There weren't too many punk groups with albums out – and that was to our advantage. The Damned were the first, as they'd been with 'New Rose'. Produced by Nick Lowe, *Damned Damned Damned* was released by Stiff in February.

I talked it over with our art director Paul Henry and said I wanted to stay clear of all the clichéd punk rock images that were being used for singles. I wanted the Stranglers' album cover image to make them look dark and mysterious rather than menacing. There'd be no strangled victims anywhere in sight. I didn't want to use any ripped clothes, safety pins and scrawled writing or something that looked like a blackmail letter cut from a newspaper. I had this idea to put a number on the title in Roman numerals. So it was *The Stranglers IV: Rattus Norvegicus*, but not explaining why *IV*, or why *Rattus Norvegicus*. The title was meant to be perplexing, not offensive but more 'What the fuck's this all about?'

The Clash album came out the week before. I was friendly with Dan Loggins at CBS and we deliberately put the Stranglers back a week. Dan phoned when he got the chart position for the Clash and said, 'You'll never guess where we've entered?' And he made me play the guessing game. I started at No. 32, then 25, and kept going further up the charts till we arrived at No. 12, and I said, 'That's a great result for a new band's first record.' I had no idea where the Stranglers album would land, although the feedback from the sales guys was good. I also used a couple of live tracks from the Nashville to copy what I'd done with *Stupidity* by shrink-wrapping a free 45 with the first 10,000 copies. We crashed in at No. 4, way higher than anybody expected. I couldn't resist phoning Dan and saying, 'You'll never guess where we charted!'

It really couldn't have gone better for the Stranglers after that. For the rest of 1977 every single charted in week one, and the gigs were all selling out. With everything else I'd ever done there'd been a slow build, so it was a mark of how the market had changed. With Hawkwind, the Groundhogs and even the Feelgoods, it took till the third album. Man took six albums to even crack the Top 30. Singles had a currency again. Prior to punk, most of the singles we put out were aimed at picking up airplay to help boost album sales. The Stranglers had more hit singles that year than the rest of the UK artists I signed put together.

Andrew's Western-style office at United Artists in 1977

Working with the Stranglers was so painless, in part because we had Martin Rushent in the studio and they continued working well with him. Dai and Derek Savage were also a great management team to deal with. The group more or less had the first two albums' worth of songs when we signed them. So we

easily jumped the punk queue because we had such a backlog
of great songs. July's 'Peaches'/'Go Buddy Go' hit No. 8 – the
A-side banned by the BBC for offensive lyrics; a month later
'Something Better Change' reached No. 9 and 'No More Heroes'
also reached No. 9 in October. That same month, *No More Heroes*
bettered their debut, making No. 2 in the album charts. Based
on chart success, the Stranglers were easily the most successful
band I'd ever signed.

They didn't go out of their way to play up to a punk image,
although JJ and Hugh had their moments. When somebody in
the accounts department did something that pissed him off, JJ
locked him in his office and threw the keys away. I thought that
was hilarious. Jon Savage had a very definite idea of what punk
was and had written something derogatory about the Stranglers.
I was talking to him at the bar in the Red Cow when JJ came
up and laid one on him. I wasn't too pleased about that. Hugh's
speciality was riling up audiences. At Glasgow Apollo a number
of the city councillors sat in the front row – arms crossed and
looking disapproving. Hugh asked for the spotlight to be shone
on them and dedicated the song 'Ugly' to them. If you were a
punk band, trouble followed you during 1977. Dates were regularly cancelled throughout the year and JJ and Jet Black spent
a night in jail in Brighton after an incident at the Top Rank. It
was another punk rite of passage.

I'd bought Buzzcocks' first EP 'Spiral Scratch' in January
1977. It was on their own New Hormones label set up by singer
Howard Devoto and guitarist Pete Shelley. After only eleven gigs,
Howard left, but that didn't put me off wanting to sign them.
Steve Diggle switched from bass to guitar and they added Garth
Smith on bass. They had already toured with the Sex Pistols,
and supported the Clash on their 'White Riot' tour in May. It
was only after I'd signed them that Steve Garvey replaced Smith
to complete the classic Buzzcocks line-up.

Buzzcocks presented a completely different image to any other punk band. They'd been biding their time and not going out of their way to make too many shock waves. I loved that they came from Manchester; I'd always wanted to sign a group from the North and it wasn't till Buzzcocks that I finally achieved that. I went up to see them at the Electric Circus at the end of May on what was an extraordinary bill with Penetration, John Cooper Clarke and Warsaw (later renamed Joy Division), playing their first ever gig. There was something special about the evening, the crowd very much as one. It was a great atmosphere that conveyed a sense of 'this is our punk rock'. And Buzzcocks played their particularly unique take on it. They were nothing like the clichéd punk prototype which had caused a lot of other labels to back off. That's what drew me to them. They had all the songs ready to record, one after another of Pete Shelly's succinct, catchy, intimate songs like 'What Ever Happened to . . .', 'Orgasm Addict' and 'What Do I Get'.

I signed them on 16 August, the day Elvis Presley died. When Judith and I got back to our hotel room a note had been pushed under the door that simply read 'Elvis Is Dead'. It had been left by photographer Jill Furmanovsky, who'd come up to Manchester with us. Judith and I looked at each other in shock, assuming it was Elvis Costello. His debut album *My Aim Is True* had only recently been released by Stiff Records to rave reviews. We switched on the radio and immediately heard 'It's Now or Never' being played so we realised it must be the other Elvis.

At the end of the month, completely unbeknownst to me, Martin Davis bought an off-the-shelf company called Cladhurst that would eventually trade under the name Radar Records. Martin had been having conversations with John Fruin, MD at WEA, about a potential deal for a new label. It wasn't till late October that he invited me round to his house for dinner. I'd never been to his house before and figured something was up. That's when he told me about the offer on the table from WEA, adding that it 'hinges round you being part of the deal'. Martin was taking a calculated risk, although he knew me well enough. It would have been interesting had I said 'no', but there was another factor in play. There'd been rumours about EMI taking over United Artists from the current American owners. So when he said, 'I don't want to work for EMI, I don't know about you', he knew I felt the same. The deal he'd struck with John Fruin was almost too good to be true. Our label was wholly funded by WEA, but with us having complete control of the repertoire. He told me the figures involved. I didn't query anything and said, 'Count me in.'

The money was good and to have our own separate office and not have to work out of WEA's building on Broadwick Street was another plus. He added that we could even take some of the United Artists staff with us. We came up with the name Radar, which implied the idea of detecting something going on out there. It had plenty of potential for a logo and I especially liked that it was a palindrome.

There was a Greek Restaurant – the Glory Kebab House – just by Mortimer Street that we went to all the time and, having agreed to accept the WEA offer, I wanted to let Jake know what was going on. Stiff Records had gone from strength to strength in the year since I began pressing the early singles. I told Jake about Radar and he said, 'That's weird, because I'm splitting up with Dave Robinson and taking Elvis Costello and Nick Lowe with me. How would you like them on your new label?' It was so unexpected that my reaction was an incredulous, 'Are you kidding?' He wasn't; Jake and I shook hands on a deal between Riviera Global and Radar Records. It was a gentlemen's agreement. I left it to Jake and Martin to sort out the necessary paperwork.

Jake and Dave Robinson were chalk and cheese in so many ways. Dave was bluff and pragmatic, Jake was quick-witted and mercurial, while both were equally headstrong, and both very driven. They'd agreed to split after the *Stiffs Live* tour (a label package involving Elvis Costello, Nick Lowe, Ian Dury and Wreckless Eric) ended at the beginning of November. Elvis was about to have his first Top 20 hit with 'Watching the Detectives' and Nick was in another league since the Brinsley Schwarz days because of what he'd done at Stiff as a producer – not least producing Elvis Costello, Graham Parker and the Damned. He'd also continued his particular brand of new wave pop on three singles released by Stiff.

I'd never met Elvis Costello or even seen him play live. Judith had first told me about him because she'd been going out with Jake and spending a lot of time at Alexander Street and Queens Gate Terrace. I hadn't heard anything till she played me his debut single 'Less than Zero', and swiftly afterwards came 'Alison'. I'd had no preconception about Elvis whatsoever and was mightily impressed. When I heard *My Aim Is True* it was clear he was a major talent.

Jake filled me in on how both Nick and Elvis had new albums more or less finished that didn't require any additional funding from us or WEA; he just wanted good points on the deal for him and them. The recording costs were taken care of by Columbia in America, where both artists were signed through Riviera Global. So we'd be getting Elvis's highly anticipated second and Nick's debut solo album for the UK and the rest of the world bar the US. Oh yes, and Sweden as a result of a separate arrangement Jake had made. Needless to say, Martin and WEA were delighted. What we didn't do, though, was to renegotiate the deal between Radar and WEA, despite it now including Nick and Elvis. Given that no additional money was required for recording, we didn't think it was appropriate.

Radar (officially trading as Radarscope) was announced in *Music Week* on 26 November 1977 as a fully funded new label that would be autonomous. WEA took care of manufacturing, distribution and running costs, and we could also call on WEA's marketing and promotional teams. The aim was that Radar would help develop WEA's British talent roster. Traditionally, much of what WEA released was coming in from America through Warners, Elektra and Atlantic; that had always been their priority. They weren't used to breaking UK acts.

Immediately before Christmas, Elvis played three nights at the Nashville with his backing band the Attractions, the group he'd put together after he'd made *My Aim Is True*. I was good friends with drummer Pete Thomas, who I'd known since his Chilli Willi days. He'd been living in California, playing with singer-songwriter John Stewart, till he got the call from Jake and Pete and knew he was on to a good thing when he heard Elvis. The gigs were sold out in advance but each night there were queues blocking the streets. Jake had agreed to put the Pop Group and Soft Boys on as supports on two of the nights. I'd been having conversations with both groups about signing them to United Artists and both had agreed to cross over to Radar instead.

It was a wrench leaving United Artists and leaving behind the Feelgoods, who were adjusting nicely to life after Wilko, and the Stranglers, who'd had such an amazing year. They were already moving on to their third album. I did at least do everything I could to complete Buzzcocks' first album while I was still there. I tried to spend as much time as possible with them in those final months. All the pieces were in place. We'd released 'Orgasm Addict' in October and had set Martin Rushent up to produce them. Their designer Malcolm Garrett was already in place too. *Another Music in a Different Kitchen* was released the following March, an ecstatically received collection of irresistible, short, sharp songs. I felt awful for deserting them.

The last band I signed at United Artists was 999. That came through Dai Davies' Albion Management, which was a factor in

taking them on. Theirs was another album we did very quickly.
Something of an anomaly, 999 were a tight, intense rock 'n'
roll band, two guitars, bass and drums who were often unfairly
dismissed as punk bandwagon jumpers. We released one United
Artists single, 'Nasty Nasty', before I departed, but they were
left a little high and dry after I'd gone. Their debut album was
scheduled too close to Buzzcocks' and it was either overlooked
or dismissed. They were left to fend for themselves, something
they were already hardened to.

I'd been at United Artists – and at Liberty Records before
that – for just over ten years and it was time for a change. The
success we'd had with the Stranglers was an indication of how
the market had changed and where singles relying on a strong
fan base and music press support had become key. Radar was
essentially geared to signing new groups to fit into that market-
place. It was the opportunity to carve out something new and
create my own roster from scratch.*

Officially Martin and I left United Artists on 31 December
1977 and as of 1 January we were operating as Radar Records.
Martin made an arrangement that we could carry on working
out of UA till our new offices were set up. I wanted it to be as
smooth a changeover as possible; I'd have hated leaving United
Artists under any sort of cloud.

---

* I'd turned down so many offers in my time at United Artists – Chrysalis,
Virgin a couple of times, and CBS, among them. I had a call from Charles
Levison, who was head of international at Arista Records, not long before
Radar was announced. They were sounding me out for the position of vice
president of Arista in the UK. I thought dealing with the label's founder and
president Clive Davies would give rise to problems, though nothing I couldn't
handle; but the prospect of meetings with Barry Manilow was another matter.
I couldn't think of any situation where I could have a meaningful conversation
with him. When the conversation got round to where I'd like my yacht to be
moored at Midem, I came to my senses.

PART THREE
Change Is Now, 1978–2022

Chapter 19
Radar Blips

We took a small posse of people with us to Radar; Judith, Carol Pini, Martin's secretary, who was married to Tim Reid, who came over as marketing manager and took on International too. I'd always got on well with Mark Anders from the O band. He was very well organised, very bright, and he became my right-hand man at Radar. Just before we moved into the new Radar offices, Mark said, 'I thought I should let you know that I'm now living with Maureen.' I had no idea, but I was really pleased.

We moved into our new offices on 21 February at 60 Parker Street, an old, four-storey shopfront that was originally a coachworks at the back of Covent Garden; we didn't need the upper floor, which we rented out to Jake's Riviera Global enterprise. That included Jake's assistant Cynthia, and he shared that space with Barney Bubbles. Pretty soon Malcolm Garrett moved in with us; we'd got to know him through Buzzcocks. So we had two of the best designers – if not the best – to call upon at Radar. The offices were a real home from home. Everybody in the building knew each other and next door was the Blitz Club, masquerading as a fairly average burger joint in daylight but by night the centre of the New Romantic subculture.

We'd done the deal with WEA based upon finding four new acts a year. There was no written agreement between Riviera Global and WEA, only between Radar and WEA. We had something to release immediately; Nick Lowe's 'I Love The Sound of Breaking Glass' charted the week we moved into Parker Street, eventually reaching No. 7 and Nick's only ever Top 10 hit. His debut solo album *Jesus of Cool* followed in March and reached a respectable No. 22.

I knew a lot of the songs on *Jesus of Cool* because it had been recorded over a period of time. It was a few years before Nick was really appreciated as a songwriter; he gave the impression of just dashing something off, which could be true but belied, as with his role as a producer, just how good he was. He was juggling his time making his own records, writing, recording and touring with Dave Edmunds in Rockpile, the group they'd formed with guitarist Billy Bremner and Terry Williams from the Man band. Rockpile undertook extensive UK and US tours during 1978. Dave Edmunds had his first hit in four years with a Nick Lowe song, 'I Knew the Bride', taken from his Swan Song debut album *Get It* featuring a band that was part Brinsley Schwarz, part Rumour and three quarters Rockpile.

Nick had become the complete all-rounder and produced Elvis Costello a second time with *This Year's Model*. It was released at the beginning of April, soon after Elvis completed a three-month US tour. *This Year's Model* reached No. 4 and went gold within months in the UK alone. All three singles from the album were hits, 'I Don't Wanna Go to Chelsea', 'Pump It Up' and 'Radio Radio' and he ended 1978 selling out a seven-night stand at London's Dominion Theatre. *This Year's Model* was cut with George Peckham. Jake had him scratch a phone number on the run-out grooves; it was the number for WEA's head of press Moira Bellas and said, 'Phone this number for your special prize.' The day the album came out she was inundated with calls from people claiming, 'I've got the special pressing.' I think she did eventually see the funny side.

I wasn't surprised that Nick emerged as a successful
producer. He'd made a lot of records with Brinsley Schwarz
and learned a lot from watching Dave Edmunds, but you have
to find your own way. Nick definitely found his by allowing his
true character to come out in the studio, which was to keep
everything buzzing and create an upbeat atmosphere. He was a
good judge of mood and knew what to do to keep people's spirits
up. Nick went on to produce the first five Elvis Costello albums
and would return to produce him again. I didn't hang out
when Elvis was in the studio because I instinctively knew that
Elvis wouldn't want anybody there without a good reason. He
could be moody and never disguised that because the recording
process was paramount for him. It was very much 'man at work
here – do not interfere or get in the way'. That was fair enough,
and I was respectful around Elvis until I got to know him better,
which I certainly did over the next ten years.

I didn't have an active role with Elvis at Radar. Barney did
the artwork – as amazing as ever – and Jake took care of co-
ordinating with Columbia in America. During that first year at
Radar, Elvis was on tour a hell of a lot, especially in America. His
spectacular success in 1978 happened quickly in the UK off the
back of his Stiff reputation, but in America it happened even more
quickly and on a huge scale. For a British solo artist, there'd been
nothing like it since Elton John's rapid rise over there. It was
breathtaking just watching it happen and admiring the results;
My Aim Is True, *This Year's Model* and his next, *Armed Forces*,
were all written, recorded and released within eighteen months.

Elvis and Nick were Jake's charges, and one side effect was that
people thought Radar was Jake's label or that he was a partner
in it. It was neither, and even to this day people refer to 'Jake
Riviera's label Radar Records'. For me, the success of Elvis and
Nick created a false sense of how Radar was perceived. That soon
switched to a feeling of panic because I needed to sign some bands

of my own and to bring in a few records from outside. Some of these definitely fell flat. Albums by National Lampoon, the power-pop Pezband and solid rockers the Good Rats were licensed through Marty Scott at Passport. I was doing him a favour and filling a few holes during a frenzied time trying to create a catalogue from scratch until we could get anything out by our new signings.

Kill City was on the mark though and sat nicely between the release of Elvis and Nick's albums. It was an album by Iggy Pop and James Williamson, Iggy's guitarist and writing partner in the final line-up of the Stooges. The recordings were actually demos recorded in Jimmy Webb's home studio in 1975 and eventually released on Greg Shaw's Bomp label in 1977. By the time I licensed it from Greg, Iggy had made his most widespread impact with the David Bowie produced *The Idiot* and *Lust for Life* using many of the same musicians from *Kill City*. I wasn't alone in preferring it to the final, official Iggy and the Stooges album *Raw Power* that was mixed by Bowie.

I also put out two albums by La Düsseldorf, including a new album *Viva*. It made sense to pick up La Düsseldorf's self-titled debut from 1976 as well, which had already been deleted in the UK. It had sold in excess of a million copies in Europe thanks to an unexpected No. 2 single with 'Silver Cloud' in Germany. As with Neu!, La Düsseldorf received belated kudos for pre-dating both punk and post-punk with its angry and primitive sounds, though neither album sold well. We were also ahead of the game with a compilation by cult rockabilly artist Ray Campi, who'd been recording since the late 1950s. *Wildcat Shakeout* was a compilation of recent recordings with a young Californian band he called the Rockabilly Rebels. I licensed the tracks from specialist rockabilly label Rollin' Rock. Campi and the band came over for a few dates. They were terrific but the interest wasn't there beyond hardcore rockabilly fans. It was a genre that was always threatening to have a revival and it came a year later with the Stray Cats.

I was feeling added pressure because the two acts I brought over from United Artists, the Pop Group and the Soft Boys, weren't going to plan with only one single between the pair of them released during 1978. The Pop Group were originally managed by Alan Jones, who was the sax player in Amen Corner. He managed PJs in Newport where I first went to see them after Kingsley at Rockfield tipped me off. The Pop Group were all around seventeen years old but were moving so fast in every imaginable direction that they were always trashing what they'd done the previous week. By the time Radar was up and running, Dick O'Dell had become their manager. Dick always talked a good talk and the group fully trusted he'd back them. I'd come across him as a tour manager for the Stranglers and Hugh Cornwell had financed and produced some of the Pop Group's early demos. As a band, they spent more time theorising and rehearsing than gigging and, unlike most young bands, never wanted to rush out any recordings. I took it slowly and could see no point in racking up too much studio time till they felt they were ready.

I spoke to John Cale about producing the Pop Group. On paper it was the perfect match. He had the right experience and breadth of musical knowledge to embrace their headful of ideas and his history spoke for itself. He had a reputation for being tricky to work with, so I set up a meeting with Dick and the band. He met them the day after he'd flown in from New York before travelling straight down to Bristol. Dick told me he was so jet-lagged and out of it he fell asleep over lunch and that was the end of it. They had their own ideas and came up with Dennis Bovell, a dub maestro with a reputation for inventive-ness at the mixing desk, working with his own group Matumbi and other UK reggae acts. Dennis was never on my list, but I went with it. They were the first rock act he produced and he was as up for experimentation as they were. It was a leftfield choice and, as it turned out, inspired.

I first heard the Soft Boys through their EP 'Give it to the Soft Boys' on Raw Records, a little Cambridge label that was one of the first to emerge out of that DIY punk movement. They didn't sound like any of the other bands around because they were so skilful and almost wilfully eclectic, capable of shifting from something that sounded like Captain Beefheart to *a cappella* doo-wop or classic British folk rock. That proved to be their undoing because I found it impossible to make anything work in the studio the way I heard it in my head. It was the first time I'd really had this kind of problem. I kept hoping we'd get it right next time, but nothing ever sounded right. And Robyn Hitchcock, who called the shots in the band, found it equally frustrating.

We only ever put out the one single, 'I Want to be an Angle-poise Lamp', which we released early in May in our first year. Singles weren't the answer. They were so great live, extraordinarily adaptable, and musically, even playfully adventurous, that only an album could fully do them justice. It was never about the musicianship or the songs, although Robyn's lyrics could be a little surreal and fanciful. I blamed myself for not coming up with the goods in the studio. I can't believe how many different studios, engineers and producers we tried between April and September 1978: Regent Park Sound, Olympic, Sound Techniques and Wessex in London, and Rockfield, among other residential studios. We couldn't figure it out and in the end I had to give up. I couldn't go on spending more and more money chasing something which kept eluding me.

Even with what we had in the can, there was nothing we could release that would do us or the band any favours. We could certainly have done with clawing back some of the £40,000 we spent. Fans ask about the legendary lost Radar sessions but they weren't good enough to release. It was as simple as that and Robyn had always said the same. The Soft Boys put out *A*

262

Can of Bees a year later, recorded back at Spaceward Studios in
Cambridge and which Robyn funded. It included a lot of songs
they'd recorded for Radar, and it was better than anything we'd
been able to get down.

I did achieve one ambition in our first year after having been
thwarted at Liberty when I tried to license the *Psychedelic Sounds
of the 13th Floor Elevators* in 1967. Ten years later they'd reached
almost mythical status and I was able to license the Elevators'
album and Red Krayola's *Parable of Arable Land* from Lelan
Rogers, who'd originally signed both bands. He was country star
Kenny Rogers' brother. We put those out in October. Pete Frame
then told me that Red Krayola's Mayo Thompson was teaching at
Leeds University. I rang him and told him what we were planning.
For all his highly cerebral theories he was very good company.

WEA saw it as a complete indulgence and, taken alongside
the Soft Boys fiasco, I needed to find something demonstrably
more marketable. To that end I signed Liverpool group the
Yachts in early summer. Stiff had released their debut single
'Suffice to Say' which earned them plenty of praise, but singer
and main songwriter J.J. Campbell then left. Keyboard player
Henry Priestman took over lead vocals and began writing with
guitarist Martin Watson, but there was never a follow-up on
Stiff. We released two singles before the end of our first year.
The first was a cover of 'Look Back in Love (Not in Anger)' by
Teddy and the Pandas, an obscure sixties Boston band. It was
one of Clive Langer's first productions.* The Yachts came out of
the same Liverpool Art College background as Clive's seminal

---

* As well as producing the Yachts, Clive produced a couple of unashamed pop
singles by Bette Bright and the Illuminations for us. She'd been the singer in
Deaf School with Clive, who Jake had signed to Rivera Global. It was a smart
move; Clive was soon making his name as a producer (with Alan Winstanley),
beginning with *One Step Beyond* by Madness, and we released a 12-inch single
by Clive Langer and the Boxes.

Liverpool band Deaf School. Having formed in the early days of punk – even supporting the Sex Pistols at Liverpool's Eric's club – the Yachts ignored the punk blueprint for witty, melodic songs with good harmonies, driven by Farfisa organ. This and a smart dress sense soon set them adrift of what was happening around Eric's during 1978 with groups such as the Teardrop Explodes and Echo & the Bunnymen emerging. The test of a great pop song is to make some impact on radio or in the charts, but the Yachts' singles did neither. Thinking it would give them more edge, I decided to record their album in New York with Richard Gottehrer, who'd recently done a great job producing Dr Feelgood.

We needed to start bringing some money into Radar; we were feeling the pinch and this was heightened by a problem of our own making when we'd done the original deal with WEA and excluded the US. We thought a separate US deal would provide another source of income for future growth and we wanted to explore other possibilities. Martin and I went to America in April to meet all the interested parties including Chrysalis and A&M, who'd licensed the Stranglers. We even did photos with Mo Ostin and various Warners execs on the assumption we were most likely to go with them.

Both sides then prevaricated too long and it was six months before Warners sent Bob Regehr (vice president) and Bob Merlis (director of press) to check us out. We took them to see the Yachts, the Pop Group and 999. You couldn't have found three more dissimilar bands if you tried, and of course Elvis and Nick were never going to be part of the package. It then went very quiet till they came back a few weeks later saying they no longer wanted to do the deal.

It was chastening once Warners turned us down because we knew we were in trouble. We'd made mistakes, first by not adjusting the deal with WEA after Jake offered us Elvis and Nick, and then hesitating about the American deal. We weren't

264

bringing in any other money and Elvis sold so many records that Martin had to ask John Fruin at WEA for additional funds to pay unanticipated royalties. When he also turned us down it became even more crucial that we secured an American deal before the New Year to shore up our incipient financial problems.

A few weeks later, Jerry Jaffe at Polydor came to our rescue. Jerry was a guy I'd met in London in the mid-seventies through Nick. He later described me as a mentor, but all I remembered was that he used to hang out in my office at United Artists and I added him to a few guest lists. He desperately wanted to get into the music industry back home. He actually had a PhD in Chemistry and, after graduating, wrote to all the major US companies giving my name and Nick's as a reference. He eventually landed a job in A&R at Polydor. When I mentioned our needing a US deal, he jumped at the chance. We weren't in a position to turn the Polydor deal down even though it was far from ideal financially. The margins between what Radar was contracted to with the artists and the terms of the US deal left us barely breaking even.

We did at least have a schedule of home-grown releases in the works for 1979, all of which Polydor committed to taking on. Once again Elvis Costello was the star turn. We released *Armed Forces* in January, for the first time also credited to the Attractions. After a year of almost solid touring, they'd developed an intuitive bond as a four-piece that's full of confidence and interrelation. Elvis had come up with an amazing body of songs, all fully bedded in. *Armed Forces* reached No. 2 in the charts, eventually selling over 300,000 copies in the UK and certified platinum. It sold almost twice that in the States, and here it yielded hits with two of Elvis' most memorable songs, 'Oliver's Army', which reached No. 2, and 'Accidents Will Happen'.

Nick Lowe's second album *Labour of Lust* didn't appear till June. It did less well than *Jesus of Cool* although 'Cruel to be

Kind', an old Brinsleys song written with Ian Gomm, would
make No. 12 in September. The album's lesser showing was more
a measure of Nick's broader focus and heavy demand from the
States. In July he began a two-month tour supporting Blondie
with Rockpile, all of whom played on *Labour of Lust*. All Nick's
and Dave Edmunds' solo output from this period was effectively
Rockpile and friends. Halfway through the dates Nick took
time out to marry Carlene Carter in Los Angeles. She was June
Carter's daughter from her marriage to country singer Carl
Smith and part of the fabled Carter Family. Her subsequent
partner, Nick's step-father-in-law, was Johnny Cash, who
recorded 'Without Love' from *Labour of Lust*.

The key to Radar's future that year was not *Armed Forces*
but the Pop Group's *Y*. The album was recorded at Ridge Farm
in Dorking, Surrey over several months. *Y* sounds unfinished at
times, however much that's masked by a heavy dub-like overlay
which managed to pull together influences ranging from raw
punk, funk, Miles Davis, Can and reggae. I knew I had to give
them their head and see what happened. They were intelligent,
headstrong and totally convinced theirs was the only way to go.
Dennis Bovell did a brilliant job of giving the disparate musical
threads a framework. He actually managed to calm them down
a bit and stopped them galloping away from themselves.

It was a long time coming but we finally released the Pop
Group's debut single, 'She Is Beyond Good and Evil' in March
1979. It's generally regarded as one of the most powerful debut
singles ever released. As somebody wrote at the time, it's as if all
five members of the band are playing something different and
came together more by accident than intent. The Pop Group had
always been backed to the hilt by the music press, for whom the
single lived up to all expectations and *Y* didn't disappoint either.
If there was a criticism, it was a suggestion that they'd bitten off
more than they could chew.

266

The Pop Group's stunning debut single was on the cusp of
post-punk

I knew more people were going to hate *Y* than love it. It was
certainly too much of a headache for WEA, and lyrically Mark
Stewart didn't miss the opportunity to berate his group's big bad
corporate label. They were always too full of themselves. They
went out of their way to alienate people but didn't understand or
seem to care that some of those people were actually on their side.

Y sold well initially – around 10,000 copies off the back of the
music press build-up – but there was nowhere to take it from
there. They set up a full UK tour, but the performances were
even more uncompromising than the record and a number of
dates were cancelled through poor advance ticket sales. I never
thought *Y* was art for art's sake, but I knew it was a difficult
record and although the term wasn't around quite yet, the Pop
Group revelled in a forward-looking post-punk approach that

placed them alongside PIL, Gang of Four and the Slits – whose album was Dennis Bovell's next undertaking.

Within a month of release the group did an *NME* interview which slated the record company and claimed there was no contract with Radar. When they left the label, Dick made a statement saying they'd pulled off a scam to rank alongside the Sex Pistols being thrown off EMI. We paid for all the recordings, which were ultimately owned by WEA, who would have won any legal battle. Instead we let them go – and WEA were delighted to see the back of them. I don't regret having made *Y*. I was proud of it, and I still am, but it wasn't what WEA were expecting. I'm not sure WEA ever even grasped the irony of the name.

I wanted Radar to be known for something other than the success of Elvis Costello and Nick Lowe. The Pop Group is the only other Radar act that has made a lasting impression. 'She Is Beyond Good and Evil' and *Y* are even more revered today than forty years ago. The stubborn streak in me took the form of recording a new Red Krayola album – *Soldier Talk* – with Mayo Thompson. It was even more extreme than *Y* with Mayo's warbling vocals, loud piercing guitar, clattering drums and Lora Logic's tuneless sax. We did a launch at the Hope & Anchor, covering the stage in camouflage netting and Red Krayola played. It was just Mayo on guitar and a drummer – very ahead of its time – and very much in the spirit of what I wanted to achieve at Radar.

It was post-punk at its most unlistenable and WEA probably thought I was taking the piss. I wanted to explore the diversity of that initial post-punk era – the more industrial, more minimal-sounding and electronic experimental groups. To that end, I desperately wanted to sign the Gang of Four and to secure a UK licence with Ralph Records to release the Residents' catalogue. Neither happened, although I did release two further albums by the Elevators and the original Red Krayola – *Easter Everywhere* and *God Bless the Red Krayola and All Who Sail With It*, but that was it for my more radical ideals. I had to find acts that would appeal to Polydor because we needed that income. Y didn't get a US release; Jerry Jaffe thought he'd be pushing his luck too far. It wasn't officially released in the US till a few years ago.

Having tried to sign them at Liberty, Andrew licensed the 13th Floor Elevators on Radar

Radar became a lot more mainstream in the second half of 1979. I thought the Yachts and recent signing the Inmates both had something different to offer, although the Yachts could never pull away from that cursed powerpop mantle that still clung to them. Polydor definitely gave the band a push though. They did a successful tour in the US, even a European tour supporting the Who. Although the Polydor deal wasn't great money-wise, they were very, very keen and Jerry worked his nuts off. The Yachts album was all over radio – even 'album of the week' in the prestigious *Record World* and *Cashbox*. Here, though, the Yachts were becalmed between quirky, new wave pop and what the press were calling the 'New Merseybeat'. That didn't stop me playing the Liverpool card, which I thought America could work with. Judith arranged an album launch in June on the *Royal Iris* ferry cruising down the River Mersey but, almost inevitably, the Yachts were upstaged by a special guest appearance by Elvis Costello and the Attractions. We'd commissioned a series of stunning cover designs by Malcolm Garrett. I like to think I did all I could, but the Yachts just didn't gel with the times. Henry Priestman did at least find success later in the 1980s with the Christians.

Jerry was also very keen on 999 to a point where Polydor ended up signing them worldwide in 1980. In the UK we released the one single, and I compiled *High Energy Plan* for American release which included tracks we licensed from United Artists. 999 went out to the States and just toured and toured, playing places nobody else ever went. For a lot of far-flung Americans, 999 was the first British punk band they ever saw playing live. Unfashionable and overlooked in this country, they built up a huge following there.

All our new 1979 releases suffered because our relationship with WEA was breaking down.* I picked up on The Inmates

---

* Bram Tchaikovsky was done totally for America. It wasn't up my street, but I was swayed because Richard Ogden managed them. There was a song called 'Girl of My Dreams' that Polydor were mad for but after a promising start at radio it went nowhere. Their album *Strange Man, Changed Man* made little impression here, although the distinctive cover by Rocking Russian often gets mentioned in dispatches.

after they released a cover of the Standells' classic 'Dirty Water' on Soho Records. I loved it so much I bought out their contract. The delay in the changeover to Radar probably cost them a hit. They were great live, especially singer Bill Hurley, and mixed their own songs with classic soul and psyche covers as diverse as Jimmy McCracklin's 'The Walk' and the Pretty Things' 'Midnight to Six Man'. I asked Vic Maile to produce their debut album *First Offence* and he did a brilliant job but, as a result, they were lazily and unfairly compared to Dr Feelgood in this country. Not so in the US where they toured heavily. It paid off with 'Dirty Water' making it to No. 51 in the US charts. *First Offence* came out in October, a few weeks before the news broke that Radar's pact with WEA was under serious review. 'The Walk' was then a surprise Top 40 hit in early December just as Martin and I were agreeing terms for our exit from WEA. The Inmates were very unlucky. There was definitely a platform there to build on, but the timing was against them.

I have very mixed feelings about Radar, and in our second year we were playing catch-up to make enough money to keep going. It smacked too much and too often of desperation – around twenty albums and nearly fifty singles in under two years.* We were definitely victims of the success of Elvis and, to a lesser extent, Nick. I still can't get a grasp on it even now. I'd worked closely with Martin Davis during the seventies, but our relationship did change at Radar. I felt Martin's enthusiasm and

---

* There were a lot of one-off singles I'm proud of releasing: by Wayne Kramer, Métal Urbain, a classic French rock record, Tanz der Youth, Brian James's short-lived group after leaving the Damned, a one-off by Richard Hell, and a four-track 12-inch EP drawn from Pere Ubu's early Hearthen singles, released as *Datapanik in the Year Zero*. The final single we released was by our neighbour Steve Strange's Visage. They recorded 'Tar' for Martin Rushent's Genetic Records. Jerry Jaffe signed Visage to Polydor and was rewarded with an immediate hit single in 'Fade to Grey' and two successful albums.

271

focus fell away as problems mounted with WEA. He probably felt the same about my level of commitment but after Y the uphill battle became unsurmountable. The most frustrating thing was not being able to get an album out by the Soft Boys; with Radar on such a roll that first year with Elvis it would have made a huge difference for the Soft Boys – but that wasn't to be.

Radar petered out and for the last few months we knew it couldn't carry on without becoming more a part of WEA. That's exactly what happened to the label in 1980 but it was without me and Martin being there. I declined to go the Warners route. Atlantic producer and founder of WEA International Nesuhi Ertegun asked me to be head of A&R at Warners, but Jake and I were already kicking around ideas for an independent label. The artist roster we left behind – the Yachts, Bram Tchaikovsky and the Inmates – was retained and the fantastic visual style of the label continued; that was one aspect of the label we did get consistently right. Radar was now being administered by the Elektra/Asylum label manager. All three acts made second albums on that basis in 1980, the Yachts calling theirs *Without Radar*, typical of their sense of humour.

We agreed the buyout just before Christmas; Martin had 30 per cent and I had 20 per cent of the 50 per cent of Radar that wasn't owned by WEA. They added a proviso that we couldn't sign any of the Radar acts to any new label either of us started up. That immediately became an issue because in early 1980, Elvis Costello and Nick Lowe moved to F-Beat, a new label I'd formed with Jake.

Chapter 20
From F-Beat to Island: What Does Chris Think?

F-Beat started up on 1 January 1980, exactly two years after Radar had begun operating. There was no plush office this time. We'd learned from that mistake and to begin with were cramped together in Jake's tiny Riviera Global office – a former travel agency – in Cheyne Walk in Chelsea. F-Beat was just Jake, me and Judith; Jake asked Andy Childs to join us as a label manager and he was there from day one. I'd known Andy for over ten years from when he produced his own fanzine *Fat Angel* and then went on to edit *Zigzag*. He worked in the press office at UA with Judith in 1976 before moving to EMI, where he became label manager for Harvest.

F-Beat was effectively the label for Riviera Global, so we had Elvis, Nick, Rockpile's only album, Carlene Carter, the Attractions, and Clive Langer, who still harboured the idea of being an artist. Jake was also managing engineer/producer Roger Becharian and soon began looking after Squeeze. Jake found a new home for us all in Horne Lane, Acton. It was above a ladies' hairdresser and next to an Indian restaurant that gave rise to an interesting blend of odours.

Andrew and Judith Riley in Hollywood

Judith and I even bought a house in Acton in 1983. We had
a cellar, so we housed Jake's wine collection which he'd started
buying. When he came over to pick up a few bottles we usually
shared at least one. People often asked how I got on with Jake
or more openly would say, 'How can you work with him?' We
never had a problem at all. There were stories about Jake
beating up journalists, most of whom he regarded as freeloaders. Famously he threw one *Record Mirror* journalist down the
stairs at the Hope & Anchor, and he could be very dismissive of
record company employees. He'd try and catch them out. If they
were after something from Elvis, he'd ask them to name three
songs off the first album or a non-album B-side, and if they
couldn't they'd be shown the door. He'd often have an argument
with someone I got on with, but it worked for us on a good-cop
bad-cop level, especially in meetings. I'd be Mr Reasonable and

Jake was Mr Impetuous. We'd spend weekends and even go on holiday together with Jake and his wife Tony. We weren't exactly desperate to get away from each other.

As at Radar, and everything I've done since, Judith was involved in every aspect of F-Beat, including some press. She'd kept in touch with most of the journalists that mattered and she did Carlene's press. Increasingly she became more involved in the management side with Jake. Press-wise with Elvis it was more or less someone to say 'no'. Judith dealt with Elvis a lot; if his calls began with 'I've been thinking . . .' she knew to sit down and get comfortable because she'd be there for the long haul. Elvis liked a sounding board. He was never difficult, although he could be demanding. It was never a case of him ringing up saying, 'Sort this out, get me this or that', although I remember one call from Elvis around two or three in the morning. He was jet-lagged and there was a giant frog in his hotel bathtub in Fiji. He spoke to Judith and she calmed him down.

F-Beat was always going to launch with Elvis Costello's new album *Get Happy* but first we had to settle an unresolved issue with WEA. Since Radar had been owned by WEA outside of the US, they considered Radar acts were technically still signed to them. It was a situation that was complicated by the fact that the contract between Radar and Riviera Global, specifically covering Elvis Costello's and Nick Lowe's recordings, had never been signed. It was a complication once things started to get a little shaky with WEA. After the buyout, Jake and I pressed on with forming a completely independent new label. As it was, no Elvis product could be released until the stand-off with WEA was sorted and it was urgent because *Get Happy* was to be simultaneously released worldwide in February.

We went to John Fruin asking for a pressing and distribution deal with WEA, which he didn't go for. He still had designs on being able to release Elvis's and Nick's records directly. So

Jake said let's go to Maurice Oberstein at CBS, who was totally up for the P&D arrangement. We knew as soon as we put the Elvis record out the shit was going to hit the fan at WEA, so we decided to be sneaky and release a single on Two Tone to test the water. Elvis was currently producing the Specials and liked the bravado of getting a single in the charts before WEA found out. Although copies of 'I Can't Stand Up for Falling Down' made it into some shops, WEA immediately served us with an injunction to cease and desist.

There was a court hearing to decide if it was an issue that could only be resolved by coming to trial. We didn't want that. Based upon the fact that *Armed Forces* had sold 300,000 in the UK, we'd already pressed up 150,000 copies of *Get Happy*. We didn't have the money for either the pressing or the sleeves. We didn't think WEA had a case, but they did have the means and intent to drag things out to make it financially draining for us. We were stymied till John Fruin agreed to the P&D deal he'd originally rejected. It was a compromise but still the best way to get F-Beat started. I was also breaking my personal legal agreement with WEA, and I didn't want that hanging over me. Little had changed. Elvis and Nick were still within the WEA fold, but it was now F-Beat instead of Radar. *Get Happy* was released in mid-February and peaked at No. 2 in the UK and 11 in the US. 'I Can't Stand Up for Falling Down' was then officially released and reached No. 4 in the UK charts, the highest singles chart position F-Beat achieved.

Get Happy wasn't as successful as *Armed Forces*. In the States its complete change of style – crammed with twenty Stax and Motown styled songs – baffled radio stations. Here, the legal wrangling almost certainly stifled the record's initial launch. The fact that we'd over-pressed *Get Happy* would have long-term repercussions. We only sold half as many copies. Ultimately F-Beat became as synonymous with Elvis's name as had been

the case at Radar. None of the other Riviera Global artists
signed to F-Beat took off. Nick didn't even release an album in
F-Beat's first year other than with Rockpile. They were fantastic
live, but I was disappointed with what was to be the only
Rockpile album. *Seconds of Pleasure* sounded like Dave had kept
the pick of his songs for his next solo album and Nick had done
the same. It wasn't the killer album we needed from them. There
were also contractual complications with Led Zeppelin's Swan
Song. You didn't want to mess with Peter Grant. Jake tried and
wasn't about to lie down easily, but he'd met his match. It caused
tensions between Jake and Dave and, as a result, between Dave
and Nick, and Rockpile broke up in February 1981 once they'd
honoured their touring commitments.

Over the summer we released *Splash* by Clive Langer & the
Boxes, and the Attractions did their own album *Mad About the
Wrong Boy*, both paid for by Riviera Global. Sales weren't great,
but Jake wanted to give them the opportunity to record albums.
Clive was by now a major producer – in tandem with Alan Winstanley. Over the next few years he produced further Madness
albums, Dexy's Midnight Runners, the Teardrop Explodes and
two albums with Elvis Costello – *Punch the Clock* and *Goodbye
Cruel World*.

Carlene Carter had already recorded two albums with Warners before Jake arranged for F-Beat to release her next two
albums in the UK. Unsurprisingly, Nick produced them. Carlene
had consciously shut herself off from the country community
she was brought up in. We spent quite a lot of time socially
with Carlene and Nick during the early eighties. They'd moved
to Chiswick from their four-storey terraced house in Shepherds
Bush where Nick still maintained his Am-Pro Recording studio
in the basement. We'd go to their house and we'd sometimes
look after Carlene's teenage daughter Tiffany. Both Carlene's
F-Beat albums – *Musical Shapes* and *Blue Nun* – featured

mostly her own songs with accompaniment by Nick and the usual suspects, including the rest of Rockpile. Both handsomely packaged thanks to Barney Bubbles' distinctive designs, they were well enough received critically but failed to connect with a new audience. The more straight-ahead country fans shunned the F-Beat records too; she was caught in the middle until she adopted a more targeted country sound again in the nineties.

The F-Beat albums only kept me intermittently busy and Andy Childs, as label manager, felt the same. That's why, first Demon, then Edsel came into being, very much as a hobby for both of us. We wanted our new venture to be properly independent. We paid for manufacturing ourselves and sheared up the distribution side with Rough Trade, Making Waves and later Pinnacle. Demon and Edsel were completely separate from F-Beat. Demon was originally a singles label in league with Clive Banks and Gary Crowley, who worked for Clive at the time. Clive had moved into the upstairs floor of the old Radar office for a while, so we got to know him well. He was really successful doing radio promotion and was married to Moira Bellas; Clive also moved into management and publishing and was particularly associated with the Pretenders. The original American Demon label had a fantastic logo I wanted to adopt. It was short-lived; its only success had come over twenty years earlier with Jody Reynold's 'Endless Sleep'.

Our first release was by Nick Kent's band the Subterraneans. Gary Crowley was always coming up with ideas, so the second single was by Glen Matlock's band the Spectres, followed by a Yachts single after they'd left Radar. Then out of the blue we found ourselves with a chart record with 'Is Vic There' by Department S – so we did a deal with RCA for that. The final single we planned was by Bananarama, but before it came out Clive did a deal with Phonogram; they bought all the copies of the single for promotion. It was kind of fun but I felt Demon

was increasingly becoming an outside A&R department for other
record companies.

Our first Edsel album was *The Ultimate Action*. The name
for the label was Jake's idea. The Edsel was a car that was a
commercial failure; nobody bought them, and they later became
very collectable. It was the perfect name for the sort of label
Andy and I envisaged and perfectly described the Action's career.
Gary had been turned on to them by Paul Weller. They were a
North London band steeped in the mod subculture and when
they came up in conversation I said I had all their singles, which
were produced by George Martin and released on Parlophone.
All the tracks had reverted to Air Productions, and they said
what about the tracks they'd recorded for an unreleased album.
I cherry-picked my favourites. Paul Weller wrote some sleeve
notes and *The Ultimate Action* sold 2000 copies pretty quickly,
and kept on selling over time. I also did a Pirates 10-inch
recording with Mick Green because the group were supposed
to be calling it a day. They went into Nick's Am-Pro studio and
recorded enough for a 10-inch LP – *A Fistful of Dubloons* –
before they finally broke up for good – which they didn't, but
that's another story. Those two releases were Edsel dipping a toe
in the water before Andy and I had to put the label on hold.

In January 1981 Elvis released *Trust* – Nick Lowe's last
production with him for five years. It was another Top 10 album
– in fact, all his albums for F-Beat, carrying through till 1986,
would make the Top 10. Otherwise, a combination of poor sales
and an accounting miscalculation meant that, fifteen months
after we'd started up F-Beat, we had serious financial problems.
Jake's solution in the short term was simple. He came to me and
said, 'You're the one with the rep so you could probably get a
top job very quickly. It would help to get you and Judith off the
payroll while we concentrate on sorting out the finances.' In the
next breath he said he'd been talking to Don Ellis, who was MD

for RCA in the UK. He'd told Jake that the Head of A&R job at RCA was mine if I wanted it.

While I was mulling this over, Martin Davis got back in touch. I'd not spoken to him since the last days of Radar. He'd been involved in something outside of music called Property Shops, so I was surprised when he said, 'I'm now the managing director of Island Records in the UK', and he wondered if I'd consider becoming Head of A&R. I had plenty of misgivings about both offers and kept wavering between RCA and Island while knowing full well that Jake was right: the only way we could get F-Beat back on its feet was to buy some time and that meant me taking one of the two jobs on offer.

After several conversations with Martin, I was inveigled into meeting Chris Blackwell at Compass Point in Nassau to discuss everything in person, lay out my concerns and clarify how best it might work for me. I flew over with Martin and of course it was a glorious place and almost immediately I felt the ball was very much in Chris's court. His first words to me were: 'It's fantastic that you've agreed to join us at Island.' As far as he was concerned, it was a done deal. So here we were in paradise – Joe Cocker and the Tom Tom Club were recording there at the time – and I'm looking at Martin trying to convey a look of 'hang on a minute' and feeling awkward saying, 'I'm only here to have a chat about it.' Martin cut in and told Chris I had a few concerns, which brought about the inevitable, 'Let's discuss it over lunch.'

I was always going to feel pressured because Chris was a renowned A&R man in his own right who had shaped Island Records, which was commonly regarded as the most successful independent label in the UK. The way I operated and the degree of autonomy I'd always had, and the sort of bands I signed, didn't fit the Island tradition. It's hard to imagine the Groundhogs, Man or Hawkwind functioning within Island. When

I finally outlined my fears over lunch he absolutely agreed and was very magnanimous, saying, 'You can have a blank canvas, paint on it whatever you want.' What could I say after that? He couldn't have made it any clearer, so I thought, 'I'll give it a go.' Afterwards, Martin said I shouldn't worry because Chris was never in the country. He said, 'You'll never see him. He's got a place in New York, he's always in Los Angeles and he's got the complex here at Compass Point with the two studios.' Despite feeling a little sceptical, I headed home having accepted the job as head of A&R and a director at Island.

Judith came too, as my assistant, and we started there in April 1981. We had our company car, drove to the office for the first time and, from day one, Chris Blackwell was in situ. Everybody was as pleased as they were surprised that he was around, echoing Martin's words that he hadn't been there in months. I didn't think it was a coincidence and I knew that everybody at Island was 100 per cent loyal to Chris. I wasn't sure how they'd feel about me coming in from the outside. There were always going to be certain things that would fall into the category of 'this is Chris's baby' and I was never going to stick my oar in there. It wouldn't be needed and it wouldn't be welcome. It was up to me to find a way to carve out my own territory or it wasn't going to work.

If you ever wondered 'What's the worst thing that could happen at Island Records?' then it was Bob Marley passing away. So on 11 May 1981, a dark cloud descended over Island's home at St Peter's Square, Hammersmith, and it didn't seem to lift for the next six months. I found it difficult not to feel I was intruding on the collective grief throughout the company. Island was already rebuilding, having lost all its seventies career acts such as Free, Spooky Tooth, Jethro Tull, Cat Stevens and Joe Boyd's folk stable of John Martyn, Fairport Convention and Richard and Linda Thompson. There were artists that were

281

Chris's priorities, such as Robert Palmer and Grace Jones, both of whose greater success was yet to come. With these projects I could only wait to be asked if there was any way I could help.

I certainly never got my blank canvas or felt I was in a position to say this is who I am and this is what I do. Chris was hard to get hold of other than through his assistant Denise Mills, who was great to deal with but very protective of Chris. In my first week there she told me that Chris had received a call from Bernie Rhodes who managed the Clash. He was keen for Island to sign Vic Goddard from Subway Sect. She said Chris wanted me to go along to the Lyceum and report back. I went along and came away thinking Vic Goddard was truly dreadful. He was trying to be a crooner but simply couldn't sing. Denise asked what I thought, and I said I didn't think it was worth considering any further. A few days later she informed me that Chris was very disappointed. I did suggest – very politely – that Chris could obviously pursue it himself if he felt that strongly.

This was exactly what worried me before I stepped off the plane in the Bahamas. To make matters worse, there was a girl in A&R who'd been my secretary at United Artists. I didn't know Annie Roseberry was now at Island and had been my predecessor Nick Stewart's assistant. I remember her thanking me when she left United Artists saying, 'You've taught me everything I need to know', but we now both felt uncomfortable. She felt she'd been passed over when I was hired. It was awkward and Annie was very into the New Romantic scene, which I always thought was totally manufactured and unconvincing. I knew that Chris had been keen to sign Spandau Ballet the year before. Out of that scene came Blue Rondo à la Turk, so-called purveyors of cool jazz pop. I hated that jazz had become a fashionable music accessory and expressed my lack of interest. Within a very short space of time I was being perceived as too negative within the company, while whatever ideas or suggestions I had were

282

greeted with a chorus of 'What does Chris think?' After a while
I became increasingly tetchy about this, countering with 'I don't
know, why don't you ask him?' The Island mantra was that if it
wasn't Chris's thing, it wasn't going to happen.

I did help bring Pete Shelley to Island early on in a deal with
Martin Rushent through his label, Genetic Records. Pete and
Martin came to see me just after Buzzcocks had split up. They
played me a very rough electronic treatment of a song called
'Homosapien' that Pete had written even before Buzzcocks had
formed. They wanted to know if I'd be interested in an album
along those lines; I spoke to Martin Davis and he was up for it.
We both thought it would be quite a coup for Island Records,
although if anybody was expecting Buzzcocks they were in for a
shock. Gone were the catchy melodies and buzzsaw guitar sound,
replaced by an early experiment in electronica with an emphasis
on dance beats and drum loops.

I was never going to jump straight into signing acts, A&R
doesn't work like that, and in the meantime Chris started giving
me problems to solve. That's how I came to work with Marianne
Faithfull. Chris was getting exasperated because they hadn't
been able to get her new record finished. Marianne was making
her follow-up to *Broken English* which had successfully dragged
her recording career back with highly personal, raging songs
from a feminine point of view. She'd found a way to reintroduce
herself to a generation that had heard all the scurrilous stories
and only knew a handful of hits she'd had in the mid-sixties
in that very clipped-voiced, baroque folk style. Marianne was
trying hard not to make it *Broken English 2* but Chris wanted
the same wrath and frankness, which the new songs lacked. His
instruction to me was, 'Go in and get this damn thing finished
because the producer is having a breakdown and Marianne is
in tears half the time.'

They were recording in Matrix Studios on Little Russell

Street, which Marianne described as a dungeon. She was using
the same producer who'd made *Broken English*. This time
around they were totally at odds with one another. I'd never
come across Mark Miller Mundy before. He had a curious way
of buoying up Marianne by being crabby and impatient and
insulting towards her. I'd never encountered such a discouraging
atmosphere in a studio before. Marianne was always on edge
and the musicians – all top, seasoned players – were so frustrated they didn't want to be there. I'd turn up every day and
they'd be moping around. It was miserable and the producer's
barbed comments certainly didn't help. He was angry about
something and with somebody all the time and it was usually
with Marianne. Steve Winwood had been at the sessions earlier
where Mundy asked him to 'Imagine playing like you are in a
field', to which he'd asked, 'What kind of field is it, and what
time of day?'

In the midst of all this I was trying to console Marianne.
That's all I could do. I wasn't going to suggest anything musically. There were already too many people arguing over that.
My main contribution was to calm the situation down. Far
from raging or being difficult, Marianne was despondent and
fatalistic. I'd take her to one side every so often and say, 'Why
don't we take a break.' We'd sit on the stairs outside. She was
in a bad state through a range of uppers and downers. I'd just
let her talk about everything and anyone from troubles with her
current husband, Ben Brierly (who'd played bass in the Vibra-
tors), to past encounters with Princess Margaret and jibes about
Mick Jagger. It was very random and often very funny. I'd listen
for a while and say, 'Let's go back in and try again' or 'Let's call
it a day and return to that song tomorrow.' I'd get home at five
in the morning and Judith must have thought we were having
an affair. How wrong could she have been! Somehow we got the
album finished and that was it for me. Chris came in and took

over. I wasn't involved in the mix and he chose the single. Not long after I was walking down the corridor and somebody said, 'Are you coming to the playback party?' I said, 'What playback party?' *Dangerous Acquaintances* was released in October. I never spoke with Marianne again after we finished in the studio.

I was pleased to work with U2. I'd heard *Boy*, which was a good first album. Before taking the Island job, if anybody had asked if there was one act there I'd like to work with, I'd have said U2. *Boy* hadn't sold well. There'd been no chart position, but expectation was growing and the band had toured extensively, including in the US. I'd met Paul McGuiness, their manager, at various gigs. He was very clued in and had a definite plan for U2. I'd also met producer Steve Lillywhite before and Judith and I knew Steve's wife Kirsty MacColl. For me it was never a case of whether U2 was going to be successful – it was how successful are they going to be? Given the management, and the collective drive, I thought there was no stopping them.

We flew over to Dublin, where they were recording in Windmill Lane Studios, and I immediately heard that Bono's lyrics for all the songs had been lost or stolen on the recent US tour. It was a major setback on the eve of going in to record. The band was almost starting from scratch and Bono was completing the lyrics in the studio. He had a bible on a lectern in the middle of the room and would dip in to find words or phrases to build a song around. That wasn't something I'd witnessed in a studio before.

Working with U2 was a whole new experience because I'd never met them before or knew how they functioned in the studio. Some groups are really relaxed; others get fired up by the tension. So I had no reference point. U2 were very agreeable and always very diligent. There was no joking around. They were definitely a group on a mission. They weren't a bunch of blokes

like Man or the Feelgoods. Three of the band were Christians
– not that I minded that in any way, but it was different. We'd
go to the pub and dine out occasionally but none of them except
Adam was a drinker. It brought home how much time I'd always
spent with groups getting stoned or down the pub, but Adam
was the only one who came along. He was a great fan of Jean-
Jacques' playing with the Stranglers so we had that in common.
The others were harder to get to know. They were so on it that
there wasn't much I could contribute.

They'd already decided to call the album *October* and it would
be released that month, which meant a yearlong gap between
the first and second albums. I suggested they put out an early
first single in July, then another just before the release date. I
made the advance single a limited edition gatefold with a second
7-inch using two extra live tracks from a gig in Boston. 'Fire'
was the obvious A-side, already recorded at Compass Point. I
told Chris what I was planning and got the distinct impression
he was a bit ho-hum about a band he'd been unsure about
signing. He was tired of being told how big U2 was going to
be. I said the limited edition should get them into the Top 40
and that would help set up the album. He may not have given
his blessing, but he didn't say don't do it. So I went ahead and
it went in at No. 35. *Boy* even re-charted, reaching its highest
position of 52 in its wake.

Paul McGuiness and the band were pleased to get their
first Top 40 single, but Chris just asked, 'What's it going to do
next week?' As usual he was unenthusiastic about anything I
proposed. Whereas I was convinced U2 would be huge, I never
got the same vibe back from Chris. I don't doubt he changed his
mind once *October* charted at No. 11.

*

Chris rang up one day and said he thought Island should have
a presence in African music. It was something I had very little

knowledge about. Charlie Gillett was going down that route and Roger Armstrong at Ace had started a label called Globe Style covering world music. Roger said I should talk to Ben Mandelson, who was in a Brighton-based punk band on Chiswick called the Amazorblades. Ben was a known authority on African music and came on board as a consultant. We came up with some good ideas. Island's art director Tony Wright designed some clever artwork based around a map of Africa to use for 12-inch singles where you could just fill in whatever country the act came from. We put together a sampler album of various tracks from different parts of Africa – Cameroon, Congo, Ivory Coast, Zaire – having done a deal with a label called Decca West Africa. We were able to draw from their entire catalogue with no payment up front on the proviso that anything we released, we'd agree a percentage. *Sound D'afrique* was the first African compilation that Island released and with an early performance by Youssou N'Dour. I figured I'd delivered on my part of the bargain. Using Ben's expertise, between us we put a lot of work into it. It was also the first compilation of African dance music to be issued in North America by a major label.

Everything we'd done was boxed up in my office until we came in one Monday morning and all the African stuff had gone. I spoke to the security guy, who didn't know what had happened. The next day we discovered that Chris was behind the disappearance. He was going out with French actress Nathalie Delon and had been spending weekends in Paris with her. African music was always popular in France, and Chris returned from a weekend in Paris having decided the African music division would best be run from the French office. I thought it was contemptuous that he'd just handed over all our work without a word. That's when I knew the writing was on the wall. Chris wasn't showing me any respect, whereas in good faith I'd delivered on all the projects he asked me to look after.

I was so fed up during the summer that I signed a couple of things that were totally non-Island Records in their objectives. The Meteors were the first UK band to combine raw 1950s rockabilly with the energy of punk, thus creating a new sub-genre called psychobilly. The Cramps were doing something similar in the States. The Meteors were building an impressive live following after Chiswick had released their debut EP; they even made the front cover of *Melody Maker* as prime movers in this new genre. I thought it was well worth doing an album because it was a happening thing. That was my motivation, not simply to piss off people at Island. We recorded it at Nick Lowe's Am-Pro studio. The Meteors' raw sound and graveyard lyrics didn't suit the Island brand, so the group came up with a label called Lost Soul Records, although to all intents and purposes it was an Island release. *In Heaven* was housed in replicated trashy pulp novel artwork; not a palm tree in sight. It sold well enough and was released on Island in some European territories. They didn't last long on the label but continued to pump out EPs, singles and albums on a variety of mostly independent labels. Had I remained at Island, I would have argued that there was really something to work on and develop with the Meteors.

My other signing was a more deliberate exercise in finding the ultimate antithesis of an Island Records release. The Lightning Raiders had released a single on Arista called 'Psychedelic Music' using Paul Cook and Steve Jones from the Sex Pistols. They were basically a hardcore, punk metal band with a line-up of pub rockers including Duncan Sanderson from the Pink Fairies, Johnny Guitar Hodge, who later regularly played with Bert Jansch and others from the Tyla Gang, and the Johnny Thunders Band. 'Criminal World' was the only single through Island, which we released on Revenge Records. Revenge was my way of making a statement about my time at Island Records. I knew it was running out by then.

In the end Chris and I had an argument over something derogatory he said about Jake. I said, 'Jake's a very good friend of mine and I really don't want to have this conversation.' I put the phone down on him. That was the last time we spoke. It was so unlike me. I'd never put the phone down any anybody before. I'd had it with Chris and Island Records. It wasn't any one thing, just an escalating mound of grievances on my part.

The next day Martin said he'd been talking to Chris, who thought 'it would be a good idea if Andrew has his own label within Island'. I was nonplussed by this. I couldn't see it working and wasn't about to make the same mistake twice. Twenty-four hours later, Martin said Chris now thought the best thing would be if we didn't work together any more. For once we agreed on something.

I left during October, the same month that the U2 and Marianne Faithfull albums were released. Pete Shelly's 'Homosapiens' single had just come out and was immediately banned by the BBC because of its explicit sexual content. Pete's album was finally released in January, by which time the Lightning Raiders and the Meteors had long since been dropped.

Chapter 21

The Demon Years – Don't Use a Racehorse to Deliver Milk

I phoned Jake the day after leaving Island and he said his long-term assistant Cynthia was ill and likely to be off for a couple of months and would Judith come in and cover for her. F-Beat and Riviera Global were in much better shape. Jake had brought in Lew Difford – Chris from Squeeze's brother – who was a recommended accountant and did a great job getting the company back on track. Jake had done a licensing deal with RCA for F-Beat, which was now exclusively representing Elvis and Nick. Elvis was about to release his album of country covers *Almost Blue*, which he'd recorded in Nashville with veteran producer Billy Sherrill. Far from being perceived as a marginal interest side-project, fans took to it straight away; the album reached No. 7 and the extracted single, 'A Good Year for the Roses', was his first Top 10 hit since 'I Can't Stand Up for Falling Down'.

Jake asked when I wanted to come back and I said I needed a break. Nothing had gone particularly smoothly since leaving United Artists and I needed to get my head straight. It was already October, so it made sense to leave returning until the New Year. Judith and I had recently moved into an apartment in Maida Vale, and I'd finally retrieved all my records from the Barbican flat where Maureen was living. It gave me time to unpack

everything and generally unwind. I already knew what I wanted
to do, which was to put out loads of great reissues on Edsel and
pick up on current recordings for Demon. There were plenty of
great records falling between the cracks, mostly by artists the
major labels had no interest in any more. I was looking forward to
working with Andy Childs again too. We still wanted Demon and
Edsel to remain completely independent, and to keep the stock at
the house in Horne Lane so we could do mail order ourselves and
ship to specialist shops and independent distributors. I wanted to
build up a catalogue I could put my stamp on, and already had
the first Demon and Edsel releases in mind.

The first Demon LP was a Dr John album of piano music
called *Dr John Plays Mac Rebenack*. It was Demon FIEND 1,
licensed from a little audiophile label in America called Clean
Cuts. We released a second Dr John album from them a year
later. Blues was always going to figure in my plans. I'd always
liked Clarence Gatemouth Brown and Johnny Copeland, and we
licensed two albums apiece by them from Rounder. These were
American labels that reflected the classic feel of blues, soul, R&B
and rock 'n' roll that would be part of my brief for Demon. In our
first ten Demon releases I put out a new album by Del Shannon
produced by Tom Petty, as well as the new Loudon Wainwright
album *Fame and Wealth*. I thought it was ridiculous that people
like Loudon and Dr John didn't have major deals any more, but
they were perfect for Demon.

We'd picked up a Lamont Dozier album called *Bigger Than
Life* through his Megaphone label, which led to us doing a separate deal with Holland Dozier Holland's HDH label for *The Hits
of Invictus & Hot Wax* and releases by Freda Payne, Chairman
of the Board, and Laura Lee, which hadn't been available for
years. I also got in touch with Al Bennett, who now owned the
HI catalogue, which gave us access to classic releases by Al
Green, Otis Clay, O.V. Wright and Ann Peebles. Very quickly

Demon was up and running with a well-rounded catalogue while Edsel was also fast out of the traps.

The first Edsel release on my return was a Screaming Jay Hawkins album which came through CBS. They insisted on manufacturing everything we did with them, which suited us fine; the points weren't great but the advances were only a modest £1000 per album. Most of the deals we did were around that figure. In the early eighties the market for licensing records wasn't flooded as it is today; we did a lot with CBS early on, which made it easier to go to EMI than Polygram, Decca and the rest. Significantly, we only had UK rights, but we could then sell to exporters.

The Screaming Jay Hawkins album surpassed all expectations. We asked Northern Soul DJ and club promoter Roger Eagle to do liner notes, colourised a black-and-white photograph for the cover, and I chose my favourite, awesome Screaming Jay Hawkins tracks he recorded for Okeh in the mid-fifties and we called it *Frenzy!* It started well enough, but Andy kept coming back saying we're running out of stock again. We'd expected sales of around 5000 but *Frenzy!* went on to sell over 50,000. There was a Jim Jarmusch film called *Stranger than Paradise* that was big in France which prominently featured 'I Put a Spell on You'. *Frenzy!* was the only record anywhere at the time that included Hawkins' most famous recording. *Frenzy!* was an exception but even some of our more obscure albums were selling between 6000 and 10,000. And these were all full price. We were never a budget label.

With Edsel we were releasing deleted albums or compilations by artists that had usually been badly treated on budget labels. The selections for Edsel entirely reflected my personal taste; the deciding factor was 'Are they records I would buy?' Andy and I instinctively knew when there was sufficient interest to make each release worthwhile and cost-effective. I'd compile records at home in the evenings or at weekends and we had an in-house artist. We knew that what people wanted was quality sleeves, comprehensive liner notes and the best mastering possible from the best audio sources available. It was a niche that worked for us, and we didn't feel we were in competition with either Ace or Charly, the other main UK labels specialising in catalogue in the UK. There was some overlap, but they were mostly ploughing a different furrow.

The early Edsel albums almost selected themselves. Having released the Action it made sense to do the Creation, the leaders in the Pop Art movement outside of the Who. The first dozen or so compilations mined the beat and Merseybeat era that I grew up loving so much. We released collections by the Merseybeats, the Big Three, the Mojos, and the Paramounts. The Artwoods meant a lot to me and I met them in a pub in West Hammersmith several times to discuss what I wanted to do. It was a good excuse for a reunion. Art did the sleeve and I had the chance to remind him about the significant part his group had played in my life. Some of those early releases sold in excess of 10,000. We could soon see the pattern in sales; some of the blues albums only sold a couple of thousand, but that still made sense for us. Almost everything we released kept ticking over.

Others surpassed our estimates. The Yardbirds' second album, the first with Jeff Beck and usually known as *Roger the Engineer* sold 25,000 copies; I did separate mono and stereo editions for fans and collectors and it paid off. Many of the Edsel releases were personal favourites, such as *The Larry Williams Show* that I'd seen at the Flamingo, and Del Shannon who I first saw play at the Sunderland Empire* in early November 1963. He later

---

*   It was a package tour headlined by Gerry and the Pacemakers. I loved so many of Del Shannon's classic singles, which he mostly wrote, produced, came up with ingenious arrangements and then sang in an assertive falsetto. He was backed by the Eagles from Bristol, one of the great but lesser-known pre-Beatles British instrumental groups featuring the classic two Fender Strats, bass and guitar.

recorded for Liberty in the mid-sixties and United Artists, where Brinsley Schwarz backed him at Rockfield on a few songs. We did a rare Edsel Deluxe release for his *Runaway Hits*. There'd been too many cheap and cheerful compilations and he deserved better.

Andy and I were like kids in a sweet shop. I never stopped releasing my favourite blues and soul records, including albums by Albert King, Major Lance, Clyde McPhatter and the Drifters, Rufus Thomas, and Sam & Dave. There was a degree of competition with Charly. We both had access to the Atlantic catalogue, so we spent an evening in the pub with Charly's Joop Visser carving up what we each most wanted. I think I got the best of the deal, our first batch including Clarence Carter, the Clovers, Don Covay, Dr John and the Coasters.

There was no way I wasn't going to focus on classic 1960s San Francisco bands. Some we were releasing in the UK for the first time, others drew from unreleased archive recordings such as Big Brother & the Holding Company's *Cheaper Thrills* through the band's drummer Dave Getz; we also put out albums by Kaleidoscope, Moby Grape (restoring its original artwork), Dan Hicks and his Hot Licks, the Beau Brummels, Mad River and Quicksilver Messenger Service's debut, which was our 200th release.

We weren't ignoring our recent past either, so Demon was the home for classic records by Ian Dury, Dr Feelgood and Suicide, while Brinsley Schwarz's *Silver Pistol* and Rockpile's *Seconds of Pleasure* were on Edsel because the bands were defunct even though as individuals they were still very much alive. A major fillip for Demon was being able to release the entire Elvis Costello catalogue before he signed to Warner Bros. Significantly, beginning with *My Aim is True* in July 1982, Elvis's back catalogue was systematically released by Demon through to *Imperial Bedroom* in 1986. It was a big help in America to be able to say that we had his back catalogue and that he part-owned the company. When we were struggling financially to pay royalties at F-Beat early on, Jake made an arrangement to pay them over a period of time. So we made Elvis a partner in Demon. Imp Records was a separate subsidiary label we gave to him.

Some of his choices were so outré they didn't sell well; ex-Radiator from Space Philip Chevron's unique, Elvis-produced interpretation of Brendan Behan's *The Captains and The Kings* was very niche. As was an album by Agnes Bernelle called *Father's Lying Dead on the Ironing Board*. It was in a sort of Brecht style and one of the few albums we released that I really didn't care for. Needless to say, I was never going to say no to something Elvis wanted to do. We got a few things through his recommendation too: The Men They Couldn't Hang's debut album *Night of a Thousand Candles* was produced by Philip Chevron and a big seller for us. He also turned us on to the Hoodoo Gurus, a band he'd seen in Australia. So we licensed their first album *Stoneage Romeos* from Big Time in Australia. That was a great contemporary garage rock guitar album.

I knew we were making the right impression when Warners asked us to release T Bone Burnett's 1983 album *Proof Through the Night* in the UK. They thought it would do better on Demon than through WEA.* Demon grew substantially over the next few years into a significant business that was turning over £2.5 million by the mid-eighties. We closed F-Beat down in 1986 now that Demon was doing so well. Elvis's *Blood and Chocolate*, which was released only on Demon, saw him back with Nick producing for the first time since *Trust*. That was the album between his Columbia deal ending and him signing to Warners and was Demon's biggest seller, shifting over 130,000 copies.

---

* T Bone and Elvis began working together in 1984, they toured colleges in the US, recorded a single as the Coward Brothers, and T Bone produced *King of America*, where Elvis reverted to his given name Declan MacManus. It was the last album released by F-Beat.

Nick was finding the eighties hard because he was still signed to Columbia, who expected a new album every year. The hits had dried up and I don't think he really knew where his career was going. He accepted that his pop star days were over but where did he go from there? He aspired to a different level of appreciation more akin to American artists like John Hiatt, John Prine or T Bone Burnett. There was no tradition in Britain where a good reputation as a talented songwriter could sustain you as a recording artist.

Working with John Hiatt was a step in the right direction. Hiatt's agent Mike Kappus came to the house in Acton to play me six tracks he'd done for Hiatt's first Geffen album with producers Ron Nagle and Scott Matthews. Ron Nagle was somebody whose work I really liked, not least because he was in the Mystery Trend, one of the early San Francisco bands. Mike wanted to try something different for the rest of the album, to record over here and with Nick producing. *Riding with the King* was released in 1983. John stayed with us for two months while they were recording at nearby Eden Studios. Our spare room had a very large wooden frame bed with a huge headboard that actually belonged to Mother Maybelle Carter. Carlene didn't have any room for it.

John was the perfect house guest. I said, 'If you're ever stuck for a release, I'll always put your records out.' He did one more for Geffen and we released the next one, *Bring the Family* in 1987. It's one of my favourite records that we released on Demon. Nick was brought in to play bass alongside Ry Cooder and Jim Keltner. It was a big deal for Nick to be in such company. John Hiatt is a musician's musician. That usually means their records are steady rather than huge sellers and that suited our thinking at Demon. I've always loved great singer-songwriters and that's another vein of releases I've carried through every label I've been involved with. There'd always be a home for the likes of John Hiatt, T Bone Burnett, John Prine, and Loudon Wainwright and by the 1990s I think that's where

Nick Lowe finally found his niche. When Warners reunited John Hiatt, Ry Cooder, Jim Keltner and Nick Lowe to form Little Village in 1992 it was a sign that he was now a member of that club.

Nick's marriage to Carlene was struggling later in the eighties but not before Judith and I were able to spend some time with his in-laws Johnny Cash and June Carter. The first time we met them was when Judith had to go through some stuff with Carlene. We turned up at the house in Chiswick where they now lived, and June answered the door. She sent us round to the back door and we thought at first she was being dismissive. She wasn't at all and when she opened the back door we noticed she was wearing an apron and was in the middle of washing the kitchen floor.

Even meeting Johnny Cash socially, it was impossible not to be a little overwhelmed and tongue-tied. He was very good at putting you at your ease, but if you sat opposite him over dinner you couldn't but be thinking, 'That's Johnny Cash.' Nick said he never stopped finding it strange. He'd come down in the morning and there'd be Johnny in his towelling dressing gown, strumming the guitar. Johnny was very fond of Nick, who was always reluctant to play him things. He never wanted to seem pushy, but Johnny would ask, 'What have you got, play me some songs.' Nick and Carlene divorced in 1990 but they kept in touch and Johnny Cash covered 'The Beast In Me' from Nick's 1994 album *The Impossible Bird*; it was one of the highlights of Cash's game-changing *American Recordings* the same year.

F-Beat and Demon were based at the Horne Lane house for a few more months after I came back from Island until we moved to a residential square in Brentford called The Butts. It was an elegant eighteenth-century house where we turned the rooms into offices. Jake's parents moved in next door and Nick bought the place from them a few years later. You can become a victim of your own success and the volume of releases by the time we

moved to The Butts meant that I could no longer be as hands-on
as I liked. The stock was all stored in the basement, but I knew
it wouldn't be long before we'd need a building with warehouse
space. I always hated the idea that any of our records were any
less than perfect. Jake once found me carefully checking all
the records in a box that had been damaged, pulling out and
replacing any copies where the sleeves were bent. Jake made the
rather droll observation that 'you don't use a racehorse to deliver
milk', but I could never stop myself.

We had various offshoot labels, but Demon Verbals was my
pet project. It was a spoken word label which took me back to
World Pacific again for three Lord Buckley albums. We also
released two by Lenny Bruce. One was from a live recording in
1961 at Carnegie Hall that United Artists had released, while
the other, *The Sick Humor of Lenny Bruce*, took me back to Fantasy in 1959. Even these were all selling upwards of 3000. We'd
launched Demon Verbals in 1984 with Viv Stanshall's *Sir Henry
at Ndidi's Krall*, further adventures with the old curmudgeon
complete with cover art by Ralph Steadman.

I'd kept in touch with Viv on and off. He hadn't released an
album since *Teddy Boys Don't Knit* for Charisma in 1981; they'd
released the first *Sir Henry* album in 1978. It was Glen Colson
who approached me about Viv. He and Viv went back a long way
and Glen had been the press guy at Stiff Records. He suggested
we just offer Viv a high percentage royalty but no advance because Viv would squander any money up front on booze. Glen had
Viv's best interest at heart. He took care of the recording, which
went well till Viv fell off the wagon, but they had enough to edit
together for an album. It wasn't as good as the original and I'm
not sure we could have got away with some of the question-
able language today. Viv signed off on it even though a few years
later he claimed to have no memory of the recording. He said
Glen had stolen the tapes, sneaking on board his boat one night

behind his back. It was the final album released in his lifetime.

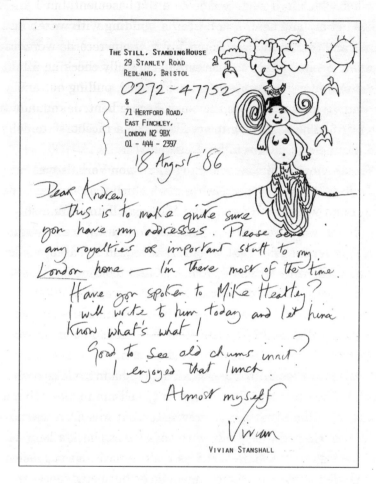

Andrew kept in touch with his old chum from Bonzo Dog
days at Liberty

A few years earlier we'd visited Viv in a flat he had in Fins-
bury Park. He invited me and Judith round for dinner and rang
every day during the week saying, 'You are coming, aren't you?'
We assured him we'd be there but on the day we were getting
no answer at his front door. We kept on knocking till he finally

appeared in a Victorian dressing gown that came down to the floor but which he'd neglected to do up. He was stark naked, looked aghast and said, 'You bastards, you came!' We never had dinner and eventually had to put Viv to bed before we left because he really needed to get some sleep. If Viv had an idea he would just stay up for days working on it. The only heating he had in the flat was one of those old two-bar electric heaters and Judith was terrified he was going to set fire to himself. And of course he died in an electrical fire in his Muswell Hill flat in 1995.

The Demon label was becoming more prominent from 1985 onwards because I was releasing more current stuff. The Robert Cray Band was key to that shift. Although Demon funded the odd album, we were never in the business of signing anybody on a long-term basis. That would have required a different level of commitment in terms of promotion and marketing. We did break a few acts and it's fair to say that we broke Robert Cray in the UK. I first discovered him when he released an album for Hightone called *Bad Influence*. We did a deal for that in 1983 thinking we'd break even. We did some dates with him starting out at Dingwalls and before long he was playing at Hammersmith Odeon. *Bad Influence* went on to sell around 60,000 and it was the album that really drew attention to his unassuming brilliance. He had a lot to do with the rise in popularity of blues again since the 1980s. Robert was a lovely guy and so modest. He married a girl from Leicester and they are still together. We only released one further album, *False Accusations*, which even topped the independent charts. The two Robert Cray Band albums are amongst the highlights for me at Demon.

There were other albums where we knew we were soon going to lose the acts, as we did with That Petrol Emotion when they soon signed to Polydor. We released the 1986 debut album by the group, which featured John and Damian O'Neill from the Undertones. That too topped the independent charts. They had a slew of

front covers in the music press and were touted as very much the
next big thing. I still think the Demon album, *Manic Pop Thrill*, is
their best. It was becoming a slight frustration watching so many
acts that started out with us sign to another label. That was certainly the case with the batch of albums we released on Zippo.
We released all the debut albums or significant early albums by
almost all the key groups in what became known as 'the paisley
underground scene' between 1984 and 1986.

Zippo was really Andy Child's baby. His initial interest was
sparked by Pete Flanagan. Pete had a record shop in Clapham
called Zippo Music that specialised in imports. He gave Andy a
bunch of new American imports by the Long Ryders, the Rain
Parade, Green on Red and True West. They were like a bolt from
the past but in no way retro, and a couple of days later Andy
came in and said, 'This is something that nobody knows about
yet over here.' I picked up on Andy's enthusiasm and totally got it
when he played the records to me; I just said, 'Go for it.' So Andy
and Pete set up a separate Demon offshoot based on approaching
all the various Los Angeles bands with a view to a UK release
on Zippo. The bands were all influenced by the kind of 1960s
psychedelia we were releasing on Edsel but all taking different
approaches to it, whether it was the Long Ryders debt to the
Byrds or Dream Syndicate's take on the Velvet Underground.

Andy contacted all the labels and the bands and went over
to Los Angeles with Pete to meet them and discuss the idea,
and we soon scheduled seven or eight albums over a fairly short
period of time. We started with the Rain Parade's *Emergency
Third Rail Power Trip*, the Long Ryders' *Native Sons*, Green on
Red's *Gas Food Lodging*, plus albums by True West and Thin
White Rope; four of them made the Top 10 albums in the Indie
Chart. We also released the Replacements' *Let It Be*; they were
more hardcore and ramshackle but with great songs. They went
to Sire soon after.

Most of the bands came over too and it was great while it lasted. The music press lapped them up, particularly the *Melody Maker*, and they all got snapped up pretty quickly. Those bands broke out of this country before making inroads back home and Zippo played a huge part in that by releasing all their breakthrough albums. We had the follow-up albums for most of the groups and extended the catalogue to include Giant Sand, the Dream Syndicate and Naked Prey.

It was in 1985 that Judith and I discovered our country retreat. We used to go down to see Jake in Cornwall at weekends. He'd bought a house by the Carnglaze Slate Caverns, which got us thinking it would be great to have somewhere of our own to escape to. I'd been in London for twenty years and it was becoming almost too social – even out in Acton. We'd be round at Nick's, or he was at ours. Pete Thomas liked a drink and was tremendous fun to be around; he and his wife Judy were great friends, but Pete would often turn up just as we were about to turn in. We were hardly going to draw the curtains pretending we weren't home.

There were too many late nights. We held a birthday party for Nick at ours, not knowing who Nick had invited. Judith's face was a picture when she answered the intercom buzzer and found Tom Petty and his wife waiting outside. We were our own worst enemies too. A band like the Fabulous Thunderbirds would be in town and we'd invite them over, get a crate of beer, wine and whatever and fire up the jukebox. It was great fun and I wouldn't change it for the world, but we needed a break.

We spent New Year's Eve 1984 with Jake and his then girlfriend. We'd rented a cottage in a country village in Somerset and drove around on New Year's Day looking for somewhere to eat. We drove through so many lovely villages and that's when we made up our minds to find a place in the country to buy – it

302

would be Judith's house, since I'd bought the one in Acton. A couple of weeks later we spent the weekend at a country house hotel in Dulverton on the edge of Dartmoor and visited a few estate agents, one of whom suggested a place in East Knowstone in Devon. It was a small cottage next to a farmhouse. It was pissing with rain and it didn't look at all inviting. A month later, still trying to find our dream house in Devon, we chanced upon a thirteenth-century thatched pub called the Mason's Arms* in Knowstone itself – the village only had the pub and a church as far as we could tell. So we went in; everyone was so friendly, especially the owners, Dave and his wife Tim. It turned out that Dave was doing the conveyancing on the cottage in East Knowstone that we'd never actually checked out. Needless to say, we went back there, completely changed our minds and ended up buying it. It needed work; we replaced the tin roof with the pantiles from an old barn and slowly but surely made further improvements over the years. We took ownership in March 1985.

There were a number of reasons why I left Demon, although even now it's hard to get a clean shot at why because it was such an incredibly enjoyable and successful time. But things were changing by 1987 and not for the better. Demon was becoming too impersonal and autocratic, and I felt we were losing sight of what made it work in the first place. By 1985 we'd outgrown The Butts and we moved to an old 1930s building on the Great West Road in Brentford on what's known as the Golden Mile. It used to be Brentford Nylons, which was one of the best-known brands of the 1970s. It never shrugged off the memory of electrostatically charged pink

---

* In his autobiography Ginger Baker tells how his dad's parents acquired a pub in Knowstone called the Mason's Arms, where he was evacuated to in 1944. He says the old man would get drunk and beat him and after a few months his mum took him home.

nylon sheets, and an advertising campaign voiced by disc jockey Alan Freeman. We'd expanded out of necessity and had brought in Andy Cheeseman, who was Jake's right-hand man and looked after all the Riviera Global bands. Pete Macklin was recommended by Ted Carroll at Chiswick, came in as sales manager, and we had a one-man art department. There was also a door through to the warehouse where we could now drive a forklift truck round.

Within two years we moved again; Jake had become very ambitious and spent a lot of money on Canal House on the Starz Industrial Estate in Brentford, creating a huge warehouse space – adding a mezzanine floor – and an open-plan office. It had big, rounded windows that looked out over the canal, and we put in huge gates at the front so you could drive an articulated lorry in and to the side there was a separate lock-up space for storing all the bands' equipment.

I accepted that we needed more people working in the warehouse. I used to like going in there and packing a couple of orders up, but there was so much stock now and systems in place that meant I could no longer do that. Just wandering round at the end of the day was my way of keeping in touch. Then one day it was locked. That's when I started falling out with Lew Difford, who was now a fellow director of the company. He said the warehouse had to be locked up for security reasons. I'd see somebody I didn't recognise and Lew would say, 'He's the new warehouse manager' – and of course he didn't know who I was.

Lew had taken to sending endless memos about things he wanted to change or tighten up. Too many people were receiving such unnecessarily officious memos. Paul Riley – one-time bass player with Chilli Willi – was an in-house engineer for the labels and he'd been working on some tapes at Nick's Am-Pro studios. Lew assumed he was turning up late and sent him a warning letter; Paul was quite rightly furious. So was I. What really galled me was that Lew hadn't consulted me before admonishing Paul.

304

Pretty soon everything Lew did started annoying me and I got it in my head that he was trying to assume control by excluding or overriding me. There were even sly comments regarding me and Judith spending too much time in Devon where, aside from anything else, I'd always worked on compilations from home. I felt I was being petty and that bothered me too. None of this would have happened if Jake had been around, but he was spending more time in America. I missed his presence and support and it left me alone with Lew, feeling increasingly aggravated and vulnerable.

Even now I wonder if I was being unreasonable. Was Lew just doing his job or overstepping the mark? Was he eroding my role in the company? It eventually reached a point where I said to Jake, 'Either Lew goes or I go', feeling let down that Jake couldn't understand what was going on from my side. The problem was that Lew had increasingly made himself indispensable to Jake, taking care of the Riviera Global side of things on a day-to-day basis. When I found out that some of our musicians were being charged for storing their equipment that really was a step too far.

We'd always managed to maintain the combination of working hard, having fun and being successful – and that had always been Jake's ethos. We needed Lew and he'd helped turn things around when F-Beat was struggling financially, but he and I were no longer compatible in our ideals and working methods. So I left. I was rightly proud of the catalogue we'd built up at Demon. Perhaps my work was done and it's likely I would have moved on from Demon and Edsel within a few years anyway, but this wasn't how I wanted to leave.

Chapter 22
Fool's Gold

My lawyer and friend Anthony Jayes knew that I was leaving
Demon. He'd been speaking to Clive Calder, one of the co-found-
ers of the Zomba Group of Companies, and my name came up in
conversation. Clive said: 'Ask Andrew not to do anything till he's
spoken to me.' Clive duly phoned me from America and said that
for all Zomba's pop success with Jive he wanted to create an
outlet for more credible projects. I don't think he had the Stone
Roses specifically in mind, although Roddy McKenna – one of
their A&R people – had already signed the band. Zomba also
had the thriving Zomba Music Publishing and they'd taken over
Morgan Studios, which had become Battery Studios, and they
had Dream Hire, a music equipment rental company. So it was
a buzzing group of companies although best known for acts such
as Sam Fox and Billy Ocean on Jive Records. Clive knew exactly
how Jive was perceived and its reputation was never going to
attract any legitimate artists. He knew it would benefit the
studio to have a more plausible label as part of their operation.

I had an initial meeting with Clive's partner Ralph Simon
and Clive's consultant John Fruin to go through a potential
deal. Clive's interest was based on what I'd done in the past and
Demon in particular, and John Fruin obviously knew me and
my history only too well. I said it would have to be a separate
label or it wasn't going to work. I also wanted to be completely

independent and have independent distribution, not through
BMG, which handled all Jive's releases. Clive Calder agreed,
after which the deal was finalised with John Fruin and Ralph
Simon. We signed the contract on 18 April 1988. I'd left Demon
at the end of 1987 but I continued my involvement till March,
completing various projects I'd initiated and retrieving stuff of
mine stored in the warehouse.

We did a modest deal, which was really good when it came
to being able to sign acts and promote them. John Fruin once
said he'd never known Clive be so compliant. I got everything I
wanted. It wasn't a particularly financially rewarding arrangement. Although I had conceived Silvertone, it was a wholly owned
subsidiary of Zomba Records Ltd. We agreed a decent salary for
Judith and a working basis for me. I was starting from scratch
and Zomba was so removed from any area I wanted to work in
that there was never any conflict. I was also able to bring in my
own press and radio promotion people and take the distribution
to Steve Mason at Pinnacle. Demon had become a major label for
Pinnacle and I wanted to maintain that relationship. Zomba had
an office in Holland and all the coordination throughout Europe
went through the Dutch company, which was run by a great guy
called Bert Meyer, and that turned out to be excellent.

Silvertone had been the name that Sears Roebuck used for all
their music-related stuff – including cheap guitars – in their mail
order catalogues from the 1930s to the '50s. I thought the name
had a timeless quality – a bit like Parlophone. It was in the paper
one week 'Lauder leaves Demon' and the next 'Lauder starts new
deal with Zomba'. The deal was exactly what I was after. There
wasn't an office we could move straight into and it was almost a
year before we took over a two-storey cottage by Battery Studios.
So to begin with we worked from home, then out of a portakabin
in what was essentially a building site behind Dream Hire. Next to
us was a Zomba-owned film music library run by producer/manager

Laurie Jay, who'd fronted the Laurie Jay Combo in the early
sixties and recorded a few singles for HMV. He had a really good
secretary who we poached as another assistant. Silvertone Records
was just the three of us: myself, Judith and Lucy Launder.

Having shaken hands with Ralph and John Fruin and done
photos for the trade papers, John said, 'Before you go, we'd like
you to listen to this tape of a band we've signed.' My heart sank.
Having been promised complete freedom, here they were offering
me a band and, given Zomba's track record, my expectations
were low. John said, 'They're called the Stone Roses.' I hadn't
even heard of them. John explained they were from Manchester,
and managed by the guys who ran the International club. John
said, 'Take this cassette away and have a listen; they've done
some demos and Peter Hook has just produced a single.' John
handed over a proof of the 12-inch sleeve which the group's
guitarist John Squire had designed for the single, which was
'Elephant Stone'. It was the first of his Jackson Pollock influenced sleeves and I thought it pretty impressive. I then noticed
a Rough Trade logo and catalogue number in the corner.

Roddy McKenna was a young Scottish guy who had been at
Polydor before joining Zomba. He'd been pursuing the Stone
Roses for a couple of months and wouldn't let go. He was the
person who signed them in early March 1988 with Steven
Howard, who ran Zomba's publishing. My only decision was
whether I wanted them on my new label. When I pointed out
the Rough Trade logo, John Fruin explained that Rough Trade
had been very keen, but they'd managed to prise them out of
Geoff Travis's clutches. He said Zomba were going to release
their records on Jive, but if I wanted the Stone Roses they would
assign the existing contract to Silvertone. He made it clear there
was no pressure on me if I didn't like what I heard.

I thought the tape was pretty good, very good at times. We sat
at home and Judith and I listened to the tape with Will Birch.

I'd known Will since his Kursaal Flyers days and we all liked
the sound of it but, given that the songs had so many familiar
sixties influences, we did wonder if it was only going to have
a retro appeal to old buggers like ourselves. I wasn't about to
jump straight in, but there were plenty of other plus points.
John Leckie was already involved – ironically at Geoff Travis's
recommendation – and he was working with them in a studio in
Stockport ahead of producing their debut album. I'd met John at
Rockfield and I knew his CV, which included XTC, Magazine, the
Fall and the LAs. He wouldn't have been involved if the Stone
Roses didn't have something going for them. The connections to
Peter Hook and Geoff Travis also helped tip the balance. Most
of all, though, the Stone Roses would give me something to start
work with immediately, but I wanted to see the group live and
meet them first.

The Stone Roses were doing their first show in six months in
Manchester at the International 2 on 30 May. It was a benefit
for the Anti Clause 28 Movement and they were supporting
James. I met manager Gareth Evans and his partner at the
Britannia Hotel. Matthew Cummins' background was in
property – we rarely saw him and only sporadically dealt with
him directly. I also met Michael Tedesco, who'd not seen the
band before either. He'd been appointed as Silvertone's man in
America – the main conduit between us and BMG.

Gareth drove us to the gig. It was a scary ride because he
kept looking back over his shoulder to speak to us, talking
non-stop and dangerously veering to the wrong side of the road.
While I wasn't a fan of his driving, I couldn't fault Gareth's
energy and enthusiasm for the band. When the Stone Roses
did their set it was obviously a very partisan crowd they were
playing to. It smacked a bit of a rent a crowd, but that didn't
bother me; it was another sign that Gareth was doing the best
for the band. The gig was very patchy because they were so

rusty and, as with the tape, when they were good, they were very good, but at times they were awful. They were impressive enough musicians and even though it was the vocals that mostly let them down, singer Ian Brown was a totally riveting frontman. You couldn't take your eyes off him. I made up my mind during the gig that I was going to take up Zomba's offer and bring them to Silvertone.

Meeting them afterwards only served to endorse that decision. We went round to drummer Reni's flat and sat around drinking and playing records – a lot of which we'd released on Demon and Edsel, such as Love, the Byrds and Sly and the Family Stone. It helped that I'd signed Buzzcocks at United Artists and we had plenty in common. They were fun to be around; John was quiet and more serious but still very friendly.

I didn't look at the contract Zomba had made with the group. I made the assumption it must be OK because 'Elephant Stone' had been slated to come out on Rough Trade. I thought, 'Well, if it was good enough for Geoff Travis . . .' then Zomba must have matched or bettered what Rough Trade put on the table. It was only much later that I discovered there'd never been a contract between the band and Rough Trade, even though they'd funded the recording of 'Elephant Stone' and had been set to release it.

Since taking on the Stone Roses management Gareth had made a lot happen that I doubt would have happened but for him. When I became involved, I never doubted that the band felt he was totally on their side. I got on well with him over most things. I did come away thinking Gareth was going to be very time-consuming and annoying at times, but I couldn't knock his determination. It was over a year before he set up an office and had any secretarial assistance, so he could be hard to get hold of at times. If he did rub some people up the wrong way it was often because of his naivety; he didn't always understand how things were done in the record business.

I found it strange that neither Gareth nor the band were bothered that their records would be released on Jive. It was a label with no credibility whatsoever. It may have been a measure of Gareth's overconfidence that it didn't matter to him if the Stone Roses were on Zomba rather than a cool label like Rough Trade. In fact, Gareth was unsure about Silvertone to begin with; he'd liked that Jive was mainstream and not an independent. It wasn't the attitude I expected.

We were ready to go with 'Elephant Stone' as the first single, although it was six months before it came out. John Leckie remixed it in Zomba's Battery Studios in Willesden, where he began recording the album on 28 July with a completion date of the end of February 1989. It was convenient that the band were recording at Battery and I'd drop by most days.*

Although Zomba never interfered, I was mindful about Roddy McKenna. It had been his persistence that got them signed and I appreciated that he wasn't about to hand everything over to me. I wasn't going to shut him out but, pretty quickly, Roddy was dispatched to Chicago to manage a studio Clive had bought, which made it easier for me.

We finally released 'Elephant Stone' on 3 October 1988; it reached No. 27 in the independent charts – mostly based on sales in Manchester. 'Elephant Stone' did what I'd expected, selling around 5500 copies. I never thought we'd be charting a single straight away. The Stone Roses had been around for three years and theirs was a stop–start career. They were little known outside of Manchester and didn't have any music press support

---

* Zomba gave us a reduced rate, which made sense till John Leckie pointed out that a lot of studio equipment – even standard stuff – had to be hired in from Dream Hire. When I looked into it, I realised that the bills from Dream Hire were greater than the reduction. So I could easily justify transferring the Stone Roses to Rockfield in the New Year because it worked out cheaper. They obviously took to it and spent the best part of a year there recording their second album.

to speak of. Peter Hook's name helped the gradual groundswell
of interest in the band. They also benefited from a timely association with illegal acid house parties and raves and the dance
culture which had been all over the press in the summer. I
was really happy John was doing the artwork, which perfectly
suited that new 'summer of love' vibe and soon came to identify
every release by the Stone Roses.

I wanted to build the right team to get behind the band, to
which end we brought in Philip Hall to handle the press and
Gareth Davies to do radio and television. I also suggested Nigel
Kerr from ABS to take over as their booking agent; I knew
Nigel from looking after the Feelgoods. He remained with the
Stone Roses long after they split from Silvertone. Come the New
Year, the Stone Roses debut album was finished on time, after
which they began touring more widely than ever before. Used
to playing isolated gigs in Manchester, they were on the road
nationwide for the next four months.

The second single 'Made of Stone' also did OK on release on
6 March, selling over 8000 copies. It still didn't make the Top 40
but reached No. 4 in the independent charts this time. Gareth
was disappointed. He always wanted everything to happen
'now', but there was no doubting that the Stone Roses were on
an upward curve even if the album didn't set the world alight
either. I was delighted with the album. It surprised me just how
well it turned out and a lot of that was down to John Leckie's
patience and expertise. The reviews were good across the board,
they got decent space in the music press and *The Stone Roses*
entered the LP charts at No. 32 at the beginning of May. It
plummeted after just one week but would re-chart five times
over the next twelve months. It never had a chart position that
reflected the eventual sales; 19 was the highest it reached but
fifteen months later it achieved platinum sales of 300,000 and
would eventually sell well over a million copies.

With Philip Hall now well on board, the band got their first music weekly cover in *Melody Maker* in early June, and a second in *Sounds* in July, so the press was building in line with an escalating live following. Gareth was still disappointed in the chart positions and in July he executed his master stroke, taking a gamble by headlining the Empress Ballroom in Blackpool to a capacity 3500 crowd. It was the first of Gareth Evans' hunches that succeeded in massively raising the band's profile. He knew the Stone Roses weren't just another Northern indie band. It was the beginning of the Stone Roses legend. There were plenty who thought they'd fall flat on their faces, but instead the Blackpool show worked to enhance the perception of the group's popularity. Blackpool was a real statement.

I knew something was already really building up. There was one gig at Middlesex Poly in early March that was a turning point for me; there were far more people than I expected and they got a fantastic reaction. The band were playing well, much more together and with Ian clearly coming into his own as a frontman. It was around that time that we decided we should have a look at the Stone Roses contract. They'd been signed to Zomba for a year, so I asked Mark Furman in Business Affairs for a copy to have on file. I didn't want to miss any deadlines where any options needed to be picked up – a band can easily wriggle out of a contract if that happens.

I was on the phone when the envelope was dropped off and I saw Judith open it up and start reading through the contract and I could see her expression darkening in front of me. With half an ear on my phone call I could hear her uttering a stream of expletives in utter disbelief at what she was reading. When I put down the phone she said, 'Have you seen this?' knowing full well I hadn't. She was almost beside herself. I could soon see why; certain clauses were jumping off the page in front of me. The first 15,000 copies in each format sold in every territory were royalty free. In a lot of territories, you wouldn't expect to reach that many copies at all. The more I read the worse the contract looked.

It was for eight albums and the percentages were low with no appropriate incremental adjustment. Zomba was taking a high percentage of the merchandising too. Although John was already doing the artwork, there was nothing in the contract to say the band had artistic control. This was a given for me and the band did already have de facto artistic control as far as I was concerned. In all my dealings going back to United Artists days I took the view that the artist would always have the right of input and approval relating to the material, artwork, sleeves, test pressings and the like; on a few occasions when the band didn't consent, we complied with their wishes.

I rang Mark Furman straight away and said I was worried that if this contract was ever challenged it wouldn't hold up. Even for a band at the Stone Roses' stage of development when they signed it, the contract was ridiculously weighted in favour of Zomba. And by now I'd have put money on the Stone Roses making it big time. So many record companies – Zomba clearly being one of them – printed up and rolled out their standard draft contract knowing it would be returned and decimated by whichever lawyer the artist hired. The initial contract was often simply a way to start discussions till you reach agreement over the various clauses and points. Only on this occasion Gareth had approved the contract without addressing anything. Mark admitted that nobody had expected Gareth to accept the contract without questioning it at all.

When I later asked Mark if Gareth had brought in a lawyer he said yes – but it was somebody who specialised in conveyancing with no music business experience. The advance was actually OK – £70,000 – split between the record company and the publishing company. But was Gareth aware that this was a deal he could easily walk away from anytime? He'd certainly never mentioned

314

any issues that he had with it until I brought it up.

Mark Furman confessed that he, too, was concerned, so I said I needed to speak to John Fruin. I told John that we were at risk of losing the band because the contract could be challenged so easily and overturned. He agreed and said, 'This is our screw-up; we'll make it right.' I knew I had to speak to Gareth about it. I didn't want him flying off the handle, but I thought it was in everybody's interest to sort this out. I told Gareth I'd raised the matter with John Fruin and Mark, and they were going to fix it. Gareth's immediate reaction was, 'Are you telling me it's a bad contract?' It was, of course, but I played it down and said the original contract reflected the group's standing at the time they signed to Zomba. The way I couched it was that the group now needed a more appropriate contract.

It wasn't my place to be part of any renegotiation because the deal wasn't with me or with Silvertone, which hadn't existed at the time. I explained to Gareth that it was up to John Fruin and Mark Furman to renegotiate with him on the band's be-half. In the months that followed, whenever I brought up the subject both sides came back saying talks were going fine. They always gave me the impression they were making progress, but the conversations dragged on. It wasn't till after 'Fool's Gold' gave the band its first Top 10 hit at the end of the year that everything was ramped up.

We needed a new non-album single and after two weeks at Sawmill Studios in Cornwall the band came back with 'Fools Gold' and 'What the World Is Waiting For'. 'Fool's Gold' was originally going to the B-side, but such was the positive reaction on radio that we made it a double A-side. Gareth Davies came to me and said we needed to put the emphasis on 'Fool's Gold' to avoid splitting airplay. He said we need to re-sticker the promos and I said, 'Go ahead'. After that, 'Fools Gold' quickly took on a life of its own radio.

315

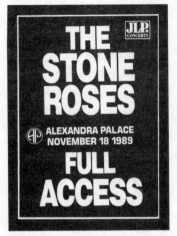

The ambitious show coincided with the Stone Roses'
breakthrough single 'Fool's Gold'

The release of the single on 13 November came five days
before the band's second high-profile gig at Alexandra Palace in
London – this time to a capacity audience of 8000 people. It was
their first live show since Blackpool and had the same impact,
although it met with far less enthusiastic reviews. The Stone
Roses tended to get away with it when they played because they
always generated such a vibey atmosphere. With the Roses it
was always 'you had to be there'. The airplay and buzz about
playing Alexandra Palace propelled 'Fool's Gold' into the charts
at No. 13, which meant they were asked to appear on *Top of
the Pops*. Earlier that week they were on BBC2's *Newsnight*.
It was a prestigious slot which was cut short when, after 45
seconds, the volume they played at blew out the studio fuses.
In the chaos Ian Brown could be heard shouting that the BBC
were amateurs. It wasn't exactly the Stone Roses' 'Bill Grundy
moment' and Gareth inevitably claimed they'd deliberately
caused the power surge, which may even have been true. After a

little persuasion over threats to pull out, they duly appeared on *Top of the Pops* on 23 November alongside Happy Mondays. Both bands were on the show for the first time. The combined impact of the two bands on the nation's flagship pop show is generally seen as the catalyst for igniting the Madchester scene. It would soon attract massive media attention with Ian Brown its poster boy. The Stone Roses even made flares fashionable again.

The following week 'Fool's Gold' rose to No. 8 in the charts. With so much happening and everybody talking about the Stone Roses, I went back to John Fruin to ask how it was going with Gareth and the revised deal. Gareth had led John to believe that three of the group had apparently signed a new contract and Reni would sign when he was back from holiday. John thought it would all be done and dusted in January. As a gesture of good faith, I suggested giving the group a Christmas bonus ahead of the deal against royalties. We agreed on £50,000 to be paid to them in advance. Gareth eagerly accepted and the money was transferred into a separate account he'd set up for all the Stone Roses' earnings. I knew nothing about the financial arrangements between Gareth and the band. As far as I was concerned it was a goodwill gesture on our part which would smooth the deal going through.

Since the whole Madchester buzz had kicked in, it seemed as if any unsigned Manchester band was up for grabs, including the Charlatans. In January I got a call from Gareth saying, 'I can't believe you would do this', and I said, 'What?' Apparently, Jive had made an offer for the Charlatans and the rumour mill around Manchester was that it was a better deal than the revised one for the Roses (Jive also made overtures to the Inspiral Carpets). Gareth was always going to find out because the Charlatans' manager Steve Harrison was a ticket agent he dealt with for the International. Gareth took the moral high ground, and I was just as pissed off as he was with Zomba. They really should have told me even though they weren't obliged to. Jive was a little jealous about the success Silvertone was having and this was not just with the Stone Roses. We were responsible for 85 per cent of Zomba's sales in Europe and by the end of 1989 had a turnover of £1.9 million from scratch.

The Charlatans episode really changed Gareth's mood in dealing with Zomba. I spoke to John and said this is going to slip away from us if we're not careful. I thought John had played into Gareth's hands because he was always going to find out. The Charlatans signed with Beggars Banquet in February but in Gareth's eyes the damage was done. It was a bad start to a year in which the Stone Roses could have had it all. As it was, just as everything was going so right, everything began to go so wrong.

In the aftermath of 'Fool's Gold' the continuing rise of the Stone Roses had a momentum you couldn't halt and couldn't readily explain. It was my idea to re-release the three earlier Silvertone singles, which I'd since deleted. All I did was to print the catalogue number in red rather than black so they could be differentiated from the original copies. Otherwise they were exactly the same – no remixes or bonus tracks or different art-work. There was no new single, so the demand was there from a growing legion of new fans wanting something they didn't have. I thought it was a way to show how popular the Stone Roses had become. I don't remember anybody having a problem about it. So in February 1990 'Elephant Stone' was re-released and reached No. 8; 'Made of Stone' followed in March and then 'She Bangs the Drum' later the same month.

Looking back, the whole saga of the Stone Roses is almost unbelievable. Aside from that period between February and June 1989 when they did the hard graft of touring round the country, the Stone Roses barely played any UK shows. Buoyed by the triumph of the Blackpool show, Gareth thought that was the way to go. Hence the six-month gaps between Blackpool, Ally Pally and the forthcoming Spike Island event. Otherwise they played only a handful of European and Japanese dates – and most significantly they never played in America at all. Several tours were organised over there but then cancelled.

Spike Island marked the breaking point between the Stone Roses and Zomba

Spike Island was to be the major rock event to end all major rock events for the baggy generation, taking place during the last weekend of May with the band drawing a crowd of almost 40,000 to a windswept estuary in Widnes, Cheshire. It took total commitment to make your way to the site, but Stone Roses fans were never going to miss out. It's unfair to say their performance was a let-down because it was no fault of theirs that the sound was so dreadful, with heavy winds making them inaudible at times. For the group's booze- and drug-fuelled fans it didn't seem to matter. As a logistical exercise, the Spike Island event was an extraordinary achievement and it grabbed headlines across the UK media and beyond, but there was no new single to coincide with it.

319

It wasn't just me as a record company man bemoaning a lost opportunity; it was typical that Gareth could organise an event on such an outlandish scale while 'One Love', the one new track they'd recorded, remained unfinished and unmixed with John Leckie in America for six weeks on another job. 'One Love' had taken forever because they kept rejecting test pressings and tinkering with the artwork. It was like pulling teeth. There were too many voices and the total cost of that single was an astronomical £70,000. 'One Love' was finally released in July but with no commitment by the band to promote it. Although it reached No. 4, they'd spent so much time over it that it sounded like an amalgam of unfinished ideas, which was reflected in the underwhelming way it was received.

I'd always had concerns about America and first addressed it with Gareth after the release of 'Elephant Stone'. I knew Gareth's manner and tactics weren't going to work with BMG in America and I thought Gareth needed somebody representing the band's interests out there. I immediately thought of my friend Greg Lewerke. I spoke to him and said Gareth was only going to ruffle feathers with his attitude. We needed a safety valve. Gareth was suspicious and his first reaction was, 'So you've done a deal with your mate', but it was only a recommendation. I told Gareth that Greg had a lot of experience in various roles at Fantasy and United Artists and he'd also looked after Don Arden's Jet Records at the point when ELO was one of the most successful bands on the planet. Secretly I thought that since Greg had been able to handle working with Don Arden, then he'd soon get the measure of Gareth.

That didn't stop Gareth blundering in. The classic was when I got a call from Rick Dobbis, one of the senior execs at RCA, who was in a right lather. He said, 'Who the fuck does this guy think he is – Brian Epstein?' I said, 'He probably does', which Rick didn't find at all funny. Gareth had told him it wasn't worth the Stone Roses coming over till they could play Shea Stadium.

Despite our close friendship, Greg always put the band first.
Soon after Spike Island, the renegotiations with Zomba were
clearly grinding to a standstill. Gareth thought pulling off something of the magnitude of Spike Island would bring Zomba
round to making him an offer he couldn't refuse. It was Greg
who arranged for Gareth and Matthew Cummins to fly to New
York to meet with senior execs at Geffen, Warners and Polygram.
Greg had also recommended John Kennedy to Gareth; John
was a damn good lawyer who was now handling the talks with
Zomba. They weren't going to get one over on him.

By August there were strong rumours that Gareth not only
wanted to get out of the existing contract but was setting up
a massive new deal in the interim. Geffen were front runners,
having declared their interest by making a provisional offer of
$4 million on a new album. That's why Zomba took an injunction
out on the band in September against recording for any other
label. It signalled the end for Zomba; they'd blown any chance of
hanging onto the band. At the same time, John Kennedy sent a
letter to Zomba saying the existing contract was unenforceable
and terminating the agreement.

Roddy McKenna had been back in London for a couple of
months; he still saw the Stone Roses as his baby within Zomba
and he didn't want to lose them. In September we decided to go
up to Manchester together to try and meet with the band and
make sure they fully understood what was going on from our
side. We had no idea what they knew or what Gareth had told
them. It was our last-ditch attempt to salvage something, because
Roddy and I both thought the band still had some trust in us.
We did manage to meet all of them over a couple of days. In the
course of the conversations it seemed as if they weren't being
fully informed about all the decisions being made about their
contract with Zomba. We tried in vain to arrange a meeting with
Gareth several times while we were in Manchester, but he kept

putting us off until eventually getting angry that we'd seen the band behind his back. I still believed that the group was happy with what we – as Silvertone and the team I'd brought in – had done. They never disputed this. In fact, when I met them at a gig in Belfast on 7 June they were asking if I was OK at Silvertone. Gareth had given them the impression that, with Roddy having returned, I was about to be ousted. They expressed genuine concern, and I assured them that was never going to happen.

Even at this stage, with a court case on the horizon, it was impossible to know where I stood with Gareth. Around November 1990 when I was in America he told me he'd been offered an enormous production deal – nothing to do with the Stone Roses – and would I like to be his partner in the business. I said I'd think about it and get back to him. Nothing came of it. A couple of weeks later he accused me of getting financial kickbacks from Rockfield for using the studio when the band recorded there. It was nonsense, but typical of how he blew hot and cold. He ended the Rockfield conversation saying, 'You're just like the rest of them at Zomba.'

More bizarre still, on the first day of the trial in March, Judith and I ran into Ian and some of the band and he said, 'We're going for a coffee if you want to join us.' Somebody from their legal team promptly said, 'I don't think that's a good idea.' The court case ran from 4 to 26 March 1991. It was Anthony Jayes who was hired by Zomba to fight their corner. I spent time with Anthony preparing what I was going to say. He thought the fact that Zomba hadn't expected Gareth to sign such a bad contract wasn't going to hold up. John Kennedy's case was based on 'restraint of trade' and the judge eventually ruled that the contract was 'an unfair, unjustified and unjustifiable restraint of trade' which was unenforceable. I never got to make a statement in court. I was essentially there to argue that Silvertone and the team we'd hired had played a crucial part in the band's success. Eventually it was decided that my appearance wasn't going to make any difference to the judge's ruling, so I was stood down.

It was a long wait – almost two months – for the resolution on 20 May when the judge ruled in the band's favour. It was what we'd expected. I just closed the office and went to Lord's Cricket Ground. I couldn't think of anything more removed from the record business. It was the final day of a match between Middlesex and one of the great West Indies sides – which they won comfortably by six wickets, but I was oblivious to whatever was happening in front of me.

At the end of May the Stone Roses were released from their contract. Zomba still had the rights to everything they'd recorded and released and proceeded to milk the group's catalogue and everything else they had rights to, including the film from Blackpool which they released on video. I could understand why, because Zomba had to pay all the costs from the trial, which may have been as much as £500,000. I had nothing to do with any of the releases post-trial which, of course, were all released on Silvertone. I wrote to John Fruin saying, 'I don't think you should be doing it this way', and I made it clear none of the releases were with my blessing.

The bugbear for me was that the case was against Zomba, not Silvertone, because it hinged around that original contract, but the way it was always reported in the press, particularly the music press, was that the dispute was with Silvertone since that was the label which released their records. It became very sensitive because people who didn't know me were always going to think I was the one responsible for such a bloody awful deal. That's still how it's perceived to this day. It was Roddy who signed them to Jive. I don't deserve the kudos of being the man who signed the Stone Roses but equally, I didn't deserve to have my name dragged through the dirt. The contract was all signed and sealed before I'd even heard of the band and before I started up the Silvertone label. It was a wretched feeling – and I wasn't at fault.

I certainly did my best to put it right once I eventually read the contract. I knew I'd played it straight. So it was all the more galling for Silvertone to be repeatedly cast as the bad guys. It takes away from so much of what was good about my association with the Stone Roses, from something that was great fun. Whether it was going along to *Top of the Pops*, the Empress Ballroom gig or just knowing we'd done a great job and been part of something that wasn't just successful but became a phenomenon. You can't live your life wondering what if, the biggest one for me being what if I had asked to see the contract immediately. I like to think I would have challenged it straight away as both unfair and unworkable.

The last Stone Roses thing I had any direct involvement with was the torturous process of releasing 'One Love'. I haven't spoken to Gareth since before the court case, nor had any contact with any of the band since it was over. Nigel Kerr, John Leckie and Kingsley at Rockfield kept me in the picture about what was happening once they signed to Geffen, but I was never pleased at the outcome. It was frustrating and depressing to see something I'd been heavily involved with falling apart and failing to live up to the promise.

That the second album was so poorly received actually made the debut album even greater. I wanted to like *The Second Coming*, but it lacked the magic, the energy and the drive of the Silvertone album. They'd also lost the moment; first Nirvana and grunge and then Brit-Pop had come along while they dithered over the recordings. How much of what went wrong was down to Gareth no longer being involved is pure speculation, because he was officially dismissed in February 1992. Had they still been on Silvertone I wouldn't have been unduly worried about rushing a second album. They were never prolific, after all. Zomba might have had other ideas but with the first album still selling well we could have released the odd single and given them time.

Chapter 23
Last of a Dying Breed

Setting up Silvertone was the result of me wanting to get back into A&R again after six years where I was never actively looking to sign acts. The deal I established with Zomba on 18 April 1988 officially ended on 18 December 1991, although we'd effectively left sometime in October. Silvertone released seventeen albums, only one of which was by the Stone Roses. It's disappointing that, for a lot of people, it's all Silvertone is remembered for. It was the same with Radar. Yet while Radar was a well-intentioned label that never fulfilled its promise, to say that Silvertone did nothing else but the Stone Roses is far from the truth. Silvertone was a broad-based label that had considerable success with John Lee Hooker, J.J. Cale and Buddy Guy in particular. It was very much an 'Andrew Lauder label' where the remainder of the roster showed a disdain for image and being hip, which were never a priority in my book. This was reflected in my commitment to blues albums, and plain good music, whether it was musician's musicians such as Brendan Croker or wild cards like Peter Blegvad and Sonic Boom. Silvertone also reunited me with three acts from my past in Loudon Wainwright, the Men They Couldn't Hang and Del Shannon.

They probably don't come more unfashionable than the Men They Couldn't Hang, a band I picked up again six years after we'd launched them on Demon. They never excited the music press, which cast them as a poor man's Pogues. But they were popular all over Europe. In 1989, before we released their fourth album *Silver Town* they played to over 250,000 people in Estonia and went down a storm at Reading that year. I'd been putting out Loudon Wainwright's records since *A Live One*, the final release on Radar in 1979. It was always like making an easy-going deal with a friend. Loudon almost became something of a mascot and Silvertone released *Therapy* in 1989, up there with his best.

I'd got to know Del Shannon pretty well over the years. We sold 70,000 copies of the posthumous album *Rock On*. It was such a shock when we heard he'd committed suicide on 8 February 1990. Judith and I were on our way to Robert Cray's wedding when we got the call. It was a great album too, lots of great songs and his voice was as wonderful as ever. The album was produced by Jeff Lynne and Mike Campbell of Tom Petty's Heartbreakers. Word was that he might take Roy Orbison's place in the Traveling Wilburys, so it was doubly sad that he didn't give himself the chance to be rediscovered the same way.

Brendan Croker was actually the first to release an album on Silvertone. We released a soundtrack album he recorded with Dire Straits' keyboardist Guy Fletcher for a British TV series *On the Big Hill* before we made his debut proper, *Brendan Croker & the Five O'Clock Shadows*. Brendan was another of those musician's musicians I really admire. He's best known as a member of the Notting Hillbillies with Mark Knopfler, which was never going to win him any extra points for credibility either. That never bothered me, and we made a second album with him in Nashville which was produced by the great Barry Beckett. *The Great Indoors* featured so many top musicians like Chet Atkins, Reggie Young, Jim Horn as well as Mark Knopfler. It didn't come cheap but sold particularly well in Europe. The only record we made for Silvertone that didn't

326

sell as well as it deserved was Peter Blegvad's *King Strut & Other Stories*, though, sad to say, I don't think any of Peter's albums ever sold that well. I've no regrets about making that one. Andy Partridge from XTC and Chris Stamey from the dBs produced it, and it's crammed with Peter's wonderfully crafted short stories set to music.

I do regret we couldn't follow through with Pete 'Sonic Boom' Kember. I loved Spacemen 3 and the idea that they were a young psychedelic band where all the members were very bright and took loads of drugs. They were all huge music fans. I was always a sucker for that. I wanted to sign Spaceman 3, but it was clear that Pete Kember and Jason Pierce were falling out. We got on really well with Pete and we'd stay at his parents' house in Rugby. They were pretty well off. The first time we stayed there his mum came to us and said, 'Sorry to inconvenience you but we have an interior magazine coming by in the morning to take photographs of the house.' The album we released was a Sonic Boom album called *Spectrum* that we gave an amazing sleeve. It was a series of moving parts – an over-the-top cylindrical cover with two revolving 'psychedelic' plastic discs fixed on a gatefold picture sleeve. Being able to indulge yourself is one of the benefits of having your own label.

It was J.J. Cale and John Lee Hooker that got Silvertone up and running as much as the Stone Roses did in our first year. I had a relationship with Mike Kappus that had begun with John Hiatt and continued with Robert Cray at Demon. It was through Mike's Rosebud management and booking agency that I began working with John Lee Hooker and J.J. Cale straight away at Silvertone. I kept badgering Mike about J.J. Cale, who hadn't released an album or played any gigs since 1983. Mike would come back saying, 'J.J. would rather go fishing right now, but if he shows any signs of doing anything I'll let you know.' I'd long loved J.J. Cale's records drawing on blues, country, rockabilly and jazz, which he amalgamated into one of the most recognisable sounds of the 1970s and '80s with vocals that epitomised 'laid-back'. He was also about as opposed to the limelight as you could be. J.J.'s new songs arrived following a delightful message from him saying, 'I'll send you some tapes and if you like them you can put them out. If you sell some, send me some money.' I chose what I thought was the best album from the tapes and released them as *Travel-Log*. I was able to send him some money from over 300,000 sales. I wouldn't have released the remaining tapes but after I'd left Silverstone, they released them as *No. 10*.

I was lucky enough to go to the warm-up shows in America when J.J. toured around *Travel-Log* and was even invited down to his new house in Escondido, in San Diego. He spent the morning putting rattlesnake protection in so snakes couldn't get into his back yard and couldn't harm his dog which was curled up in the case for his new Martin guitar. He had a couple of Metallica CDs lying around. Seeing my look of surprise, he said, 'I like to listen to what other people are doing.' He was a wily old bird but great fun.

Festival and club appearances aside, John Lee Hooker wasn't visibly active in the 1970s and '80s until *The Healer* marked the first of his albums that rounded up long-term fans such as Carlos Santana, Bonnie Raitt and Robert Cray. I picked it up in 1989 from a small California label called Chameleon, which had already released it in the States. It was a modest deal and in the first year alone we sold around 150,000 copies. When *Mr Lucky* came along two years later it just took off. This time the famous guests included Ry Cooder, Keith Richards and Van Morrison, but it surprised everybody when it went in the charts at No. 2 in September 1991. That went some way towards making up for the recent woes over the Stone Roses. Three months later when

I left Silvertone we'd sold 711,000 copies.

Disappointingly, RCA came back with a very dismissive 'Oh, is he still alive?' and *Mr Lucky* ended up with Virgin's Point-blank label in the US and Canada. RCA had really missed a trick. Then, on top of having my name muddied by the Stone Roses' case, Zomba really screwed up when their accounts department contacted John Lee about overpaid royalties on *The Healer*. They'd added the VAT to what they paid him and were demanding it back. They didn't inform me. I'd just arrived in Los Angeles where, ostensibly, I was meeting Mike Kappus to talk about doing another album with John Lee. The morning after I'd arrived, the first phone call I received was from Mike saying, 'What the fuck is going on?' He'd just heard about the demand for overpaid royalties which, although out of my control, could have damaged my relationship with Mike. It left me thinking, 'What next?'

It was such a downer, especially as on my previous trip to the States with Judith we went to visit John Lee in his house just outside San Francisco. We'd taken along a car boot full of silver, gold and platinum discs from the various European territories, which he was delighted to receive. He liked getting those things which all went up on the wall. He never expected them just as he never expected to get decent royalty cheques. He'd missed out on so much since the 1950s by recording for small labels that made one-off payments and came with dodgy publishing deals on classic songs covered time and time again. He was so pleased about how well we'd done with *The Healer* and *Mr Lucky*, which only made us feel worse about Zomba's bungling accounting mistake.

The pioneering John Lee Hooker's success on Silvertone
was one of Andrew's proudest achievements

That same trip we also paid Willie Dixon a visit. I'd licensed
his 1988 album *Hidden Charms* and released it in 1991 through
our friend Dan Bourgoise, the founder and CEO of Bug Music,
which had done a label deal with Capitol Records. *Hidden
Charms* was produced by T Bone Burnett, who'd managed to
recreate the sound of Willie's early Chess recordings. We spent
a wonderful afternoon with Willie and his wife. She apologised
for the scraps of paper littered around the room and said she
daren't throw anything away because he'd scrawl lyrics on the
back of envelopes or cigarette packets and get mad when he
couldn't find them. He was still writing. He'd been ill with dia-
betes and had recently had his leg amputated. It was so great

to meet another of my all-time heroes; he died in January the
following year.

As well as the huge success we had with *Mr Lucky* in 1991,
earlier that year we'd delivered Zomba an album by Buddy Guy
called *Damn Right, I've Got the Blues* featuring guest appearances by Eric Clapton, Jeff Beck, and Mark Knopfler. It was one
of the first albums John Porter produced after moving to Los
Angeles. Despite having made his name producing indie bands,
most notably the Smiths, John was as much a blues fanatic as
I was. That album completely revived Buddy Guy's career and
had sold 365,000 copies by the end of 1991. We'd managed to
get him out of clubs and into concert halls. RCA didn't make the
same mistake twice and now in his mid-eighties all Buddy Guy's
subsequent albums have been released by Silvertone worldwide.
When I look back on Silvertone now, I would have been happy
and proud about what I'd achieved even if I had passed on the
Stone Roses.

The decision to leave was difficult but the fuck-up over John
Lee's royalties was the last straw. Soon after the release of *Mr
Lucky*, I was approached by Polygram about my setting up a
new label for them. I wrote to John Fruin saying I wanted to
change my arrangement with Zomba, knowing Clive Calder
wouldn't go for the amendments I laid out. He understood how
much the court case had impacted on me and that I could no
longer carry on. Zomba still owned the Silvertone name and the
label shifted its operation to America.

In the last years at Demon, Judith and I bought a place in
Brentford, not anticipating the problems that led to me leaving
Demon. We were living there during our time at Silvertone but
getting away to Devon kept us sane during that final year there.
It was another world, being able to mix with the locals, most
of whom accepted us straight away. Some took longer to make

up their minds. There's a lovely Devon expression that they'd 'winter and summer 'em' before deciding whether newcomers were OK. We never made a big thing of what we did in London except when asked. I remember the crazy day we did *Top of the Pops* with the Stone Roses and Happy Mondays and all we said in the pub was that it had been a busy week. We'd always ask, 'How's your week been?' and the answer was usually something like 'I've been de-horning rams.'

Having sold the place in Brentford, we moved into a rented mews in Kensington. We'd just done our first deal with John Prine's Oh Boy label and they were asking, 'What's the new label called?' We were surrounded by unpacked boxes of records with This Way Up written on the side. Why not, we thought? This Way Up started up in 1992 based on a five-year deal with Polygram as part of Mercury. Polygram essentially wanted me to set up a label that mirrored what I'd done at Silvertone. I didn't rush the deal this time and it was completed at a very leisurely pace. It was the first time I ever received any kind of royalty. Payments still come through twice a year – not huge, but well worth having. If I'd had such a deal for Silvertone I'd be laughing. The brilliant Lucy Launder came with us to This Way Up, since when she's been at Abbey Road Studios for over twenty-five years, where she is currently head of mastering services.

The deal for John Prine's recent catalogue was a good way to start This Way Up. He was one of the first Nashville-based songwriters to form his own independent label in 1984. I'd already released Oh Boy's first two John Prine albums on Demon and we picked up a new live album which we released in 1993 alongside *The Missing Years*, which had won a Grammy for Best Contemporary Folk album and rebooted his career in the 1990s. His vocals were less abrasive, befitting a more relaxed sound that was perfect for more mainstream American radio stations. That didn't translate here, where steady sales didn't make up for not being able to take John Lee Hooker and J.J. Cale with me to This Way Up. Mike Kappus was having problems with Polygram over Robert Cray, and J.J. Cale had actually bought his way out of his previous Polygram deal so he wasn't about to go back there.

The first acts we picked up and began releasing in 1993 were Ian McNabb and the Tindersticks, and the following year we released Otis Rush's first album in sixteen years. Ian had already made *Truth & Beauty*, which he recorded and paid for himself. I was immediately taken with its raw emotional songs; it's probably his best body of work. The simple production was a long way from his former band, the Icicle Works. Ian was a Neil Young fanatic and we joked about him recording with Crazy Horse. Their schedules were always one year on/one year off working with Neil, so we were able to record four tracks for *Head Like a Rock* with Neil's famed rhythm section of Billy Talbot and Ralph Molina in Burbank, California. It was easily Ian's most critically accepted work and he was even nominated for a Mercury Prize. It was frustrating that his singles only ever brushed the bottom of the Top 75. After a final album, the wittily titled *Merseybeast*, we had to let him go. I already had a feeling that after the initial five-year period that would be it for the Polygram deal.

We brought Dave Bedford into This Way Up. We'd first met him when he was at Fire Records when I was trying to sign Spacemen 3 and it was through Dave that we signed the Tindersticks. We released their self-titled debut album halfway through 1993 to glowingly appreciative reviews in the music press that continued across all their albums we put out. The Tindersticks struck an immediate chord with the kind of discerning fans who were into dark, dense and dramatic songs and half-spoken, melancholy, literate lyrics. Lead vocalist Stuart A. Staples had a deep baritone to rival even Leonard Cohen, while multi-instrumentalist Dickon Hinchcliffe's orchestrations were wonderfully immersive.

We released three studio albums as well as two live albums from Amsterdam in 1994 and the Bloomsbury Theatre in 1995. All these albums made the Top 40, their second eponymous album in 1995 reaching as high as 13. The splendour and moodiness of their music gave the band such a cosmopolitan appeal that Tindersticks increasingly sold records in countries where I've never sold records before, such as Israel, Czechoslovakia and Portugal. The sales were never spectacular but always quietly impressive like the band's music.

Halfway through our third year, Mercury Records pulled out of managing This Way Up and we were unable to release anything for months until Island stepped in. We lost momentum in that time and never really recovered. We did a deal with John Silva at Gold Mountain, whose charges included Nirvana, Beastie Boys, and Sonic Youth, among others, to release two albums by Los Angeles underground band Redd Kross beginning with *Phaseshifter* in 1993. It was as close to grunge as they got. Having pre-dated the alternative rock explosion by almost ten years they defied categorisation. We brought them over to tour regularly and play festivals and they built up a loyal following, but they never really caught on in the way Silva had hoped.

Otis Rush's *Ain't Enough Comin' In* failed to repeat the success we'd had at Silverstone with Buddy Guy. Produced by John Porter, now becoming a blues specialist, Otis Rush's sizzling guitar and an emphasis on choice covers from the pens of Sam Cooke, Ray Charles and Louis Jordan won over blues fans and critics without crossing over further. Otis always had his problems. He was certainly a lot less amenable to work with than Buddy Guy and less of a showman. We'd set the tone for blues artists winning Grammys and Otis duly got his a few years later, but he'd signed to the House of Blues by then.

As I expected, Polygram pulled the plug, with Island keeping This Way Up afloat for a brief while. Judith and I knew that whatever we did next was going to be run amidst the Devon countryside. We were already speaking to Dai Davies, who was now at Sanctuary, about a new label we could run from our village when John Porter came up with an intriguing proposition. It was a potential project with financial backing from Forbes-listed multimillionaire and internet pioneer Rick Adams. John had been speaking to photographer and music-ologist Timothy Duffy, who'd founded the Music Maker Relief Foundation in 1994. Tim had been documenting forgotten southern musicians in a series of field recordings and had set up the foundation to help them meet their basic needs, arranging medical care and access to affordable housing. Aside from raising money through his field recordings he was also organising and promoting gigs for them. The idea being floated was to start up a new label to record albums with some of the Music Makers' country blues artists as well as other overlooked blues musicians.

Instead of putting my feet up in Devon, I was flown out to New York a week later to meet with John, Tim Duffy and Rick Adams. I agreed to do some detailed costings for a label. I knew we'd struggle to make money recording unknown seventy-year-old bluesmen and recommended we try to add a couple of contemporary acts as well. Rick never said much in the meeting or any of the subsequent meetings, and it wasn't till after our fourth get-together that I was able to push him on a decision. He finally said, 'I guess so', which we took as a green light. It was a little crazy before we even got that far. All our meetings were in different parts of the States. One coincided with John's fiftieth birthday, celebrated at Ernie K-Doe's Mother-in-Law Lounge in New Orleans, another was the morning after a night at the Palace Theatre in Los Angeles where Rick paid

$25,000 for a table at B.B. King's eightieth birthday concert. Judith came along to both those and was particularly chuffed to get Dr John's autograph. We definitely racked up the air miles and had plenty of fun times during the Cello episode.

Having got the go-ahead based on the figures I'd come up with, John said he'd need a quarter of a million dollars to cover his loss of earnings and he said I should get the same. So John took care of the recording side while I set up the record company, registering the name Cello Recordings Ltd in the UK. Then it was down to me and Judith to arrange studios, producers, engineers, other musicians, flights, hotels and the like, all run from the Schoolhouse in Knowstone. We rented it from Pete and Judy Thomas, who'd followed us down to Devon but were back living in America. I did a deal with Seymour Stein to distribute the label through Warners in the US and Canada and with Pinnacle for the UK. I also made use of a subsidiary label called Jericho, which I owned as the outlet for contemporary acts, and we began releasing albums in 1999.

We released first-time albums in 1999 by John Dee Holeman, Neal Puttnam, Guitar Gabriel and Cootie Stark from Tim's Music Makers' roster of blues unknowns beginning with a compilation called *Expressin' the Blues; Reconstructed History of the Blues*. I asked Mike Vernon to produce *This Stuff Just Kills Me* by singer and harmonica player Jerry 'Boogie' McCain and *Back in Business* by Beverly 'Guitar' Watkins. They were easily the best known and bestselling of the bunch. Beverly Watkins had been in Piano Red's Dr Feelgood and the Interns and she'd played with Ray Charles and B.B. King. Jerry McCain was a big name among harmonica fans and I had singles by him on Excello and Trumpet. Tim's blues acts even did a tour sponsored by Winston cigarettes. They had girls in miniskirts unashamedly handing out free packs of cigarettes. Tim was based in North Carolina, which was at the heart of tobacco country, where

Judith and I visited Tobaccoville, and we went along to shows in
Winston Salem and a club in Chicago. Jericho initially released
Two Bulb Twilight by harmony rock band Cal Hollow and *Time
to Burn* by young Texan guitarist Jake Andrews. He was the son
of guitarist John 'Toad' Andrews from another of my favourite
Bay Area bands, Mother Earth, who were fronted by Tracy
Nelson. I also acquired *More Oar: A Tribute to Skip Spence. Oar*
was the only solo album by the troubled co-founder and guitarist
with Moby Grape, and among those participating were Robert
Plant, Mark Lanegan and Tom Waits.

I was paying for everything up front. Judith was doing all
the accounts and we'd scrupulously itemise everything for Rick
each month – usually averaging around $100,000 dollars. He'd
then transfer the money over. I was a little twitchy about the
arrangement because it was so hard to get Rick on the phone.
There was one occasion when he'd agreed to buy a major Southern blues catalogue from collector George Mitchell, who was
a contemporary of John Fahey in the early 1960s. I went with
John to Atlanta to pick up all the tapes, but the money hadn't
come through. When I finally got hold of Rick he grumpily re-
sponded with, 'Do you think I'm made of money?' He was fine
once I reminded him he'd agreed to the transaction a couple of
months before, but it made me a little wary about what I was
paying out each month.

There was talk about finding a bigger act to start bringing in
money. I flew out to see a band called Wonderland that John was
keen on, but I couldn't get past the singer sounding too much
like Freddie Mercury. By then I'd spent most of 1998 and '99 on
the project and I wasn't sure about its future direction. I'd also
involved Sanctuary in setting up a New York office for Cello, so
I decided it was time to bail out. The label petered out after a
few more years with some of the titles reverting to Music Maker.
Cello was me doing my bit for the blues again and I won't

pretend it wasn't enjoyable and definitely eventful. They were the kind of blues records that nobody was making any more and we did OK exporting some of the titles in the UK but the market wasn't really there for such an undertaking.

I'd also postponed setting up my new label with Sanctuary and I needed to turn my attention to that. Evangeline Recorded Works was run along similar lines to Demon; Evangeline was for artists who were still recording and we had the Acadia label for reissues. Evangeline released two new albums by Richie Havens through his Stormy Forest label; *Wishing Well* was particularly good. We did three albums with Graham Parker, who even if he'd been ignored by major labels for a decade never stopped making great records. Hammel on Trial was one-man anti-folk/folk punk style act Ed Hammel and, inevitably, there was a new Loudon Wainwright album, *Last Man on Earth*, which was one of his finest and most personal albums. Our biggest sales were across seven albums by Govt Mule, a Southern jam band which began as an Allman Brothers' spin-off. Govt Mule sold over 100,000 albums across Europe, but we couldn't get anyone interested in the UK.

We released over a hundred CDs on Acadia in eight years; we'd started out with an album by Doug Sahm and later released albums by the Sir Douglas Quintet. Otherwise the focus was on country rock and Americana and plenty of San Francisco acts, including Hot Tuna, Jorma Kaukonen, Sons of Champlin, the Charlatans, Joy of Cooking, Dan Hicks plus a triple set of the complete Kaleidoscope recordings. It wasn't the right time for a reissue label like Acadia. The market was saturated with major labels and well-funded specialist labels, which left little for us to license or that we could afford. There were less outlets to sell the records, too; Tower Records and a lot of the other chains were going bust or, like Virgin and HMV, were shrinking, so we couldn't get the pre-orders to make it work. I don't think we fully exploited online sales either; that was still something of a no man's land.

Both labels were CD only. Pete Macklin was in London doing sales, but the rest of it was run from our village. Judith took care of the accounts from home while I was running the label from the schoolhouse. Our friend Sarah was full-time, with her mum helping out when we were busy. Joss Stone, who spent her teenage years in the nearby village of Ashill, did work experience with us before she rose to fame in 2003. We had a local designer doing all the artwork and were able to do our mastering in nearby Taunton with John Dent, who I knew from Trident Studios. I enjoyed Evangeline being hands on and I really liked that we were a presence in the village; there was the church, the pub, the local builder and three local farms; we were the only other business in Knowstone.

Once we made the permanent move to Devon in 1997 we bought some land off a neighbouring farmer and extended our cottage in East Knowstone. The view out of our window was stunning, stretching straight out to Exmoor. Three quarters of a mile down a country lane, Knowstone was a village with less than 250 people, and we knew them all. There were no shops and even the post office closed down soon after we made the permanent move. Judith's mum lived there after her dad died. I bought a house for her at the other end of the village and she became parish clerk. For a few years Judith ran the parish council, which was a surprising amount of work. People would drop by the house at all hours. We were very at home there and village life was important, whether it was trying to help prevent the village being surrounded by wind farms or in 2001 anxiously monitoring the foot-and-mouth epidemic that was really distress-ing when it spread to a nearby farm.

The Mason's Arms was very much the centre of village life. A few years before we left Knowstone, the pub was taken over by Mark and Sarah Dodson, who turned it into an award-winning Michelin-starred restaurant. Mark was a top chef who had worked for Michel Roux. When we first met him he said straight away, 'I know who you are', and a couple of days later he showed me a photograph; it was a picture of the Stiff Records office in Alexander Street with Jake and Cynthia and everyone we knew at Stiff. He wanted me to identify them all, but I said, 'I don't know this person on the left-hand side.' And he said, 'That's me.' He'd entered a 'win a day in the Stiff Records office' competition in *Melody Maker*.

A few years after Judith and I had moved to France we went back to our old village and to the Mason's Arms. Mark came out and said, 'Wilko's in the other bar with his band.' He was playing in Barnstable that night. So – tentatively at first – Wilko and I had a grand reunion where, thankfully, Mark didn't have to hide the cutlery. I hadn't seen him since he'd left Dr Feelgood twenty years earlier.

It was getting harder running a day-to-day business from Devon and Evangeline was struggling to sell enough records. I hadn't taken anything out of the company for seven months, so it was time to stop. I called it a day in 2008. Pete Macklin kept it going as Floating World, although he's also now retired. Devon was changing too. More and more people from London were buying houses while others were moving away and selling to weekenders. After twenty-five years it was ironic that we'd become locals complaining about 'people coming down from London with all their money and with their fancy London ways'. The big farms are still there but they are now run more as businesses, often by the kids who we used to give odd jobs to.

It was idyllic for a long time – as it is where we now live in France in another charming village called Seillans, in Provence. We discovered it after two of the former landlords of the Mason's Arms – Edouard and Antoinette – moved there and invited us over for a family wedding. We fell in love with the place, kept on coming back and finally moved to France in 2010. It was a clean break and moving to France made it harder to get sucked back into the music business again. Not that I've been tempted. Our old life – that's gone now. Instead we opened up a wine and local produce shop in Seillans. I do have a rack of classic CDs on sale, although I won't stock anything I don't like, which means customers will only find records by the likes of Del Shannon, the Artwoods, Jefferson Airplane or Howlin' Wolf.

I'm still a fan of the things I was into before but I've been building up a collection of people I particularly like now. I'm constantly looking. I really like Jason Isbell, Drive-By Truckers and Wilco, and a lot of harder to find stuff. It's mostly country that's rough around the edges and steeped in rock 'n' roll. Turnpike Troubadours, a band from Oklahoma, and American Aquarium from North Carolina were both a revelation when I discovered them. Chris Knight's another who now releases his own records. He had a hit twenty years ago with 'It Ain't Easy Being Me' and was a friend of John Prine. He sounds like a really angry old man. He's been described as the last of a dying breed. I can relate to that. Once this thing gets its claws in you there's no breaking away. I was a music fan first and ended up doing it for a living. That's definitely behind me now.

Our wonderful life together was seriously shaken when Judith was diagnosed with cancer in 2014. She lived with it, apart from two significant periods of remission, until the cancer returned last summer. Sadly, Judith died on 3 January 2023. That was barely two weeks ago. I can't begin to describe how devastated I feel right now, but I'll always remember the good times, so many of which Judith and I shared.

January 2023

Epilogue: Once Upon a Time in West Hartlepool
by Mick Houghton

There's still a sense of wonder whenever Andrew Lauder reflects upon his first day in London in January 1965. The chain of events began when Andrew's mum went into J.G. Windows' music shop in Newcastle under instruction to buy him the Artwoods' debut single 'Sweet Mary'. Barely a month later he'd almost inadvertently become an invoice clerk at Southern Music where, beneath him, was the studio where 'Sweet Mary' was recorded. And that was the beginning of a streak of luck or good fortune or whatever you choose to call such providence that continued throughout Andrew's life and career. Was it luck or more a result of Andrew being prepared and ready to take advantage of situations that presented themselves?

Either way, within three years of those surreal events unfolding, Andrew had assumed the duties of an A&R man at Liberty Records' UK outlet. A&R is often mistakenly understood to be only about discovering an artist and signing them, whereas, if anything, it's more about nurturing them, enabling the creation of the music, and then overseeing artwork, marketing, everything through to the eventual release. Andrew's particular strength after discovering a band – and he was invariably signing bands – was backing his judgement, and sticking with them, however unfashionable.

Anything written about A&R before the millennium would automatically have used the term 'A&R men'. 'You can't get round the historical fact that the music industry was very male-dominated,' recalls Andrew, 'and that was only beginning to change towards the time I got out. In America there were exceptions like Florence Greenberg at Scepter or Vivian Carter at Vee-Jay. Women in the record business here weren't given much credit for what they did and it was hard for them to climb the promotion ladder.'*

Back in October 1973 *Melody Maker* ran a feature about A&R, describing Andrew as possibly the best 'A&R Man' in Britain. 'He's made silk purses out of sow's ears at United Artists, an autonomous company with the least budget of all those companies represented here [the others were CBS, Island, EMI and Atlantic]. He's made initially unpromising material like the Groundhogs, Hawkwind and now Man successful.' Talk about damning with faint praise. If you consider all Andrew's silk purses at United Artists, then Can, Dr Feelgood and the Stranglers would also make the list; nobody expected any of them to become successful or influential. Such was Andrew's knack for seeing something others failed to see.

His biggest stroke of luck was probably in not becoming a journalist on one of the four weekly music papers. He would never have been exposed to the opportunities that Southern Music offered in an era so alive with possibilities. The job may have been routine but what he learned at 8 Denmark Street or by soaking up the hustle and bustle around him was nothing less than a crash course in how the record business worked. His already impressive knowledge and enviable collection of singles,

---

* The first female A&R person I remember was Carol Wilson at Dindisc, a Virgin label, where in 1979 she signed Orchestral Manoeuvres and later Monochrome Set.

EPs and LPs notwithstanding, he knew little about how those records ultimately made it into the various retail outlets.

It's fitting that Andrew's life would eventually centre on the business of releasing records. Despite the clichéd notion of A&Rs or their scouts going to gigs every night in search of the next big thing, or ploughing through a daily mountain of cassettes, it was more about who you knew. A&Rs relied on tip-offs from producers, agents, promoters, journalists, managers and musicians, the kind of people who'd regularly be in and out of Southern Music or who Andrew might have come across at the Giaconda or the Crown. Andrew's unassuming, affable personality ensured he was readily able to build and maintain good relationships.

Writing about Andrew and Silvertone Records in the *Independent* in February 1990, Andy Gill observed that: 'It's extremely rare, in a world as competitive and catty as the music business, to find a successful operator who is also universally liked . . . yet Andrew Lauder is blessed with an unfair share of luck and foresight, and seemingly unable to put anyone's nose out of joint.' Andrew was renowned for being friendly, helpful and generous with his time and expertise. Unlike most record company folk, he never tried to bend anybody's ear about a new signing or a new album he had coming out. He'd most likely be raving about something that was nothing to do with him. When the first Little Feat album failed to get a UK release by Warner Bros in 1971, Andrew bought multiple copies to give away. 'I never treated people as useful contacts,' he explains. 'If they were into music that was enough for me, and United Artists very much thrived on those informal relationships I'd made – and that continued down the years.'

Managing C-Jam Blues was a very different learning experience. 'Just to have managed a group that had a single out on EMI was something and, for a while I had to stop thinking this just might take off. Only later did I realise how much I'd learned

344

about the stress, pitfalls and demands of managing a band. It gave me a lot of respect for them and I learned to think twice about any band that didn't have a good manager. I always got on well with awkward and difficult people that others struggled with. So many people in the business ended up at odds with managers. That almost never happened with me.' The 'almost' is a reference to Wilf Pine, who muscled his way into mismanaging the Groundhogs. 'He was somebody who could ruin your day. I'm usually very calm but I smashed a few telephone handsets because of him. Gareth Evans could be annoying and frustrating, but we got on well for the most part. It was only leading up to Stone Roses' court case that he became impossible.'

Desperate for a job in a record company after the disappointment of C-Jam Blues he couldn't have got a better break than being offered a job at Liberty Records or a better mentor than Bob Reisdorff. His A&R philosophy of 'go sign some bands and sell some records' may have been simplistic but it fits. Bob Reisdorff's tutelage crucially demystified the process of making, releasing and marketing records for Andrew. The circumstances of the takeover of Liberty by Transamerica in 1968 were a bitter blow at first, but resulted in Andrew being elevated to an A&R position by the end of that year and effectively running the label. 'I was never officially an A&R man at Liberty, but I found myself in a situation where there was no one for me to report to or to question anything I did. If I wanted to put out a record, the only person I'd speak to was Brian in accounts. He was always happy to go along with it.

'There wasn't any one person who stood out as an example to follow aside from Bob. I still looked up to Andrew Oldham, who was running Immediate Records [founded in August 1965 with Tony Calder]. It was a very cool independent label but ultimately it was overly ambitious, very creative in outlook but without taking care of the business side. Immediate released far too many singles and in that sense didn't differ too much from the majors.

345

'Then there was Guy Stevens, who I totally identified with as a blues and R&B fan. By 1967 he'd jumped into the psychedelic thing big time when he was doing A&R. They were both strong and charismatic characters who contributed to their own downfall. Mavericks like them may have inspired me, but the way Chris Blackwell ran Island Records was closer to the way I was doing things at Liberty. It wasn't a conscious thing. I was inherently more level-headed. I see nothing wrong in that. I was always trying to do right by the bands I signed.'

A&R men in Britain used to be referred to as recording managers. They'd match the song to the artist and pick the best arranger for the recording, which they often produced themselves. That's how it was in the rock 'n' roll years and during the beat and R&B boom from 1963 to 1965. The British music business was dominated by EMI and Decca, which had 95 per cent of the market, while the Dutch-owned Philips and former electronics company Pye fought over the remainder. 'A lot of the A&R men at the majors were musicians or could read music or had music credentials of one sort or another. They were usually producers or engineers working out of in-house studios and weren't role models for me. I never thought about becoming a producer. I didn't really know what an A&R man did until I went to Liberty.' If he related to anybody, it was risk-takers such as Leonard Chess, Ahmet Ertegun at Atlantic, Art Rupe at Specialty or Sam Phillips at Sun. In America in the late 1950s at least half of the rock 'n' roll and R&B hits of the time came from independent labels.

'George Martin was obviously an incredibly successful producer and Parlophone was his label within EMI. It was best known for comedy records and was the least successful after HMV and Columbia before the Beatles came along. In those days the engineers had to dress like boffins in white coats and attitudes were still formal and square compared to what we were doing at Liberty

346

or what Island was doing.' Gone was the attitude typified by John Schroeder at Pye that 'our job was to make hit records. What was the point otherwise? We didn't retain an artist for longer than three singles without a hit.' Within months of launching in May 1967, Liberty Records began building a roster of mostly album-oriented bands. Bob Reisdorff could see that the balance was shifting from singles to albums and towards a more eclectic and adventurous path, allowing Ray Williams and Andrew to follow their instincts by bringing The Idle Race, The Bonzo Dog Doo-Dah Band, Family, Aynsley Dunbar's Retaliation and the Groundhogs to the label. None of them were fettered by the lack of hit singles.

By the 1970s Island had become the frontrunner among the independent labels alive to this transformation with bands such as Traffic, Jethro Tull, Free and Spooky Tooth. Aside from the faux independents set up by the majors – Harvest (EMI), Deram (Decca), Vertigo (Philips), and Dawn (Pye) – a spate of genuine independents was emerging. Among these were Tony Stratton Smith's Charisma label, Chrysalis, which came out from under Island's wing having tried to poach Andrew, and Virgin in 1973. It says a lot for Andrew's reputation that Virgin which, on principle, wouldn't hire anyone who had already been in the music business, tried to recruit him more than once.

The record business was changing rapidly as pop music gave way to rock in all its forms. The German-originated Polydor was known as Deutsche Grammophon's export label until 1967 when it took on distribution for Robert Stigwood's Reaction (and later RSO) and Track Records, founded by the Who's management. Through these two labels alone Polydor snaffled the Who, Jimi Hendrix, the Bee Gees, Cream and later Eric Clapton's solo career. CBS – the UK arm of US Columbia Records – had the best American roster with the likes of Dylan, the Byrds, and Simon and Garfunkel, and now rivalled the other American giants Warner, Elektra and Atlantic.

Despite more limited funding, United Artists was able to compete. It operated in an area between an independent and a major where, having been promoted to head of A&R, Andrew's new boss Martin Davis was prepared to let him do things entirely his way. Martin knew that Andrew had a knack of being one step ahead of the next trend. In hindsight it's easy to identify the changing eras in music during the 1970s, but underground music, pub rock and punk in Britain evolved quite seamlessly and it was visionaries like Andrew who, instinctively, saw what was coming and helped bring about those transitions.

Andrew knew that marketing his bands at United Artists was going to require ingenuity. They all adhered to Frank Zappa's assessment of his own music as having 'no commercial potential'. As a record fan, Andrew knew how much a striking album cover and great packaging captured the imagination. He loved the look of Jac Holzman's Elektra label. Jac understood that the 12-inch format was the perfect showcase for his LPs in record racks. Frank Zappa also made sure that early Mothers of Invention LPs came in deliberately shocking and grotesque sleeves that played to his notoriety.

So Andrew definitely wanted a voice in originating artwork, whether it was the comic art that adorned the Groundhogs' *Thank Christ for the Bomb* and particularly *Who Will Save the World* or Man's *Be Good to Yourself at Least Once a Day* – the one that opened out as 'Man's Map of Wales' which drew on Man's history and easy-going humour. And of course he had genius designer and illustrator Barney Bubbles to call upon in creating compelling visual dimensions for Hawkwind. Barney was also on hand at Radar and F-Beat and no less adept at presenting captivating visuals for Elvis Costello and Nick Lowe.

Hawkwind and Man were both hard-gigging psychedelic adventurers, but while Hawkwind were gaining attention Man went unnoticed. A different strategy was required. Budget or

348

mid-price albums had been pioneered by Pye's Golden Guinea and Marble Arch series. At a third of the price, I remember buying Marble Arch LPs by the Kinks, Donovan, Searchers and even Chess collections by Chuck Berry and Muddy Waters. Then, in 1968, it was the CBS sampler *The Rock Machine Turns You On* – priced at fifteen shillings – which started a new revolution in samplers geared to underground music. Everybody I knew bought it. It's where we all first heard Leonard Cohen and were blown away by Spirit's 'Fresh Garbage'. It's hard to think of any label that didn't get in on the act.

Greasy Truckers Party was a different kind of underground sampler, featuring four acts recorded live at the Roundhouse, three of which were Hawkwind, Brinsley Schwarz and Man. It was the first in a number of limited edition, budget price, live albums where Man were the chief beneficiaries. Andrew had hit upon a way of generating and then maintaining momentum behind Man as a great live band. In quick succession he released *Live at Padget Rooms, Penarth, Christmas at the Patti* – a sumptuous double 10-inch gatefold, no less – that also featured Help Yourself, and the half live/half studio recorded double album *Back into the Future*. As a result, Man won over a legion of new fans. Andrew even purloined Liberty's mainstream budget line Sunset with more impenetrable, contemporary offerings such as Captain Beefheart's *Strictly Personal, Hawkwind*, Amon Düül II's *Phallus Dei* and even a Can sampler titled *Opener*. Whether it was through cool packaging or competitive pricing, Andrew's bands were making waves. 'You had to find ways to get underground bands heard, because if John Peel didn't like a band you couldn't get played on the radio.'

Andrew's resourceful methods at United Artists definitely made him a progenitor of the indie label boom that sprang up during 1977. He'd been something of a midwife in the birth of Stiff Records, where Jake Riviera outrageously tailored many of

Andrew's ideas, enhanced by Barney Bubbles' audacious designs. You name it, Andrew had already done it: picture sleeves (early Hawkwind singles all came in picture sleeves; the 'Sonic Attack' promo came in a cloth bag); coloured vinyl (remember the red vinyl *Hapshash and the Coloured Coat* album in 1967); customised record labels (Dr Feelgood's releases were given a distinctive black label with silver lettering to give them a period feel); and bonus 7-inch singles on initial runs of LPs which Andrew utilised for Dr Feelgood's *Stupidity*. These were all incentives and inducements for fans and collectors. It takes one to know one, after all.

Not everything in Andrew's career was smooth sailing. Launching Radar, F-Beat and his interlude at Island Records were reality checks. Andrew's reaction to those setbacks was to start up a stream of new labels under the Demon Records umbrella, all independently manufactured, distributed and marketed. Andrew's first forays into catalogue had begun at Liberty, where he released his first compilation, *33 Minits of Blues and Soul* in 1968, but it was at United Artists that he and label manager Alan Warner began expertly exploiting what they had in the vaults. Drawing on his love of vintage movies, Alan released the memorable *Golden Age of Hollywood Musicals*, a gatefold featuring spectacular pop-up Busby Berkeley dancing girls. I still treasure his three themed *The Many Sides of Rock 'n' Roll* compilations, which came in gaudy gatefolds with four-page illustrated inserts. Andrew's two labours of love, *Mersey Beat '62–'64* and *The Beat Merchants*, are stand-outs for me. I was made up when Andrew asked me to do research on all the groups and write the copy for *The Beat Merchants*' inner spread. The cover illustration by Tony Wright is superb; it depicts a period music shop in resplendent colour and faultless detail.

Working with Andy Childs at F-Beat, Demon Records and its reissue arm Edsel Records were given a trial run in 1980 and were reactivated a year later. What started out filling in time between F-Beat releases grew to an operation with a £2 million-plus turnover within five years. The key to their success was intuitive licensing of contemporary artists discarded by major labels or through labels such as Rounder and Hightone. They were also unearthing back catalogue most labels could see no value in exploiting, and doing deals with the likes of Hi and HDH for classic gospel and soul recordings. Demon and Edsel had no qualms about straddling different genres and different eras of music; they knew where there was a demand, however niche.

The mid-eighties saw Demon become something of an A&R to the industry by breaking a number of current artists such as That Petrol Emotion, Rain Parade, the Long Ryders and Robert Cray, and even funding albums by US singer-songwriters such as John Hiatt and the Blasters' Dave Alvin who found their way back into the American Hot 100. Demon thrived because they uncovered a series of holes in the market, until the majors and other independent labels eventually caught on, here and in the States. Gary Stewart, who was head of A&R for Rhino Records, said Demon and Edsel were the benchmark and the blueprint when Rhino shifted from releasing novelty and surf records and local new wave bands to focusing on classic vinyl reissues in the mid-eighties.

Silvertone Records was Andrew's response after Demon didn't end well for him personally. He says himself that Silvertone was probably the apotheosis of 'an Andrew Lauder label' – reviving the careers of J.J. Cale, John Lee Hooker and Buddy Guy as well as initiating the Stone Roses phenomenon. Andrew effectively ceased to be an A&R man after This Way Up folded twenty-five years ago, although the extraordinary episode with Rick Adams, John Porter and Cello Records proved to be a crazy last hurrah. It was fun while it lasted and fittingly it was another testament to Andrew's commitment to the blues which he'd begun thirty years earlier at Liberty.

His final venture setting up the Evangeline and Acadia labels was a much lower key operation but after eight years he knew that his small Devon-based independent couldn't compete either financially or to the standards he'd long upheld. Technological advances were already changing the way people consumed, discovered and listened to music in the digital era. There's an almost romantic cachet about A&R during the three decades Andrew was actively involved, since when the landscape for live music has seriously diminished. Today it's no longer enough to be inspired by the music and take a chance on a gut feeling without having data and analytics to back it up. Andrew certainly didn't need an algorithm to make up his mind about Hawkwind or the Pop Group. I'd like to think there's still a place in A&R for somebody as obsessive about music as him. He's always retained a fan's perspective, which, combined with an exceptional knowledge of music, meant he was at ease around musicians and others who were as passionate about music as he was – and still is. He's never happier than spending time talking about music.

Acknowledgements
by Andrew Lauder

As I sit here on the cusp of my seventy-sixth year, most of my thoughts are about Judith Riley, my partner in love and life for the last forty-four of those years, who died on 3 January 2023. I can't imagine life without her; she'd be sitting beside me now, shouting out the names of this or that person I need to mention. There have been so many friends, colleagues, collaborators and inspirational people in my life and, not least, all the artists and musicians I've signed, or been associated with, and who are featured throughout *Happy Trails*. Thanks to them all and to the many producers, engineers, designers and other talented people who were part of the process of putting out records.

Growing up in West Hartlepool was very easy-going thanks to Mum and Dad who were so understanding and always there for me, and to Nigel and Simon who were the most incredibly obliging elder brothers you could wish for. My boarding school days didn't start well but Ian Sutherland, at the Craig School in Windermere, played a significant part in my coming down to London where we shared a flat together. In my first week at Wellingborough School, I met Simon Thirsk (my oldest friend, then and to this day), and our fellow bandmates in the Deacons, Kevin Laker and Mick DeVetta. One master stands out for his enlightened attitude; the sartorial John Elwick was a top man.

In the first week of January 1965 I lucked immediately into
a job in the music business as an invoice clerk for a leading
music publisher in Denmark Street. At Southern Music I'd like
to thank Peter Foss (for giving me that job), Peter Austin (my
co-manager of C-Jam Blues), John Merritt from Burlington Music
and Wayne Bardell, the first and best friend I made in London. I
also met Andrew Oldham at Southern – another former pupil at
Wellingborough; it was Andrew and Guy Stevens whose maverick
methods laid down a marker for me in the future.

My career as an A&R man evolved at Liberty Records where
I owe a considerable debt to Bob Reisdorff (a true mentor and
the second man to offer me a job). I learnt the ropes from him
as part of a convivial team that included Ray Williams (the
ideal flatmate), the experienced and kindly Ronnie Bell and our
publisher's in-house writer/arranger Mike Batt. It was Liberty's
US boss Al Bennett who thankfully stopped me from going to
Apple, and Lee Mendell in the Los Angeles office who made
my deal with Creedence Clearwater Revival possible. It was
at Liberty that I signed my first band, the Groundhogs, little
knowing how much of a bargain the original £52 advance was.
Blues enthusiast and top guitarist Tony McPhee helped me in
releasing a series of blues albums on Liberty.

Whatever trepidation I had at first, United Artists was another
welcoming place to work throughout the '70s. So huge thanks to
Martin Davis (for letting me get on with it without interference),
catalogue-king Alan Warner, Dennis Knowles (for being supportive
and fun), Pierre Tubbs (for the artwork), Barney Bubbles (the gifted
designer for Hawkwind and so much more), fellow Hartlepool FC
supporter Richard Ogden, Tim Read, Kick Van Hengle, Martyn
Smith, Martin Rushent (producer and engineer supreme) and Andy
Childs. Andy became my major co-conspirator at Demon and Edsel
Records in the '80s. Managers should never be undervalued and
much of what I achieved at United Artists would not have been

possible but for Doug Smith, Wayne Bardell, Roy Fisher, Barrie and Jenny Marshall, Dave Robinson, John Eichler, Chris Fenwick, Dai Davies, and Richard Boon. As 'the man who signed Can' (not strictly true), I was indebted to Siegfried 'Siggy' Loch and Gerhard Augustin from Liberty's Munich office.

It was during the United Artists years that I met Maureen O'Donnell in New York on my first visit to America; she came over to the UK where we lived and worked together for much of the '70s. I always got on well with Mark Anders from A Band Called O. Maureen and Mark, to my delight, became a couple and we're still great friends to this day. Among my closest friends from that time are Jean-Jacques Burnel and his wife Dorothy (now near neighbours in France) and Pete and Judy Thomas. I've known Pete since he was the drummer in Chilli Willi and the Red Hot Peppers and later in the Attractions. They've all been enormously supportive since Judith died and are true friends.

Rockfield Studios became something of a second home; Kingsley and Anne Ward were fun to be around and it was at Rockfield that I first met Dave Edmunds. I forged so many enduring relationships during the '70s including *Zigzag* founders Pete Frame and John Tobler, Charlie Gillett, Mike Leadbitter, Mike Vernon (who I first met in Southern's basement studio producing the Artwoods), Andy Dunkley, Ted Carroll and Roger Armstrong, Ian and John from *Musicland*, Paul Fenn and Paul Charles at Asgard, Nigel Kerr and Will Birch. I made so many American friends too: Seymour Stein, Greg Shaw, Harold Bronson, former Charlatans' bass player Richard Olsen and his wife Susan, Ralph Gleason, Rick Griffin and Greg Lewerke. I first met Greg when he came to London during my days at Liberty. When I made my first pilgrimage to Los Angeles and San Francisco in 1970, we sealed a friendship that lasts to this day.

I also met Jake Riviera back then and our paths kept crossing through his involvement with Nick Lowe, Dr Feelgood and

Stiff Records which led to Nick and Elvis Costello being signed to Radar Records. We formed F-Beat together in 1980. Judith and I spent a lot time with Nick, his then wife Carlene Carter and her teenage daughter Tiffany who lived nearby; it was generally party time at our then house in Acton. From the '80s onwards, I started up a number of other labels, namely Demon, Edsel, Silvertone, This Way Up, Cello, and Evangeline. There's a host of people I worked closely with and shared more happy times during the next two decades. So thanks to Henry Priestman, Clive Langer, Alan Winstanley, Andy Cheeseman, Paul Riley, Cynthia Lole, Malcolm Garrett, Jerry Jaffe, Pete Flanagan, Phil Smee, Gareth Davies, Richard Wootton, Steve Mason, Pete Macklin, my lawyer Anthony Jayes, Loudon Wainwright (whose records I released on four different labels), Mike Kappus, Dan and Kelly Bourgoise, Robert Cray and his wife Susan, Dave Alvin, John Hiatt, the Fabulous Thunderbirds, Richie Havens, Richie Hayward, John Prine, John Silva, Jean-Luc Epstein, Lucy Launder, Dave Bedford, James Endicott, Ian McNabb, Tim Duffy, John Porter and Linda Keith. Although Silvertone became known for the Stone Roses (where I always got on well with the band), I'm particularly proud of releasing records and spending time with some of my all-time heroes — John Lee Hooker, JJ Cale, Buddy Guy, and Willie Dixon.

It was in 1985 that Judith and I discovered our country retreat and bought a cottage in the small village of Knowstone in Devon; we made the permanent move there in 1997. Life in the village very much revolved around its sole pub - The Masons Arms. Judith and I became great friends, from both sides of the bar, with all four couples who ran the pub: Tim (Elizabeth) and David Dodd, Paul and Jo Stretton-Downes, Edouard and Antoinette Van Vliet (and their children Hugo, Stephen and Eline), and Mark and Sarah Dodson who turned it into a Michelin-star restaurant. Sisters Emma Lock and Sarah Adams both helped out at Evangeline; their parents and brother John were all part of our extended Devon family. I finally called time on the record business in 2008 and in 2010 Judith and I moved to another charming village, Seillans, in France. We took Chip, the first of our two Lakeland Terriers with us, who made way for Gibson.

I'd been talking for years about telling my story but it was only after a series of conversations instigated by Andy Childs, between Jeff Barrett, Lee Brackstone and Mick Houghton, that *Happy Trails* became a reality. Mick came on board as my co-writer; I've known him since 1970 from sending him records when he was writing for Leicester University music magazine Fast 'N' Bulbous. The book finally got underway in 2020. Mick and I talked for hours and hours, week after week after which he went away, pieced all the threads together and brought my story to life. It was always a fun talking to him; he even follows the mixed fortunes of Hartlepool FC now.

People often ask what my favourite record is and, if pushed, I'd say *Happy Trails* by Quicksilver Messenger Service. So it's a fitting title. I only wish that Judith, and far too many others in *Happy Trails*, were still here to read it.

Andrew Lauder

January 2023

Acknowledgements
by Mick Houghton

I'd like to extend special thanks to Andy Childs, Heavenly
Records founder Jeff Barrett and White Rabbit Publisher Lee
Brackstone. It was a conversation between Andy and Jeff that
sparked off this book. Andy was amazed that Andrew and Jeff
– two modest men, two generations apart, driven by a passion
for music – had never met. Andrew now lives in France so they
spoke over the phone and Jeff came away buzzing; he called Lee
straight away and said Andrew's story would make a great book.
My name came up as a potential co-writer, not least because
I've known Andrew for over 50 years. I knew what a fascinating
story he had to tell although there was a lot more to come that
definitely surprised me.

Lee gave us the go-ahead and Andrew and I began our
weekly conversations just as the first lockdown kicked in. They
offered a sense of normalcy in those strange times. We spoke
every Friday afternoon for the best part of a year; our chats only
concluded when the battery in Andrew's phone beeped and cut
out at around three hours.

So thank you Andrew for all our congenial conversations
and for tolerating a certain amount of prying and persistence on
my part to burst the bubble on your self-effacing nature. I can't

359

forget Judith Riley for helping to keep the wheels spinning. She and Andrew were inseparable at work and play and in life for over forty years. It's her story too. I'd particularly like to thank Richard Williams for writing the Foreword. Thanks also to Stuart Batsford, Mark Cooper, Julian Cope, Nigel Cross, Daryl Easlea, Ian Harrison, Michael Heatley, Lucinda McNeile at Orion, Tim Read, John Reed, Terry Staunton and my ever-supportive and loving wife Sara.

Mick Houghton

January 2023

Picture Credits

p.22   Getty/RB/Staff

p.37   Alamy/Pictorial Staff

p.50   Courtesy of Andrew Lauder

p.65   Courtesy of Andrew Lauder

p.73   Courtesy of Andrew Lauder

p.88   Ray Williams/Coleman-Rayner

p.90   Courtesy of Andrew Lauder

p.96   Alamy/Pictorial Press Ltd

p.102 North News and Pictures Ltd

p.116 Courtesy of Andrew Lauder

p.124 *Zigzag*/Courtesy of Andrew Lauder

p.160 Alamy/Pictorial Press Ltd

p.182 Courtesy of Andrew Lauder

p.188 Alamy/Victor de Schwanberg

p.212 Courtesy of Andrew Lauder

p.217 Courtesy of Andrew Lauder

p.240 Courtesy of Andrew Lauder

p.248 Getty/Erica Echenberg

p.267 Courtesy of Andrew Lauder

p.269 Courtesy of Andrew Lauder

p.274 Courtesy of Andrew Lauder

p.299 Courtesy of Andrew Lauder

p.316 Courtesy of Andrew Lauder

p.319 Courtesy of Andrew Lauder

p.331 Getty/Paul Natkin